WILLIAM SMITH

WILLIAM SMITH

WILLIAM SMITH

Educator and Churchman

1727–1803

By

ALBERT FRANK GEGENHEIMER

UNIVERSITY OF PENNSYLVANIA PRESS

PHILADELPHIA

1943

FOREWORD

WILLIAM SMITH represented the already old conservative political tradition in late American colonial history; he also represented the new liberal cultural movement in the fields of belles-lettres that developed, particularly to the south of New England, in the last half of the eighteenth century. A churchman of distinction, probably America's most gifted pulpit orator of the pre-Revolutionary period, he nevertheless largely owes the preservation of his name to the fact that he capably presided over the destinies of the new Academy of Philadelphia, which under him evolved into the College of Philadelphia and then, finally—but after his forced resignation of the provostship —into the University of Pennsylvania. Smith was in most respects admirably fitted for this responsibility: He had been trained in a Scottish University, was well versed in literature, was possessed of real talents for promoting such a cause as that of the education of youth, even to the raising of funds, and, finally, was full of enthusiasm for the new Philadelphia institution. With a strong leaning toward poetry and the dramatic arts, he succeeded in gathering about him a group of talented students who came to share his interest in these fields and some of them, to achieve fame. Dr. Gegenheimer has for the first time presented with fullness this interesting aspect of the life of Smith.

Loyal to the Crown as well as to the Anglican establishment, and therefore looking askance at the rise of American hostility to both; committed at the same time in loyalty to his new home in America in a variety of ways, both spiritual and material, William Smith felt impelled to attempt to reconcile attitudes that in themselves had little enough in common. As a result, he was accused of equivocal conduct and he certainly temporized —seeking some golden, middle road such as lured perhaps most conservative Americans with the advent of the crisis of the Revolutionary War. In good conscience he could pray for his

King and in equal good conscience, we may believe, he pointed out to Washington and his officers their high responsibilities as American patriots. Fervently as he hoped for the preservation of the unity of the English-speaking people, he at the same time defended the principle of colonial political autonomy. That he fell under suspicion of extreme radicals and equally extreme reactionaries is not to be wondered. But he was not all things to all men, for he had convictions; and the respect that he enjoyed from the more moderate patriots in Pennsylvania and Maryland made it possible for him to enjoy even in the course of the war a large measure of freedom of action.

William Smith was not only a churchman, an educator, and political controversialist as is especially stressed in this volume, he was also a business man. In fact, his business interest during the latter years of his life—particularly after the conclusion of the Revolutionary War—increasingly absorbed his time and energies; he speculated in a large way in western lands, laid the foundations of towns, and, as the result of careful investment and the wise administration of his holdings, became a man of considerable wealth. However, one cannot but feel that his absorption in more mundane affairs came through a conscious effort on his part to bury his deep disappointment over the fact that he was neither permitted to reëstablish himself, at least effectively, in the institution that, in spite of his faults of character and weaknesses, he had for years adorned, or to enjoy the position that his talents seemed to have entitled him in the newly established American Protestant Episcopal Church.

In welcoming Dr. Gegenheimer's contribution to the "Pennsylvania Lives," it should in justice be pointed out that the rounding out of this study was made possible not only through the generosity of Justice Jasper Y. Brinton of the Cour d'Appel Mixte, Alexandria, Egypt, but the zeal of Bertha Sprague Fox of Cornwall Bridge, Connecticut. The latter became interested in the life of William Smith some years ago and ultimately succeeded in working out arrangements whereby the great collection of Smith Papers, inherited by Judge Brinton, was sent from Alexandria to America to permit her to utilize them in her investigations. Out of the latter came two excellent papers: "Provost Smith and His Quest for Funds" and "Provost Smith and His Land Investments in Pennsylvania," both of which were published in *Pennsylvania History*, before domestic cares compelled Mrs. Fox to turn reluctantly from her contemplated larger project of a well-rounded biography. Thereupon the Brinton Collection was transferred from the Lehigh University Library to that of the Historical Society of Pennsylvania, where it is now on deposit.

While to some students of colonial history, Dr. Gegenheimer's life of William Smith may seem to stress too greatly the beginnings of literary activities in Pennsylvania and literary criticism, one may be quite sure that this emphasis would not have been displeasing to the genial Provost of the College and Academy and Charitable School of Philadelphia. The book in fact measures up to the high standard set for "Pennsylvania Lives" and deserves a warm welcome.
delphia.

LAWRENCE HENRY GIPSON

Lehigh University
March 1943

CONTENTS

WILLIAM SMITH   *Frontispiece*
  *Copy of a Gilbert Stuart Portrait by E. D. Marchant at the
  University of Pennsylvania*

I

EARLY LIFE

THE date and place of a man's birth are considerably more than statistics. When William Smith was born in Aberdeenshire on April 20, 1727, two of his most essential characteristics were determined for him: he was a Scotsman and a citizen of the eighteenth century. His father, Thomas Smith, a small landholder, was the son of James Smith, a physician and astronomer, who had been the first of this branch of Smiths to be born in Scotland, the family having previously resided in England. On his mother's side, William Smith was descended from an old Scots family; Elizabeth Duncan was a daughter of Alexander Duncan and a sister of Admiral Adam Duncan, who became Baron Duncan of Lundie and Viscount Duncan of Camperdown after his victory over the Dutch fleet of Admiral De Winter in 1797. William Smith had one sister, Isabella, who later joined him in America. A half-brother, Thomas, a son of Thomas Smith's second marriage, also migrated to America, where he eventually became a member of the Supreme Court of Pennsylvania.

According to an autobiographical account of William Smith's life, which his great-grandson Horace Wemyss Smith claimed to have seen and which has since disappeared, Smith entered the parochial school at the age of seven, but remained there only until March of 1735, at which time his training was entrusted to the Society for the Education of Parochial Schoolmasters. Its care of his education ended with his entrance into college. While little factual material relating directly to William Smith's schooling can be given, it must have followed the general rather stern pattern of the day in Scotland. Long hours of study and long terms were, however, happily broken up by intervals of vacation, when young Smith resorted to the neighboring countryside. Undoubtedly his love of nature was cultivated by walks and rambles through the valley of the Don, and through the beautiful Deeside, then as now one of the outstandingly beautiful regions in a somewhat bleak and austere part of the country. The far northern location of Aberdeen gives it exceptionally long days in the summer; one may be sure that the youths of the eighteenth century appreciated this bounty of nature, sorely needed to compensate for the miserable shortness of the raw winter days when the winds of the North Sea blew through every bone.

In 1743 William Smith entered King's College, Aberdeen, the older of the two colleges which form the present University of Aberdeen. King's College, though not known by that name until some time later, was called into official existence under the sanction of a Bull issued by Pope Alexander VI on February 10, 1494/5. Legend carries its history back to earlier times, even as early as 1157. The nature of the education which Smith received at Aberdeen is important to the student of his life, since Aberdeen's influence was always strong upon him. Consideration will be given to this subject in a later discussion of Smith's own ideas on education, but it should be mentioned here that the outstanding feature of King's College during Smith's student days, and indeed during the history of the college from its beginning down to 1798 (with the exception of a period from 1628 to 1641), was the system of "regenting," under which, as Robert S. Rait has explained, "Each teacher was confined, not to a certain subject, but to a certain class, directing its studies from beginning to end of the curriculum." Smith's class at Aberdeen was under the regentship of Professor D. Bradfut and of Alexander Raut. The study of Greek was alone exempted from the system of regenting. A Parliamentary commission, appointed in 1690 to visit the Scottish universities, had decided in 1700 that "it would conduce much to the better learning" of Greek if the teacher of Greek stuck to his Greek rather than took a class through all its subjects.

The University of Aberdeen has no record that it ever

granted William Smith an undergraduate degree. He is listed as having been a student for the four years from 1743 to 1747 and as having been successively in those years bajan, semi, tertian, and magistrand (the Aberdeen equivalents of freshman, sophomore, junior, and senior), but there is no indication that he received a degree in course. Smith was listed, however, as a bursar. In Bishop Elphinstone's original foundation for King's College, thirteen bursars were among the thirty-six persons whose residence within the college was to be covered by the endowment. Rait explains that "the students in arts who were specially provided for were thirteen bursars proceeding to the degree of master." Apparently, then, William Smith enjoyed a somewhat superior status as a student, even though he may not have proceeded to a degree.

Smith's immediate activities upon leaving King's College are shrouded in the same obscurity which surrounds his apparent failure to take a degree. That this should be so is perhaps no great wonder; the lives of most men soon become lost in the hazy mist of the forgotten. The interesting thing about Smith is that, with the energy and forcefulness which were always distinctive of him, he so soon reëmerged from this area into that of record. The October 1750 issue of the *Scots Magazine,* that northern counterpart of the *Gentleman's Magazine* of London, carried a letter signed by Smith as president of a committee "impowered, by the late general meeting of Scots schoolmasters, to apply to parliament for an augmentation of their livings." After a short preface, the body of the piece was introduced under the resplendent title of "Some reflexions on education, with a modest scheme for augmenting schoolmasters livings. Humbly offered to the impartial consideration of the publick." The actual six-point scheme offered on behalf of the Scottish schoolmasters is of little interest; minimum stipends and various other details of providing a sufficient living were dealt with. Of much greater interest are the "reflexions on education," which reveal the touch of Smith's hand and show that at the age of twenty-three William Smith

had already thought much about education and already possessed in germ ideas which were later to be expounded more
fully and to be put into practice on a much wider scale than
he could have dreamed of when he put his signature to this
letter at Abernethy, Scotland, on November 5, 1750. The very
first paragraph of the reflections referred to a previous memorial issued by the committee on September 14, 1749 (in
which it must be presumed that Smith also had a part), which
had emphasized that "the glory, happiness and safety of human society, in a great measure depend on the fidelity and
ability of those who are instructed with the education and
publick institution of youth." The 1750 letter offered an even
more explicit definition of the aims of education:

> . . . it is plain, that to teach children languages either dead
> or living, is but the least part of their [the schoolmasters']
> duty. They must also, and above all, form their taste and man-
> ners aright, distinguish the true from the false, regulate their
> passions, and make the first and strongest advances toward the
> training them up reasonable and social creatures.

"Training them up reasonable and social creatures" was one
of the aims of William Smith throughout his life, though he
was able later to find apter words to express his ideas.

A postscript to this letter in the *Scots Magazine* added that
one of the committee was to go up to London to petition for
leave to bring in a bill to put the proposed scheme into effect,
and that he would set out about the twenty-fifth of November.
It is most natural that the president of the committee should
have been the one to go. And in fact the *Scots Magazine* for
December reported that "Mr William Smith schoolmaster at
Abernethy, set out for London on the 20th, as commissioner
appointed by the established schoolmasters, to apply to parliament for an augmentation of their livings." The end of the
year 1750 therefore saw William Smith again in London, going through that routine of waiting upon committees and upon

persons supposed to be of influence which was to become painfully familiar to him in later years.

Horace W. Smith wrote of his great-grandfather: "The whole of the year 1750 he passed in London, and I have every reason to believe that during that time he acted as clerk for the Honorable Society for the Propagation of the Gospel." This statement cannot be entirely correct. The letter in the *Scots Magazine* indicates that Smith was at Abernethy in November; and the Society for the Propagation of the Gospel in Foreign Parts has nothing in its records to show that Smith acted as a clerk to the society in 1750 or at any other time. Furthermore, the statement of the *Scots Magazine* makes it clear that Smith was teaching school at Abernethy in 1750 and suggests strongly that from his leaving King's College in 1747 he had been himself trying to train the youth of Scotland as "reasonable and social creatures." The movement to improve the lot of the underpaid and overworked teachers brought out in Smith his natural talent for leadership, and one of the youngest of their number became president of the schoolmasters' committee.

Probably with the idea in mind of furthering his efforts for his fellow teachers, Smith took with him to London letters to various people of importance, among them the Archbishop of Canterbury. While these contacts were apparently not strong enough to give success to the immediate scheme upon which Smith had come to the capital, they were to prove of use to him personally on several later occasions.

It was in London, no doubt, that Smith learned of an opportunity to become the tutor of two young boys about to return to their home in America. Bearing letters from the Archbishop of Canterbury to James De Lancey, Lieutenant-Governor of New York, and others, Smith left England with the two sons of Colonel Josiah Martin on March 3, 1751, and arrived in New York the first of May. For the next two years he lived at the Martins' Long Island estate, Hermitage, in his

capacity of tutor. His duties in that position were not strenu-
ous enough to content his lively mind or to weary his strong
Scottish body. Matters educational, political, and literary absorbed some of his excess energy.

Apparently Smith's first publication in America came early
in 1752. The *Pennsylvania Gazette* for March 24 and the *New
York Gazette* for April 6, 1752, each carried "The Mock-Bird
and Red-Bird; An American Fable," an extremely didactic
poem which has little interest other than historical. Although
the evidence that Smith was the author is circumstantial, it is
fairly conclusive. Less didactic, one suspects, were "On Seeing a young Pair blush during their marriage" and "On the
Month of May 1752," early poems which are now known only
because their titles are on a list of his own writings made by
Smith.

The writing of verses was a common enough pastime among
eighteenth-century gentlemen with a literary turn of mind.
More typical of Smith's serious interests was a prose piece, "On
the Liberty of the Press. (A Letter to the Printer of the New
York Gazette; when he stood presented for printing an Indian's Speech on the Subject of Revelation & ye Incarnation of
Jesus Christ. July 28th 1752)." The letter was not published,
though Smith undoubtedly sent a copy to James Parker, publisher of the *Gazette;* a manuscript in Smith's handwriting is
still extant. Perhaps it is prophetic that the subject should have
been one of which Smith was to have considerably more—
and considerably more personal—knowledge. The general remarks in the first half of the letter Smith acknowledged to
have been largely developed from one of Hume's essays; but
he went on in his own way to a vigorous defense of liberty
of the press, closing with an admonition to Parker to change
his mind about not printing unsigned articles:

. . . how pernicious wou'd this Method be should we ever
be in that Situation in which the Liberty of the Press would
stand us in most Stead! Were Men to subscribe pieces written
in Order to lash powerful Vice, or arrouse their Country to

stop the Progress of growing Tyranny, they would frustrate the very End of their own Writings by exposing themselves to certain Destruction: & depriving their Country of her firmest Patriots & surest Protectors.

It is interesting to observe that even in this obviously apprentice work there is present considerable strength of feeling and conviction, along with a commensurate force of expression, a force which increases greatly when Smith strikes out for himself and leaves Hume behind. One thing the letter clearly illustrates: When William Smith saw a cause in which he was interested being attacked, he could hardly wait to jump in and deliver his blows. In spite of the fact that his ancestry was not 100 per cent Scottish, Smith was pure Celt in his love of a fight.

Within a month after writing this letter, young William Smith turned his hand again to verse and in August 1752 composed an "Epitaph on a Young Lady deceased." The short poem expressed conventional religious sentiments, with just a trace of romantic morbidity; it is neither exceptional nor very exceptionable. When it was published in the *New York Gazette* on August 10, 1752, the manuscript title was changed to "Epitaph, on Miss Philipse."

Smith soon appeared in a capacity in which he was better qualified, that of a writer on education. On October 24, 1752, there was issued (if the advertisement in the *New York Gazette* for October 23 announcing its publication "to-morrow" is correct) a pamphlet of forty-two pages, bearing the title:

Some Thoughts on Education: With Reasons for Erecting a College in this Province, and fixing the same at the City of *New-York: To which is added,* A Scheme for employing Masters or Teachers in the mean Time: And also for raising and endowing an Edifice in an easy Manner. *The Whole concluding, with* A Poem: Being a serious *Address* to the *House of Representatives.*

In addition to ten lines of Latin quotation and the information that the work was printed and sold by J. Parker at the

New Printing-office in Beaver Street, New York City, the title-page bore the good news that the price of the pamphlet was only one shilling. But no mention of an author can be found on the title-page, and the dedication to James De Lancey was signed merely "Philomathes." It is clear beyond doubt, however, that William Smith wrote *Some Thoughts*, for in a copy owned by the Historical Society of Pennsylvania there are many alterations in Smith's handwriting, and the copy was marked by Smith "To be printed for Vol. 3 New Edit." The work is also included in two different lists of his writings in Smith's own hand, both of which are preserved in the Brinton Collection of Smith Papers. Further proof, if needed, is to be found in the fact that Smith referred to the piece as his in a speech delivered in 1773, and that in 1770 he adapted part of the poem which formed an appendix to *Some Thoughts* for use as an exercise at the College and Academy of Philadelphia.

Smith's 1773 judgment of this poem of twenty-one years before was that it was "juvenile." With that criticism one cannot disagree. In the prose preface to *Some Thoughts*, Smith offered an interesting defense of the inclusion of the verses. Because literature and education had been "sadly neglected" in New York, he felt that his duty, far from ending with the mere setting forth of proposals, required him "to excite his Countrymen to a Speedy Execution of them." "The most pathetic Manner of doing this," it seemed to him, was to show the happy state which might prevail if the proposals were put into practice. He chose to show this happy state in verse, not only for variety and relief from the preceding prose, but also because "anticipating distant glorious Scenes naturally warms the Fancy, distends the Soul, and raps it into the Enthusiasm of *Poetry*."

Avoiding the easy witticism that Smith's verse was indeed "the most pathetic Manner" of presenting his subject, one is still aware that the whole performance, both in prose and verse, was generally weak and unoriginal. By far the greater part of the nineteen pages of prose was given to a defense of

New York, or any large city, as a location for a college. Concern was shown lest anyone should believe that a college in a large city might tend to the corruption of its pupils' morals. Smith even discussed the question of the relative price of firewood in different locations and ventured on the bold assertion that perhaps in another fifty years coal would be a more general fuel than wood. He had little to say about the actual conduct of the proposed college. Parenthetically, in a discussion of the moral issues involved, he suggested that the students should lodge together within the walls of the college. The curriculum received equally scant attention, being mentioned only in reference to financial problems. On the subject of finances, the discussion reached its most adult level and, almost alone, gave promise of better things to come from the author. At this time £3,443/18/— had been collected in New York toward the erection of a college. Smith very properly suggested that "we begin at the wrong End, if we apply the Money already rais'd, to the immediate Rearing of a Building." It would be far better, he thought, to apply the interest of the sum at once "as Salaries for two sufficient Men, each to teach two Classes at first; *viz.* the one GREEK and LATIN, with the most useful Branches of the MATHEMATICS; and the Other moral PHILOSOPHY, and what is comprehended under the general Name of PHYSICS."

Smith was now twenty-five years old, and not all his thoughts were as weighty as *Some*. Several letters that passed between him and Mrs. Phila De Lancey, wife of Governor James De Lancey, during November 1752, have been preserved and may be taken as proof that Smith had developed considerable social grace, especially when the matter of writing letters to ladies was involved. The correspondence was stilted, polished, and urbane, in the best eighteenth-century manner, full of protestations on the lady's part that as a mere female she should not be expected to understand all about so profound a study as literature, and full of polite rejoinders on the part of the gentleman. Included in the series was "An

Essay to Fix the Idea of an American Pastoral," which Smith wrote and sent to Mrs. De Lancey for her perusal. The essay in itself is of no particular literary value, but the fact of its having been written at least shows Smith's interest in such a subject.

It is not possible to say just when in 1752 Smith's volume in prose and verse, *Indian Songs of Peace*, was issued; indeed, it may not have been published in 1752 at all, even though the title-page bears that date, for the *New York Gazette* on March 12, 1753, announced that the book would be out "To-morrow." Regardless of the exact date of issue, the work of composition was undoubtedly done in 1752. By far the most interesting part of the volume is its preface, which occupied twelve of the twenty-seven pages. Addressed to "Sylvanus," this prefatory epistle, as it was described on the title-page, commented at length upon a problem which was long to occupy Smith's attention: the education of the non-English groups in the English colonies, in this instance the Indians. Politics and religion were closely associated in his thoughts on the subject:

> To civilize our Friends and Neighbours;—to strengthen our Allies and our Alliance;—to adorn and dignify Human Nature;—to save Souls from Death; to promote the Christian Faith, and the Divine Glory, are the Motives.

These were the motives that were to move men to institute schools for the education of the Indians. No very specific plans were offered by Smith; his intent was rather to stir up interest and to urge the appointment of a committee to make a thorough investigation and proper recommendations. Smith contented himself with suggesting that persons be selected to go among the Indians and learn their languages, that these persons should then be placed as teachers in a school for Indians, and that the Indian graduates of such a school should themselves become teachers in other Indian schools:

> Should not Schools and Oratories be set up in sundry Parts of the *Indian Nations*, or, at least, as has been said before, one

or two Principal Ones, from whence others might derive, as from some beneficent Springs-Head flows a Stream, which becomes a great River to refresh an extensive Country, and make glad the Hearts of a populous Nation?

If proof were wanted that William Smith had the instinctive outlook of the educator, here it is. He was not alone in realizing the Indian problem, or in wishing for the education of the Indian, but he was distinguished for the whole-hearted reliance which he placed upon education as the means to achieve the desired end. This attitude is not only the mark of the educator, but of the statesman with a long-range view of things. Smith took an evolutionary view of social development, and in 1752 that amounted to a revolutionary point of view.

Smith began his literary activity for 1753 early in that year; in fact, he must have been working on his *Ode on the New Year, 1753* during the last month of the old year in order to have published the sixteen-page pamphlet at the proper time. The prose preface displayed a bumptious self-assurance scarcely justified by the text:

. . . The Critic that resolves to see nothing in a Book but its Blemishes, betrays a Heart as bad, and a Taste as perverse, as a Painter that Searches a whole Kingdom in order to expose only the Deformities and Distortions of human Nature; they equally insult Humanity, and must equally be detested by Mankind.—I shall just add, that without intending it, they effectually forward my Interest, if in nothing else, at least in obliging me to give as little Room as possible for finding Faults.

As to the following Piece, I shall prevent their Remarks by telling them, that I question whether there was any Thing new, in a New-Year's Ode these Two Thousand Years, and that the Thoughts in it are perhaps as old as the Subject from which they flow, *Time* itself.—However, if there is any Merit in the Numbers and Conduct of the Piece, that at least Envy itself must allow me.

I have put my Name to it, which I faithfully promise to do, shou'd I ever publish any Thing more in this Place, being ambitious of no more Praise or Blame than I am justly entitled to. And I hope I shall be so far believed, as to have no anony-

mous poetical Piece, in any Paper whatever, for the future
ascribed to

WILLIAM SMITH

Before bursting into song, the young author felt obliged to let
his readers know what he intended to sing about, and hence
"The Argument":

Morning. Subject propos'd. Progress of the Year. An Incen-
tive to Gratitude, moral Order, and Harmony. A Thought on
Eternity. The Security of the Virtuous Man: His Serenity, Joy,
Faith, Intrepidity and Death.

After this exposition of his themes, the versifier (one would
hardly wish to use the sacred name of poet on this occasion)
began in earnest:

I

NIGHT's *Sentinel,
With Silver Bell,
Has shrilly rous'd the slumbering Day!
The Stars wax pale,
And down yon Vale
The scatter'd Shades swim dusk away.

* The Cock.

II

And now, behold!
With fluid Gold,
Approaching *Phœbus* gilds the *Morn!*
And Nymph and Swain,
From Hill to Plain,
Sing round,—"*Another* YEAR *is born.*"

III

The Year! the Year!
Whose great Career
Begins, is warbled from each Tongue!
The Year! the Year!
And its Career!
Shall be the Subject of my Song!

IV

My Song inspire
With all thy Fire,

O *Muse*, and dignify with Thought!
        Yet, as the Stream
        Of *Time*, (my Theme)
Smooth let it flow from Note to Note!

V

        And while I sing,
        And from each String,
Each trilling Harmony explore;
        O may my Heart
        Bear high its Part!
Be warm'd! be ravish'd! and adore!

VI

        'Tis done!—The Muse
        Her Favour shews!
Lo! from the Skies she comes confest!
        Her Presence charms!
        Deep Transport warms,
And sacred Ravings swell my Breast!

The modern reader may be pardoned if he chooses to adopt the descriptive noun of the last line without its qualifying adjective.

Apart from an impeccable correctness of sentiment, there is little about this poem that is worthy of praise or even of mention. That William Smith wrote it must be admitted, for although the signature might belong to someone else, and the poetic style might well have been shared by half a hundred other William Smiths in New York in 1753, the prose of the preface bears the unmistakable mark of Smith's impress. Corroboration is to be found in the inclusion of a copy of the poem among the Smith Papers and its mention on several lists in Smith's hand of his works, among them a codicil to his will referring to republication of his writings.

It is fitting that Smith should have greeted the year 1753 with a literary offering, infelicitous though it was, since that year was to be one of considerable literary activity for him. And indeed, one thing he wrote was to have far-reaching influence.

THE COLLEGE OF MIRANIA

ADVERTISEMENTS by the firm of J. Parker and W. Weyman in the *New York Gazette* for April 2 and April 9, 1753, preceded its publication on April 11, 1753, of a new work by "Mr. Smith of Queens County":

A General Idea of the College of *Mirania;* With a Sketch of the Method of teaching *Science* and *Religion*, in the several Classes: And Some Account of its Rise, Establishment and Buildings. Address'd more immediately to the Consideration of the Trustees nominated, by the Legislature, to receive Proposals, &c. relating to the Establishment of a College in the Province of New-York.

The title-page also bore quotations from Horace (*Quid Leges sine Moribus vanæ proficiunt?*) and from Seneca.

The importance of this eighty-six-page pamphlet in Smith's life cannot be overestimated, since it undoubtedly led to his choice as head of the Academy of Philadelphia. And that *Mirania* was to serve as a model for other than the intended college at New York may be seen from the preface which Smith added to the work upon its republication in the 1759 and 1762 editions of his *Discourses*, and which also appears in the version given in his posthumously published *Works:*

The following Idea of a Seminary of Learning, adapted to the circumstances of a young colony, was drawn up and published, at the desire of some gentlemen of New-York, who were appointed to receive proposals relative to the establishment of a College in that province; . . . it contains a pretty exact representation of what the author is now endeavouring to *realize* in the Seminary over which he has the honour to preside in another colony. [The College and Academy of Philadelphia.]

Mirania, of course, never was on sea or land, but the adoption of the utopian method of presentation gave Smith a better opportunity to enunciate his views than almost any other could have done, and in itself represents a distinct advance over his previous literary efforts. That Mirania was hypothetical was made clear by the designation of the verse prologue as "Supposed to have been spoken at the Opening of the College of Mirania." Early in the prose text, the author explained that while ruminating on the constitutions of those colleges with which he was familiar, and being unable to find one entirely suited to the needs of the day, he happened to meet Evander, "a Person of some distinction of the Province of Mirania," who described the Miranian college to him. Before recounting Evander's description, Smith again emphasized the hypothetical character of Mirania; all that the reader knows about the place is that it was "one of the Provinces of the *New-World* first settled by our Country-Men, the English, above a Century ago. In what Degrees of Lat. &c it lies, is of no Importance."

The verse prologue was a noticeable improvement over the halting lines of the New Year's *Ode*, but it was in its prose that *Mirania* more especially reached a new level of excellence for Smith, attaining at times to genuine eloquence. The increased dignity of expression accorded with the greater profundity and importance of the ideas expressed. An example of this improved style is to be seen in a passage which is also important for its content:

The Object they kept always in Sight, was the easiest, simplest and most natural Method of forming Youth to the Knowledge and Exercise of private and public Virtue; and therefore they did not scruple to reject some Things commonly taught at Colleges; to add others; and shorten or invert the Order of others, as best suited their Circumstances. They often had this Sentence in their mouth, which I think, in other Words, I have read in Tillotson,—That the Knowledge of what tends neither directly nor indirectly to make better Men and better Citizens, is but a Knowledge of Trifles; it is not Learning, but a specious and ingenious sort of Idleness.—We must not then, said they, wilder ourselves in the Search of Truth, among the Rubbish contain'd in the vast tomes of ancient Rabbies, Commentators and Schoolmen; nor in the more refined Speculations of modern Metaphysicians

. . . nor yet in the polemic Writings about Grace, Predestination, moral Agency, the Trinity, &c. &c. . . . The Years of *Methusalem* would be far too short to attain any Proficiency in all the Disputes and Researches of this Kind, which have so long puzzled the learn'd World, and are still as much undecided as at first. Almighty God seems to have set the Knowledge of many Things beyond our present Ken, on purpose to confound our Pride, and whisper to us continually the Degeneracy and Imperfection of our Nature, and when we consider such Things in this Light, we make the only proper Use of them: For, suppose we could live long enough to become as well vers'd in all these Points as the most subtle Doctor that ever breath'd, what would it contribute to the main Point, the making better Men and Citizens? Why, just nothing at all! We ought then, continued they, rejecting Things superfluous and hypothetical, to mount directly up to fundamental Principles, and endeavour to ascertain the Relations we stand in to GOD *and universal Intelligence*, that we may sustain, with Dignity, the Rank assign'd us among intellectual Natures, and move in Concert, with the rest of Creation, in accomplishing the great End of all Things.

Regardless of the academic question whether there is any knowledge that is altogether useless to the making of better men and better citizens, it is still true that such a distinction was particularly valuable and not a little daring for a college to be erected in a new colony and in 1753. Smith made another distinction, quite as valuable and even more daring, when he went on to say that for educational purposes the Miranians divided the whole body of people into two "grand Classes," the first consisting of those designed for the learned professions ("Divinity, Law, Physic, Agriculture, and the chief Offices of the State") and the second of those "design'd for the Mechanic Professions, and all the remaining People of the Country." Since the object of education was to train youth to act as good men and good citizens "in their proper Spheres," it was necessary that different training should be given to those intended for different walks of life. For example, a knowledge of the classical languages as a means of acquiring further useful knowledge was essential to those intended for the learned professions, while, for the mechanic class, time spent on such languages would be considered as almost wasted.

At first glance, this appears to be an undemocratic scheme of education, in that it necessitated an *a priori* judgment on the all-important question of which people were to be trained for which spheres. But Smith, it must not be forgotten, was writing in a British colony in the year 1753. At that period and place, the proposal undoubtedly had a less aristocratic sound than it would have today, for choice of the learned professions was determined by social and financial standing to a far greater degree then than now. Indeed, Smith's scheme probably seemed exceptionally democratic to most of his readers and probably radical to some. He very properly argued that, granting the existence of the two "grand Classes," any scheme that proposed to teach the members of both in the same manner or that was wholly devised for the needs of one of them, without regard to the other, could not be effective. "Colleges," he rightly proclaimed, "are almost universally calculated for the First Class; while a collegiate School for breeding Mechanics, is rarely to be met with." That the most numerous class, "the Hands and Strength of every Government," should be thus overlooked and forced to depend upon ill-regulated private schools or upon colleges for which they had no time and for the courses of which they had little use, seemed not only unjust to this class but also inherently bad for the state itself. The education of the mechanic class was therefore entrusted by the Miranians to the "Mechanic's School, or Academy," which operated in this fashion:

In this School, nine Years compleat the Mechanic's Education; proportionable to which are nine Forms or Classes. In the Three lowest, *English* is taught grammatically, and as a Language, with Writing. In the six higher Classes, *English* and Writing are continued, at the same Time that Accompts, Mathematics, Ethics, Oratory, Chronology, History, the most plain and useful Parts of natural and mechanic Philosophy, are taught; to which is added, something of Husbandry and Chymistry, which, as improv'd of late, they esteem of great Use to every Mechanic.

A further democratic safeguard was supplied by the provision that all the youth attend the same school for the first three years. At the end of that period, "such of the youth as discover Genius, and are intended for the learn'd Professions" were entered into the first of the five classes of the Latin School. The first four years of this school were "given wholly to the Latin Tongue, and improving the Boys in English and Writing at leisure Hours." In the fifth and final year, the day was divided between Latin and Greek, so that at the age of fourteen, "well vers'd in the Latin-Tongue, with some Tincture of the Greek," the students entered the first year, or "Greek Class," of the college. Here, forenoons were devoted to Theocritus' *Idylls*, with selections from Hesiod, Homer, and Xenophon; afternoons were occupied by arithmetic, "vulgar and decimal," "Merchant's Accompts," algebra, and the first six books of Euclid.

The second-year students were put under the direction of the professor of mathematics, who "carries the Youth forward in Algebra; teaches the eleventh and twelfth Books of *Euclid*, Geometry, Astronomy, Chronology, Navigation, and the other most useful Branches of the Mathematics." Theoretical training in mathematics was augmented by "practical geometry," surveying, and map-making. Some logic and metaphysics were included with this mathematical schooling, but not very much, since mathematics itself was felt to be the best method of training in logic. A weekly exercise in Latin and Greek served to keep those subjects fresh in the minds of the students.

The third year was spent under the direction of the professor of philosophy, whose work was divided between ethics and physics. "Under the latter, the *Miranians* comprehend Natural History; Mechanic, or corpuscular Philosophy, and experimental Philosophy." Plato, Cicero, Locke, and Hutchinson are among the writers whose works were studied in the division of ethics.

Evander impressed upon his listener that the fourth and fifth college years were the most important of the whole scheme, because in them all that had been taught before was brought "home to the Business of Life." The chief aim of the first three years was to teach the students to think well, "that is, closely and justly." This basis, however, was held to be useless without its superstructure, which was no less than teaching the students to be masters of their thoughts and able to use them in "writing, speaking, acting, and living well." The first two of these four noble ends were the particular concern of the master of the fourth class, the professor of rhetoric and poetry. To achieve them, it was felt that nothing contributed so much as an ability to appreciate properly what others had written or spoken. "Hence the proper Studies of this Class, are Rhetoric and Poetry, from which arise Criticism and Composition."

The students were first given a "general notion of the Precepts and different Kinds of Rhetoric," following which Cicero's oration in behalf of Milo and that of Demosthenes for Ctesiphon were closely read and analyzed. Three other orations, one each in Greek, Latin, and English, were studied in a somewhat different manner: At one meeting of the class, the instructor would assign a certain portion of the oration, upon which the students were to write out their observations as to its conformity with the rules of rhetoric, its plan, and its thoughts. These observations were brought to the next class meeting to be examined and corrected by the instructor.

Much the same method was followed in the study of poetry, although the Miranian students, having already had philosophy and rhetoric, were supposed to be capable of dealing with this subject in the rather short space of two months. About two weeks were spent on "all the lesser Poems"; drama and pastoral were allotted a similar period; and the second month was devoted to the epic poem or "Epopæa." The remaining six months of the fourth year were spent in composing and delivering orations. Each day one oration composed by a class member was corrected, while another, previously corrected, was delivered. Supposing a class of twenty, each member would thus perform once in ten days. Smith made a point which might well be kept in the minds of any who have to pass upon youthful work, and which might also be remembered when one is tempted to criticize some of Smith's own earlier attempts, both in prose and verse:

In correcting the Compositions of Youth, however, the Professor is sensible, that great Judgment and Art is requir'd: Always remembring that they are Youth, he is greatly careful not to discourage them by too much Severity. If ever he seems displeas'd at any Thing, it is when he discovers a Sort of Stiffness, Precision and Judgment in their Pieces above their Years, which he considers as a certain Sign of Coldness and Sterility; while, on the other Hand, Redundancy of Thought, and sprightly Sallies of Imagination, share his distinguish'd Indulgence. These he calls the blooming Shoots of Genius; and, tho' exuberant, thinks they are no more to be lopp'd off at an improper Season, or in an unskilful Manner, than the luxuriant Growth of a thriving young Tree. It is dangerous for any Hand, but that of Time, to reduce these wholly within their proper Bounds.

The teaching of youth to appreciate critically the great works of literature was defended for both personal and social reasons. The Miranians believed that the man who has been trained to appreciate the beauties of order, harmony, design, and the other merits of the best art "finds, within Himself, an unexhaustable Fund of the most noble and rational Amusement." They went further in their praise for "this Taste for polite Letters," holding that it "not only teaches us to write well, and renders Life comfortable to ourselves, but also contributes highly to the Cement of Society, and the Tranquility of the State." No one who could feel the charms of literature and the fine arts could be a bad man or a bad citizen.

The fifth-year students were under the direct supervision of Aratus, the principal of the college, who gave them instruction in agriculture and history. Agriculture as Aratus understood and propounded the subject was something considerably more than mere agronomy. The knowledge of nature, or "natural philosophy," gained in the third year was reviewed preliminary to this study. Aratus was careful to give his students "a good Tincture of Physic and animal Anatomy," which not only helped them to know the "proper care of their own Health and Bodies," but was essential in explaining "the Œconomy and Mechanism of Plants, the Structure of their Vessels, their Generation, Manner of Life and Accretion, Perspiration, Circulation of Sap, &c." The class also examined the mineral strata of the earth and "the Nature of those saline and aqueous Juices that constitute the nutritious Matter or Food of Vegetables." The whole course of "agriculture," which has been seen to have included botany, some biology, and a dash of geology, was "illustrated by a Course of chymical and statical Experiments."

As an historian, Aratus was quite as unorthodox as he was an agriculturist. His students did not read history merely to satisfy their momentary curiosity with a series of single and unrelated facts. (Smith claimed that this was all the advantage gained by the usual method of handling the subject in other colleges of the day.) By the time the Miranian youth had reached the last of their collegiate years, they had obtained a fairly complete knowledge of the principal events "that happened in the World before they were born." The task of the fifth year was "to review those Events in the calm *Light of Philosophy*." Immediate and remote causes and consequences of events were sought out, not for their own sake, but in order to make them lessons in ethics and politics and to provide "an useful Rule of Conduct and Manners thro' Life." Wisely was it thought:

It is dangerous to send raw unpractis'd Virtue abroad into a World where Right and Wrong are too often confounded; and nothing can obviate this Danger but the giving Youth a previous Acquaintance with the World, and making them behold Virtue and Vice with all their Consequences painted in genuine Colors by the Historian.

To accomplish this estimable end, Aratus first reëxamined the principles of ethics, which his students had studied previously, and demonstrated the advantages and disadvantages of various forms of government. Following this, Greek and Roman history was studied. A jump was made from Augustus to the beginning of the sixteenth century and a study of modern European history which emphasized England and those nations the histories of which were closely connected with hers. The restriction of the study of history to Greek, Roman, and modern European was justified in several ways. It was as much as could conveniently be included in the curriculum, and more than usually was. The graduates so educated were well acquainted with the history of the modern nations most likely to be of concern to them, as well as with that of Greece and Rome, which was regarded as "the History of *Heroism, Virtue* and *Patriotism.*" History thus did its part in the making of the better citizen. Individuals not satisfied by the restricted field might extend it at their leisure, since an important part of their training had been the method by which they might pursue any historical studies that interested them.

Almost as an afterthought, it would seem, Smith added that "Every Sunday Night about an Hour is spent in the Study of the Bible History."

It was held essential to the Miranian scheme that one master should have charge of a class for an entire year rather than that different instructors should teach the class in separate courses. Too many teachers and studies at a time were deemed inadvisable. Instead, related branches of knowledge were grouped together and studied under the same teacher before the students proceeded further. By this method the subjects could be arranged in a natural order, so that the completion of one study led logically to the beginning of the next.

A characteristic of the College of Mirania was the holding

of public exercises performed by the students. Saturdays throughout the school year (which ran for ten months of the calendar year) were devoted to these functions, which included such feats as the *extempore* translation into English, by a member of the first-year class, of a Greek passage set by a member of the third class, who corrected any errors. Sets of theses were offered and impugned, and speeches were given by members of the fourth and fifth classes. Great stress was laid on the fact that these exercises were conducted in the English language. Even more important were the exercises performed on the night of the King's birthday by the fourth, or "Class of Rhetoric," for then its members "entertain the Town with some of our best dramatic Performances." The fifth class did the same at commencements.

The social graces were esteemed in Mirania and were not neglected by its educational institutions. A dancing master was available in the lowest classes of the Latin and Mechanics' schools, while in the college, masters in French, Italian, Spanish, and German gave instruction at private hours, as did a fencing master, who also taught "the military Exercise." These courses were not compulsory, and a rule required those who took them to do so before the fourth year of college, since the work of the last two years was deemed too important to allow other studies to interfere.

Evander left the matter of religion for separate treatment, not only because of its importance, but also because religion and morals were the "chief Object of the Studies of every Class, and consequently cou'd not be brought into the Account of any particular Class." In every subject that was offered, the masters were careful to stress the moral and religious point of view. The microcosm and the macrocosm of physics, for example, were both called upon to furnish instances of the omnipotence of God and His goodness to men. Aratus, particularly, emphasized the moral and religious note and fulfilled the design of the founders of the college, who had looked for more than learning in the men they selected as masters. They

had sought men whose lives should be "a daily Comment on
their Precepts," and whose consciousness of the weight of their
responsibility should make them indefatigable in the discharge
of their duties. The founders realized that upon the securing
of such men depended the reputation of the college and "in
a great Measure, the *Morals* and *Genius,* of the Country to
latest Generations."

In the versions of *Mirania* republished in his *Discourses* and
Works, Smith omitted all that followed Evander's account of
the College of Mirania, since the rest was given over largely
to such temporary concerns as the plan of the buildings, the
methods of raising money, and the choice of a location for
the new college proposed at New York. Pages 73 to 81 of the
original pamphlet were devoted to a conclusion, signed "W.
Smith" and dated from "*Hermitage* on *Long Island,*" March
2, 1753. A postscript was added, under date of April 10, 1753,
being occasioned by a letter which the author had received
from a gentleman in the West Indies "in Return to one sent
Him with my former Pamphlet, in *November* last." The
former pamphlet was undoubtedly *Some Thoughts on Education,* and the postscript dealt largely with one of the major
considerations of the *Thoughts:* the advisability of choosing
New York City as a site for a college. The success of any such
plan depended upon the enrollment of students from a larger
district than the city or even the colony; consequently, the
coöperation of persons outside New York was essential. Smith
quoted the West Indies gentleman as giving his approbation
of the New York site and indicating that many British plant-
ers in the West Indies would rather send their children to New
York than to England. In commenting upon the letter and in
further urging the advantages of New York, Smith was led
by his zeal to include a quotation from the *Monthly Review*
for November 1750, in which the two great English universities were said to be rendered useless by idle doctrines and
corrupt manners. Evidently Smith quickly regretted his im-
petuosity, for the quotation was not allowed to stand in most

of the copies of *Mirania*. A few copies got abroad unchanged and occasioned some criticism of Smith. Smith was on better ground when he spoke of the comparative risk and expense involved in sending children from the West Indies to England or to New York.

The natural question to ask about the *College of Mirania* is: "Where did this young man get his ideas?" Some of them, as one might expect, had been running about the world since the time of Plato. Closer examination is required to discover the sources of the more specific suggestions which constitute the real value of the work. One of the striking features of Mirania was the existence of the separate Mechanics' School. Smith freely acknowledged in his text that this plan owed much to the English School at Philadelphia and to Benjamin Franklin's plans for it, although he did not refer directly to the *Proposals Relating to the Education of Youth in Pensilvania* or to the *Idea of an English School*.

A greater influence on Smith was the two colleges at Aberdeen. It so happened that 1753 was a year in which Marischal College made considerable changes in its system of instruction and King's College, though finally deciding to hold on to the old ways, at least formulated a statement of what those ways were. Anyone familiar with the manner in which universities generally go about making changes cannot doubt that proposals had been in the air for some time before 1753. The introduction of college or house plans and of a semi-tutorial system in several of our universities was discussed for many a year before the innovations were effected. It is improbable that Aberdeen in 1753 was vastly different. Smith must have heard much about the proposed changes, perhaps even as early as his own student days.

The changes of 1753 in Marischal College are covered in an extract from the faculty minutes for January 11 of that year, a transcript of which has been deposited in the library of the University of Pennsylvania. The old order, it was held, was wrong in that it taught the most abstract subjects first; it required the students to master "the Theory and Foundations of Evidence and Reasoning" before they were acquainted with the subjects in which examples could be found to explain or illustrate the abstractions of pure logic. The difficulty of bringing students to conceive abstruse subjects before they were prepared for them was such that it took up a great share of time and left none for "some very useful parts of Knowledge." The faculty found themselves unanimously of the opinion that "the gradual openings of the human mind, as well as the natural order of things" made it proper to begin with the study of particular facts, thence to ascend to general reasonings on these facts, and only then to proceed to the "abstruser inquiries concerning the operations, natures, and states of the mind, the Deity, and Moral and Natural Philosophy founded on them." It was hoped that a change to this natural order would not only make the course more valuable to the students but might even remove "the prejudices some have entertained against University Education as useless." The new order did not involve an entire displacement of the old. The first year was to be spent under the professor of Greek, as it had been previously, and all classes were to continue their customary Sunday evening meetings, with "discourses on such subjects of Natural and Revealed Religion as the Professors shall judge most useful and adapted to the capacities of their Students." The rest of the curriculum was reconstructed:

. . . the semi year, or second of the course, shall be spent in the most useful parts of Natural History, in Geography, and the Elements of Civil History; . . . the tertian, or third of the course, shall be employed in the Scientific parts of Natural Philosophy, Mechanics, Hydrostatics, Pneumatics, Optics, Astronomy, and such other branches not reducible to any of these, as either are in some measure invented already, or may be invented and improved hereafter, as Magnetism, Electricity, &c. . . . the magistrand, or last year, shall be taken up in the Abstract Sciences, or the Philosophy of Spirits, Pneumatology, Ethics, and Logic.

The principal and masters also agreed that it would be to the greater advantage of both teachers and students to have one teacher in charge of a class for a whole year; to this end three members of the faculty were appointed to teach "constantly" the semi, tertian, and magistrand classes, respectively.

In addition to the detail of Sunday evening meetings (which probably were not unique to Marischal), Smith obviously drew more upon Marischal than upon his own King's College for his idea of assigning a single teacher to each year of the course, because in the same year of 1753 the masters of King's College, after long and deliberate consideration of whether the students should "through all the three years of their Philosophy course, be under the care of the same Professor," or whether "the three Professors of Philosophy should confine themselves, each to a different Branch of Philosophy, and the Students to pass a Session under each of them successively," decided to continue their "antient Practice." The extra labor which the ancient practice of regenting imposed upon the professors was thought to be more than balanced by the benefits of greater intimacy between student and professor.

One feature of his system, however, Smith seems to have taken from King's College:

That the Students may have the benefit of those Parts of Education, which are not commonly reconed Academical, such as Dancing, Writing, Book-Keeping, French, &c. without losing Time in attending Masters at a distance from the College; the Sub-principal and Regents, shall appoint Rooms in the College, and proper Hours when these things may be taught, and Shall bespeak Masters of the best Character and Qualifications, for instructing those who choose to attend them.

Most of the King's College rules of 1753 were given over to the statement of formal and administrative regulations rather than to educational policy, but it was noted that the professors of philosophy had unanimously agreed to spend much less time upon the "Logic and Metaphysic of the Schoolmen," which seemed to them designed largely to make men subtle disputants, and to spend more time upon those subjects "which may qualify Men for the more useful and important Offices of Society." Like their brethren at Marischal, the faculty of King's was agreed that "those parts of Philosophy, which are conversant about objects of sense ought in the Order of teaching to precede those which have the mind and its Faculties for their Objects." The course of study ran closely parallel to that of Marischal.

It is apparent then that, although Smith was indebted for certain features of the College of Mirania to the influence of Aberdeen, the hypothetical college was essentially the product of his own richly imaginative and original thinking. The duality of outlook which laid emphasis upon both the personal and the social justifications of the study of literature is typical of the whole conception. Better men and better citizens were to be made by his plan. As better men, they were to be of more use to themselves, if one may so phrase it—more able to understand and appreciate the physical and intellectual world that lay about them. As better citizens, they were to be of more use to the world. The two rôles are to some degree concomitant, but Smith was right in his sureness that they were not altogether or necessarily so, and that both needed emphasis in a well-rounded plan of education. Too often was the old-fashioned scholastic mind, even when able to elevate itself out of the dust of minutiæ, merely concerned with trying to produce a better citizen and a better man in an almost exclusively moral sense, with little regard to the happiness of that man or to his future intellectual development. Smith was quick to see that education was rightly the affair of a lifetime rather than of a few juvenile years. Thence came his emphasis upon teaching his pupils a method by which they might learn for themselves, and his small concern over whether they knew all the facts of history. More important to him than how to teach a subject was what subject to teach, and what effect the subject would have upon the students. It was the human product of the educational machine, not the workings of the cogwheels of the machine, that appealed to Smith. Of course cogwheels are necessary to a machine, and at times Smith entered into what may seem like small detail. But his chief concern, though not dissipated or grandiose, was for the larger aspects of the educational problem. In reading *Mirania*, one notices the details, but carries away with him a picture of the whole and a conviction of a large mind animating the whole.

Mirania was not especially fruitful in immediate results, for as Smith himself said later of the New York scheme, "A very laudable and promising seminary was opened about six months afterwards in that province, on a plan somewhat different." The Reverend Dr. Samuel Johnson was to become the first president of the seminary—King's College (the present Columbia), popularly called the College of New York. That Smith was welcome to a position there is shown by a letter which he wrote to Dr. Johnson in May of 1753. "I am infinitely obliged to you for what you write about the College," Smith told Johnson. "If anything could prevail on me to alter my resolutions, it would be to be brought up at the feet, or might I fondly add, to live in the bosom of Dr. Johnson. But I am fixed, and rationally fixed, in my purpose as I hope I shall be able to convince you." What this purpose was Dr. Johnson must already have known, for Smith did not mention it further except to say, "I shall sail about the 10th June." Smith acknowledged in this letter some remarks by Johnson on *Mirania*. Johnson's query about the omission of Hebrew, Smith answered with as great candor as another Dr. Johnson replied to the lady who questioned his definition of pastern: "The Hebrew I quite forgot and some things else. It should in my opinion be taught in the fifth class at leisure hours, to such as are designed for Holy Orders."

The usefulness of *Mirania* was not, however, at an end. The day it was published, Smith had sent a copy to Benjamin

Franklin at Philadelphia, probably because he wished to acknowledge his reference to Franklin's plan for an English school and also because he was aware of Franklin's general interest in matters educational. On the nineteenth of April 1753, Franklin replied:

I received your Fav^r of the 11th Instant, with your new Piece on Education, which I shall carefully peruse, and give you my sentiments of it as you desire, by next Post.

I believe the young Gentlemen, your Pupils, may be entertain'd and instructed here, in Mathematics & Philosophy to Satisfaction. Mr Allison (who was educated at Edinburgh, or Glasgow) has been long accustomed to teach the latter, and Mr Grew the former, and I think their Pupils make great Progress. Mr Allison has the Care of the Latin and Greek School, but as he has now three good Assistants in that School, he can very well afford some Hours every Day for the Instruction of those who are engag'd in higher Studies. The Mathematical School is pretty well furnished with Instruments. The English Library is a good one, and we have belonging to it a midling Apparatus for Experimental Philosophy, and propose speedily to compleat it. The Loganian Library, one of the best Collections in America, will shortly be opened; so that neither Books nor Instrum^{ts} will be wanting; and as we are determin'd always to give good Salaries, we have reason to believe we may have always an Opportunity of choosing good Masters; upon which, indeed, the Success of the whole depends. We are oblig'd to you for your kind Offers in that Respect, and when you are settled in England, we may occasionally make use of your Friendship and Judgment. . . .

If it suits your Conveniency to visit Philadelphia, before your Return to Europe, I shall be extreamly glad to see & converse with you here, as well as to coresp^d with you after your Settlement in England. For an Acquaintance and Communication with Men of Learning, Virtue and Publick Spirit, is one of my greatest Enjoyments.

I do not know whether you ever happen'd to see the first Proposals I made for the Erecting this Academy. I send them enclos'd. They had (however imperfect) the desired Success, being followed by a Subscription of £4000 towards carrying them into Execution. And as we are fond of receiving Advice, and are daily improving by Experience, I am in hopes we shall in a few Years see a perfect Institution.

> I am very respectfully, Sir,
> Your most hum¹ Servᵗ
> B FRANKLIN

The second paragraph of this letter confirms the impression afforded by other Smith correspondence that Smith was originally interested in the academy at Philadelphia as a place in which his two young charges, the Martin boys, might continue their education after his contemplated return to England. In the letter to Dr. Johnson, already mentioned, Smith regretted his inability to accept an invitation to visit Johnson until after his return from Philadelphia, "whither I propose to go the 24th inst. to fix my pupils in the academy there." Yet between April 19 and May 3, 1753, there seems to have occurred a change in Smith's relationship to Philadelphia, judging from the advice Franklin gave him in a letter written on the latter date:

. . . you may depend on my doing all in my Power to make your visit to Philadelphia agreeable to you. Yet methinks I would not have you omit bringing a Line or two to Mʳ Allen [a trustee of the academy]. If you are more notic'd here on Account of such Recommendation, yet as that Recommendⁿ will be founded on your Merit, known best where you have so long resided, this Notice may be esteemed to be as much *"on the Score of something you can call your own,"* as if it were merely on Accᵗ of the Pieces you have written.

The implication certainly is that Smith was interested in more than merely fixing his pupils in the academy. Other remarks in this letter indicate that *Mirania* had begun to make an impression in Philadelphia:

Mʳ Peters has just now been with me, and we have compar'd Notes on your new Piece. We find nothing in the Scheme of Education, however excellent, but what is, in our Opinion, very practicable. . . . We have both receiv'd great Pleasure in the Perusal of it. For my Part, I know not when I have read a Piece that has so affected me, so noble & just are the Sentiments, so warm and animated the Language. . . .

Mr Allen . . . directed me to procure him 6 of your Pieces, tho' he had not and has not yet seen it. Mr Peters has taken 10. He purposed to have wrote to you; but omits it as he expects so soon to have the Pleasure of seeing you here.

The exact date of Smith's arrival in Philadelphia is unknown, but he probably reached the city shortly after May 24, 1753; he remained at least until the fifth of June. The visit was a great satisfaction to him. It gave him an opportunity to inspect the academy—which he did with enthusiasm—and to discuss theories of education with men actively engaged in the conduct of a school. As the author of *Mirania*, he enjoyed attentions which must have been gratifying. Before leaving the city, he honored the trustees with *A Poem On Visiting the Academy of Philadelphia, June, 1753*, acknowledging in the preface, dated June 5, "the undeserv'd Notice many of you were pleas'd to take of me during my short Stay in your City, and the Honor the Academy (when I first went into it) did me, in making one of the Youth speak a Copy of Verses, which I lately wrote to promote the Interest of *Science*." Smith described the poem which he was offering the trustees as one which modestly hinted at the virtues to be inculcated through education. Admitting that the performance was inferior to the subject, he asked their acceptance of it as it was, since he had no time to improve it "during my Stay in *America*." This remark makes it appear that Smith's intention still was to return to England, either for a temporary stay or for permanent settlement.

On June 7, 1753, an advertisement in the *Pennsylvania Gazette* announced that there would be published the following week a volume of *Prayers, for the Use of the Philadelphia Academy*. Thomas H. Montgomery, in his *History of the University of Pennsylvania*, suggested that these prayers were composed by Smith at the time of his visit to Philadelphia. This ascription does not seem altogether tenable, particularly with regard to the first item, "A Morning Prayer, To be used by every Scholar in his Chamber at rising from Bed," the tone of which is a bit more pietistic and, one might almost say, servile than one is accustomed to expect from Smith. On the other hand, the "General Evening Prayer" not only sounds more in Smith's usual vein, but actually recurs in a revised form in a volume known to be his, of somewhat later date. What is probably true is that Smith was asked to contribute to a volume of prayers already undertaken by others at Philadelphia, perhaps by the Reverend Mr. Richard Peters, who was greatly interested in the academy and was one of its trustees.

During his visit in Philadelphia, Smith undoubtedly discussed with Benjamin Franklin and some of the other trustees the hopes which they had of raising their academy to a college. The author of *Mirania*, full of ideas about colleges, was just the person to expand on the subject. Franklin was quick to see in this young man a zealous worker, who would be indefatigable in the pursuit of a plan which he favored. And certainly he would favor no plan more than one which he had himself devised. Franklin probably suggested to Smith that Philadelphia's Aratus might well be William Smith; the idea fell on fertile soil. But, Franklin felt it necessary to add, although he was eager to see a college at Philadelphia, his enthusiasm was not generally shared. Even those who agreed with him about the desirability of a college could not see where the financial support would come from. If the Penns, the proprietaries of Pennsylvania, could be prevailed upon to give financial aid, the story would be quite different. It seems very likely that Franklin not only told Smith about this phase of the situation, but went further and said that if Smith would use what influence he might be able to bring to bear (through his church connections) on the Penns, a successful issue of such an appeal would be followed by his appointment to head the new college. Whether he went this far or not, Franklin certainly must have told Smith that he hoped to see the academy enlarged into a college and that he looked favorably upon Smith to head the institution. Smith could not have been at all averse to the prospect. Yet he was wise enough to realize that not all prospects mature. As late as July 23, 1753, in a letter to Dr. Johnson, he said that a return to America was not his "present resolution."

Nor was it his resolution to return to schoolmastering in Scotland; that, at least, was behind him. Whatever Smith's plans in England were, it is made clear by letters he took with him that he intended to enter the orders of the Church of England, but whether as a basis for a career in the church or in education, one cannot be sure. It would be pleasant to be the master of an English college, and the way to such an eminence was through the church. The church itself offered a promising field to such men as Smith. Indeed, the Archbishop of Canterbury was later to remark that if Smith had remained in England, he would have been under the archiepiscopal eye: that distant sound is the rustle of lawn. The Philadelphia offer now intruded itself upon a situation that was already fairly complex, for there were at least two other possibilities in America which must have appealed to him, despite his resolution not to return. Dr. Samuel Johnson was still eager that Smith should assist him in the College of New York whenever it was started. And there was always the prospect of settling in New York as a clergyman. Smith was on good terms with the leaders of the church in New York and had served them well with his pen. The nature of the so-called "church controversy" in New York in 1753, Smith's part in it, and the regard in which he was held by his associates there may best be seen in a letter which Samuel Johnson wrote to the Archbishop of Canterbury on June 25, 1753:

Among other pernicious Books the *Independent Whigg* grows much in Vogue, & a notable Sett of Young Gentlemen of Figure in New York, have of late set up for Writers in that Way, in a Weekly paper called the *Independent Reflector.*— Several worthy Gentlemen of the Church in that province have of late been embarked in a Design of erecting a College as a Seminary of the Church, tho' with a free & generous Toleration for other Denominations.—Upon which these Reflectors have been indefatigable in their paper, & by all possible means both public & private, endeavouring to Spirit up the people against us, & to wrest it out of the Churche's Hands, & make it a Sort of free-thinking or latitudinarian Seminary, as your Grace will see by several of these papers Mr Smith will lay before you.

We have several of us been writing in the Churche's Defense against them, & endeavouring, not without some Success to defeat their pernicious Schemes.—Among others, I beg leave to inform your Grace how much we are obliged to this young Gentleman for his excellent Labours, whose behaviour hath been very virtuous inoffensive & amiable in all respects, & who hath exerted himself with great Zeal & Industry, & no less good Sense & Discretion in the Churche's Cause, & hath wrote several Things with very good Advantage for promoting that College, & for the Advancement of Learning in these parts, & particularly an excellent Draught of a College, a Copy of which I herewith send your Grace, by which you will see to how good purpose he hath spent his time, & with what a benevolent & affectionate public Spirit he hath been consulting the best Interest of this Country, tho' a Stranger in it.—We are extremely loth to part with him, as he would make a very excellent Tutor in our College, especially in the Belles Lettres, & I humbly beg your Graces Influence with him that he may return again to us for this purpose.—

When Smith wrote to Johnson on July 23, 1753, he mentioned that "We sail on Thursday for certain, as the captain says, but probably it will be Sunday." The actual date of the sailing is a matter of conjecture, but it must certainly have been earlier than October 13, 1753, the date given by Horace W. Smith. Likewise, it must have been later than July 26, the first Thursday after July 23, for Smith took with him a letter from Governor James De Lancey to the Archbishop of Canterbury dated from New York on July 27, 1753. He also carried letters from Henry Barclay of New York to the Archbishop and to the Bishop of Oxford. In the latter letter, under date of "July ye 25th," Barclay told "My Lord of Oxford" that Smith proposed "soon after his arrival at London to visit Oxford, and devote some Time there to the Study of Divinity, in which your Lordships Countenance and Recommendation will be of great Service to him." Apparently Smith did not follow out this proposal, since the Bishop of Oxford (Thomas Secker, later Archbishop of Canterbury) wrote to Samuel Johnson from the Deanery of St. Paul's on March 19, 1754, that if Smith "had pursued his intention of residing awhile at Oxford, I should have hoped for more of his company and acquaintance," adding that Smith was "indeed, a very ingenious and able, and seems a very well-disposed young man."

Having left New York on or shortly after July 27, 1753, Smith could not have been in England long before reporting to the Archbishop of Canterbury, who wrote on his behalf to Thomas Penn from Croydon House on September 19, 1753. The Archbishop was genuinely interested in young Smith, whom he had first known as a lobbyist for the schoolmasters of Scotland. Some months later, in a letter to Franklin and Peters, Smith revealed with remarkable candor the advice he had received and his reasons for following it:

. . . He [the Archbishop] has been very kind to me. I have seen him oft, & he said he would provide for me. But when I let him know the project for my return, he press'd it, & writ to Mr Penn on the subject. He said I would have an opportunity of doing more good with you than in England; & that the Encouragement would be better than I could expect at first setting out in England even if I had the greatest friends. This, with the precariousness of the Archb^p's life, as he is in a very bad state of health, determined me; for if he should die, he is the only person I know that bestows his favors on unfriended Merit.

The good Archbishop, probably unaware that the state of his health as well as his advice had influenced Smith, had this to say of him to Thomas Penn:

He is a Scholar & ingenious, & what is of the highest consequence of a temper fitted, as it seems to me to pursue a Plan of Education upon the large & generous footing of aiming at the Publick Good, wth no other Biass or partiality but preserving his Duty to the Constitution of his Mother Country, consistently wth a warm regard to the service of the Colonies,

& the universal benefit of the various People that compose them. I think I am not mistaken in him.

In replying from Braywich on September 23, 1753, Penn took the occasion to state that "Mr Smith appears to me of a Temper and disposition fit for the office, some of the Trustees have desired him to accept, and shal have my countenance and friendship—whenever that can be of service to him."

The countenance and friendship of Penn were doubly important to Smith. In the first place, it was becoming increasingly clear that the plans for a college in Philadelphia would fail without financial help from the outside. As Franklin wrote to Smith on November 27, 1753:

A Majority of the Trustees, I find, would be glad to see a Rector establish'd there, but they dread entring into new Engagements 'till they are got out of Debt; . . . Thus, unless the Proprietors shall think fit to put the finishing Hand to our Institution, it must, I fear, wait some few Years longer before it can arrive at that State of Perfection which to me it seems now to be capable of; and all the Pleasure I promis'd myself in seeing you settled among us, vanishes into Smoke.

The "finishing Hand" was of course the giving hand. To secure Penn's interest in the plan for a college sufficiently to earn not only his approbation but also some of his money was a task in which Smith joined the efforts which Franklin and others were directing toward Penn. Secondly, Smith needed to secure Penn's approval of him as the head of the institution. Penn's reply to the Archbishop, quoted above, shows that Smith made an immediately favorable impression. Smith's success in this double-barreled project he related in a long letter to Franklin and Peters. Although undated, this letter (now in the possession of the American Philosophical Society) shows by internal references that it was written in February or March of 1754.

The loss of a very large packet (which took me up above a week's writing) sent by Capt Davis, is the reason why I have not communicated to you before now, the Success I have had in several Schemes for your Province. My whole time has been spent this way, & you'll see by those papers I send you that I have been pretty constantly employed. There are 3 or 4 letters of great importance, I cannot now send you, the originals being lost with Davis, unless I should trouble Mr Penn to take them from his Copies. It would have been well if you had seen all the steps taken, with the Archb^p's, Mr Collinson's & other letters; but this you shall know by word of mouth. Those I send will make you master of the Schemes. The one of them I just borrowed from Mr Collinson & copied with some assistance. It is the 2^d Part of a long letter to Mr Penn, & contains the Scheme for your Academy & the Arguments for it, which I hope are conformable to your own Sentiments. You'll see it must be kept private. Mr Penn has come in to every part of it, & he will give a yearly Sum for some time, & when he comes to Pennsylvania intends to give a Manor to the Academy for the purposes I have pointed out. He ask'd me at first what I thought would be the best way of bestowing his donation, & you'll see how disinterested I was to propose a new object for one half of it, when the whole might otherwise have been applied for a philosophy Prof^r But I shall always glory to prefer private to public good, & I rejoice exceedingly to have been the Means of two such Foundations, which, being once made by the proprietor, he will not desert for the sake of a small additional expence. It would not become me to say how many Arguments I used to bring these Schemes to bear. The proprietor was not at first satisfy'd that such liberal institutions were useful in an infant Country. Your Academy also interfered with a Design he had in view of his own, & of which he intended to be the Founder. These & many other Circumstances were obstacles. But when I was able to shew the worthy Gentleman the necessity of such a seminary in a political light, he generously agreed to ingraft his Scheme upon yours in the two Foundations proposed, provided I would undertake to be the person to execute them. Tho' I had not, nor have not yet, heard from either of you I agreed to this, hoping that the person who had been the great Means of such an Union (which otherwise might have been the work of Years) even if not personally known to you, would be welcome to all the Trustees, when he comes recommended by the proprietor, with an order for foundations, by one of which, he will be in a great measure supported, with small addition from you. . . .

It is indeed unfortunate that Captain Davis' ship was lost, for otherwise one might know what the "two Foundations" were that Penn made and just how much was to be applied to the salary of the "philosophy Prof^r." All that existing records show is that an annual donation of £50 to Smith's salary was made by the proprietors for several years, until the promised grant of a manor to the college was substituted. The incompleteness of such material as has been saved from the perils of the sea and the subsequent perils of time makes it impossible to say just when Smith and Penn came to their agreement and Smith determined to return to Philadelphia. Smith's ordination to the priesthood is a significant clue. In the *College of Mirania* Smith had specified that the principal was to be a clergyman of the established religion, and he probably felt that he should exemplify as far as he could the qualifications he had himself set up for the head of a college. The Philadelphia trustees may have set up a similar ideal for their Aratus, should they have one. Accordingly, on Friday, December 21, 1753, "at the chapel within the palace at ffulham," Smith was ordained a deacon by John [Thomas], Lord Bishop of Lincoln, acting for Thomas [Sherlock], Lord Bishop of London. On the following Sunday, December 23, in the same chapel, Richard [Osbaldeston], Lord Bishop of Carlisle acted for the Bishop of London in ordaining Smith as a priest. It is interesting to notice that Samuel Seabury, later to become one of the prominent figures of the church in America, was also ordained on these occasions. Smith must have been virtually certain of Philadelphia by December 23, for not only did he obtain ordination from the Bishop of London, whose diocese included the colonies, but he also, on the day he was raised to the priesthood, secured a license from the same prelate entitling him to exercise his clerical functions in Pennsylvania.

On the last day of the eventful year of 1753, William Smith preached in the church in which he had been baptized. If family and friends at Aberdeen were sorry at his decision to cast his lot in the new world, it was only because he was going so far away; like him, they realized the opportunity which awaited him there.

The *Gentleman's Magazine* of London for December 1753 contained "A brief Account of the Academy in the City of Philadelphia." In the light of what Smith had been working for during the preceding months, the closing passage of this account takes on particular interest: ". . . it may reasonably be expected that such additions will be made to the present fund, as will improve it into a collegiate institution, and a seminary for every kind of science." According to the custom of the *Gentleman's Magazine*, the name of the author was not given, but one cannot be far wrong in suspecting that William Smith somehow had a hand in the piece. He may even have been anticipating the day when he would make a general appeal to the English public for financial aid.

Another Pennsylvania project that enlisted Smith's services while he was in England was the education of Germans in Pennsylvania, about which he conferred with various interested persons and with the Society for the Propagation of the Gospel. Other tasks helped to keep Smith extremely busy. Some of his time was taken up in arranging for an English edition of one of his own works. The *Indian Songs of Peace*, printed in New York in 1752, was now revised and took its title, *The Speech of A Creek Indian*, from an addition Smith made to its contents. This was published in 1754 by Ralph Griffiths, a bookseller in St. Paul's Church-Yard, London. Another edition was published that year from the same plates, under the more prosaic title of *Some Account of the North-American Indians*.

Smith also prepared for the press a London edition of the *Elementa Philosophica* of his good friend, Samuel Johnson of New York. The preface which Smith wrote for the new edition again demonstrates his interest in all that pertained to education. "That a right education of youth is of the very highest importance to society, is a truth as universally acknowledged as it seems little attended to," he proclaimed, and went on to say that of all parts of education, that which regarded the morals of the people was worthy of the greatest attention, "for upon this depends all good government and social advantages." Smith made a number of alterations and some additions to Johnson's text, following, at least partially, suggestions made by Johnson himself, although the author later felt that his editor had been perhaps overgenerous with changes. At the end of the book, Smith substituted a prayer which he had written himself for one which Johnson had taken from Wollaston's *Religion of Nature*. He also appended "A Letter containing Some Impartial Thoughts Concerning the Settlement of Bishops in America. By the Author and Some of his Brethren," dated July 13, 1753. In writing to the Bishop of Oxford on October 25, 1754, Johnson stated that this letter was largely of Smith's composition, although based upon papers and letters furnished by Johnson. The subject of obtaining the episcopate for the colonies was one that was to concern almost every clerical and lay member of the Church of England in the colonies. The letter emphasized one of the more tragic aspects of the lack of an American episcopacy: the fearful loss of life on the part of candidates for orders in that day of perilous ocean crossings.

Smith, at any rate, made a safe and reasonably rapid return trip from England to America, leaving London on April 5, 1754, and reaching Philadelphia on the twenty-second of May. Three days later, this minute was entered in the records of the trustees of the Academy of Philadelphia:

The Question being put, Whether it be necessary at this Time to provide a Person in the Academy to teach Logick Rhetorick Ethicks and Natural Philosophy? it was carried in the Affirmative by a great Majority.—

It being proposed that Mr William Smith, a Gentleman lately arrived from London should be entertain'd for some time upon Trial, to teach the abovementioned Branches of Learning, in Case he will undertake it; the same was agreed to and Mr Franklin and Mr Peters are desired to speak with him about it.—

With his acceptance of this offer, the "Gentleman lately arrived from London" entered upon a new phase of his career. Previously he had engaged in devising schemes of education; now he was to try to put theory into practice. The College of Mirania had existed in an unspecified degree of latitude. Now it was to be called forth into actuality in a red-brick town on the Delaware, far removed from that gray granite city on the North Sea where the original idea for Mirania had probably entered Smith's head.

III

THE COLLEGE AND ACADEMY
OF PHILADELPHIA

WILLIAM SMITH had neither the advantages nor the disadvantages inherent in starting an educational institution *de novo* when he arrived in Philadelphia. The academy which he was to serve and in which he had previously placed his charges, the Martin boys, was able, even in 1753, to look back on a little history of its own. In 1740, during the height of the enthusiasm aroused in Philadelphia by the preaching of George Whitefield, a movement was undertaken to provide him with a meetinghouse, since most of the clergy of the city had seen fit to close their pulpits to him. Jonathan Price on September 15 of that year deeded a lot on Fourth Street to four persons, as trustees, with a dual purpose in mind:

A considerable number of persons, of different denominations in religion, having united to erect a large building on the lot, intending that the same should be appointed to the use of a charity school for the instruction of poor children *gratis*, in useful literature and of the Christian religion, and also that the same building should be used as a house of public worship . . .

The four persons named as trustees accepted their appointment in a deed of November 14, 1740. On February 1, 1749, they conveyed the property to another set of trustees (substantially the same names as those listed in the charter of the Academy and Charitable School in 1753) for use as a school, specifying that the building should be kept available for its original religious purposes and that it should particularly be available to Whitefield "whenever he shall happen to be in the city, and desire to preach therein."

The new trustees enlarged the original plan to include not only a charity school but also an academy for paying students. The academy opened on January 8, 1750/51, on which occa-

43

sion the Reverend Mr. Richard Peters preached a dedicatory
sermon from a text perfectly suited to such an occasion: "And
ye shall know the Truth, and the Truth shall make you free."
The charity school was opened in September 1751. Governor
James Hamilton issued a charter incorporating the school under
the title of "The Trustees of the Academy and Charitable
School in the province of Pennsylvania" on July 13, 1753, in
the name of Thomas and Richard Penn, "true and absolute proprietors and governors in chief of the province of Pennsylvania."

It was this institution, then, that William Smith found await-
ing his return from England. He found an academy; he erected
upon it a college, and a college based upon larger principles
and a wider conception of the means and ends of education
than any other at that time extant in America.

Smith entered upon his active duties at Philadelphia in May
of 1754. Less than a month later he gave way to his youthful
penchant for versifying; new situations and new ideas were to
him as the grain of sand is to the oyster, though he did not
have the same faculty for producing pearls. Philadelphia at the
time was graced by the presence of Lewis Hallam and his company of actors, playing under a permit issued by Governor
Robert Hunter Morris. On June 19, 1754, five nights before
the close of the season, a special benefit performance of the
Careless Husband and *Harlequin Collector* was presented. The
next day's *Pennsylvania Gazette* spoke of the audience as "very
crowded and polite." The interesting thing about the performance is that it was given, in the *Gazette's* words, "for the
Benefit of the *Charity Children* belonging to the Academy of
this City." Mr. Rigby, of the actors' company, spoke a specially
written prologue. If William Smith, in two different lists of
his works drawn up by himself, had not included this prologue, one might not attach much interest to it. Under the
circumstances, as Smith's first literary production during his
Philadelphia residence, the piece acquires a certain significance:

Our humble *Prologue* means not to engage
Candor for Scenes that long have grac'd the Stage;
Nor vainly strives to pay with Words, at last,
For cheering Smiles, and kind *Protection* past.
Weak is the Power of Language to explain
The sacred Feelings, or th' ingenuous Pain
And silent strugglings of the virtuous Breast,
Beneath the Load of *Gratitude* opprest.
But tho' no Words can picture what we feel,
Our *Aims* may speak it, and our *Actions* tell.
To Night we glory in the double View
Of pleasing soft-ey'd CHARITY—and You.
For this our cheerful Service we bestow,—
'Tis all our slender Fortunes will allow;
"And those who give the little in their Power,"
The *Skies* acquit—and *Earth* can ask no more!
Thrice happy you, whom kinder Fates have given,
With liberal Hand, to ease the Care of Heaven!
To raise the drooping Head of modest Worth;
From Fortune's Blast to shield the *Orphan-Birth,*
To pierce the dark Retreats where Mis'ry sighs,
And wipe the trickling Tear that dews her Eyes;—
If Deeds like these can bid the Bosom glow
With Joys sincere—what Bosom glows not now?
For sure, if aught be *gen'rous, great* or *fair,*
It must be—TRUTH and *public* WORTH to rear!
Where *Virtue* blooms in yonder hallow'd *Ground,
With each ennobling Science op'ning round;
How many †*Maids* and *Youths*, with kindling Fires,
Now grow in all that living Worth inspires,
Whom Fortune, in their Dawn, neglected laid,
To pine untutor'd in the barren Shade,
Where *Wisdom* never did her Page unrol,
And Want still froze the Current of their Soul;
Till, by your bounteous Hand, redeem'd from Fate,
You bade them rise to grace a rising State.
Thus pinch'd beneath stern Winter's rigid Reign,
The Flowers lie mourning thro' the frozen Plain,
Till *Spring*, soft issuing from her southern Hall,
Sweeps o'er the Dew-bright Lawn, with breezy Call,

* *The Academy.*   † *The Charity Children*

And wakes them into Life:—They straight unfold
To th' orient Sun their vegetable Gold;
And in Return embalm the fost'ring Air,
Or grace the lovely Bosoms of the Fair.

The benefit was markedly successful; the trustees voted to accept "upwards of an Hundred pounds" which had been raised thereby.

Before his first summer in Philadelphia was over, there devolved upon Smith the sad duty of preaching the funeral sermon for one of Colonel Martin's sons, William Thomas, who died August 28, 1754. "And as the Preacher seem'd sensibly touch'd with his Subject, and was known to have loved the Deceased, who had grown up under him for several Years, and was a Plant reared by his own Hand, the Discourse had a very great Effect upon the Audience." So reported the *Pennsylvania Gazette*. The sermon displayed a teacher profoundly interested in his pupils and their welfare, particularly their moral welfare. There was nothing macabre or overly marmoreal about it. A touch of great interest was added to the published sermon by the inclusion of verses addressed to Smith by five of his pupils—Francis Hopkinson, Samuel Magaw, Jacob Duché, Thomas Barton, and Paul Jackson—testifying to the effect upon them of his sermon. The verses show the authors' affection for their fellow student and for their professor of philosophy. Also included with the published sermon was a hymn composed by Smith as a sort of recapitulation of the points established in the sermon. While by no means to be ranked among the great hymns of the world, the piece has few conspicuous faults and represents a marked advance over much of Smith's earlier versifying, as perhaps the first of its five stanzas may indicate:

Father of *all!* still wise and good,
    Whether Thou giv'st or tak'st away;
Before thy Throne devoutly bow'd,
    We hail thy *providential* Sway!

The sincere and mutual affection which seems to have grown up between Smith and his pupils almost at once, to judge by this sermon, the pupils' poems, and Smith's mention of his pupils in the preface, must have convinced him that he had made no mistake in coming to the Academy of Philadelphia. As late as May 27, 1754, Samuel Johnson was still hopeful that Smith might assist him at New York, but by June 10 he had to concede to a correspondent that "Smith is like to settle at Philadelphia so that I know not what we shall do."

On Tuesday, November 12, 1754, occurred the first instance of what was to become familiar in the affairs of schools under Smith's charge: a public exercise by the students. "The Exercises were ushered in," the *Pennsylvania Gazette* for November 14 told its readers, "with a Prologue, which (excepting the Lines mark'd with inverted Commas) was written by the ingenious young Orator who spoke it. The marked lines were added or altered by the Hand that wrote the Epilogue, and digested the Whole." The "ingenious young Orator" was Jacob Duché, and any doubt that "the Hand which digested the Whole" was that of William Smith is dispelled by the fact that Smith himself so stated in a codicil to his will listing some of his writings. In the epilogue, spoken by Master Billy Hamilton ("under 9 yrs of age"), the audience received this prophecy and promise:

> 'Tis gen'rous thus, with your applauding Smile,
> To fire their Souls for Fame, and sooth their Toil.
> When some few Years have ripen'd them in Knowledge
> And Time subdues the Stiffness of the College,
> In humble gratitude—they bid me say—
> For all your kind indulgence shewn To-day— }
> They'll act for You—some more *engaging* play.

Prologue and epilogue framed a series of orations by various members of the upper classes of the academy. Several of the orations were published in successive issues of the *Pennsylvania Gazette*, although a promise made in the account of the exercises to print all of them was never fulfilled. Francis Hopkinson delivered the first oration, "On Education in General," and showed that he was a true pupil of William Smith, for he declared that the "proper education of Youth" was the only means by which good government could be assured, and closed with the assertion that:

. . . it is the Business of a right Education, to train up a Succession of Men for becoming fit Members of the Kingdom of GOD, as well as good Citizens of this World!

Samuel Magaw delivered "An Enquiry into the several Branches of Education, in order to ascertain the just Importance or Moment of each," Josiah Martin delivered an address to the trustees and the governor, and John Hall spoke simply "On Logic." The names of the speakers "On Method" and "On Moral Philosophy" were not recorded, since their speeches, though mentioned in the account, were never published. Either the *Gazette* ran out of space or its readers of patience before the whole of the contemplated series was printed. An account of the exercise also appeared in the *Gentleman's Magazine*, London, for January 1755, with a prefatory letter signed "Philo-Americanus."

It was natural that the author of *Mirania* should have wanted to erect a college at Philadelphia. The feeling that he would be able to do this had been one of the strongest inducements for returning to that city. Mirania's college had depended upon an academy, the pupils of which in turn progressed through the higher school; Philadelphia, provided with academy and students, lacked only the college. Francis Alison, rector of the academy, and Smith represented to the trustees at their meeting December 10, 1754, that it would be an advantage to be able to grant degrees. The trustees asked them "to draw up a Clause to be added to the Charter for that Purpose." Instead of a clause, they drew up a new charter, which they brought to the trustees' meeting of January 14, 1755. After some revision by a committee of the trustees, the document was accepted by the board and the government was petitioned to grant it. The new charter provided for a college as well as an academy, and specified that the new institution was to be headed by a provost and vice-provost. The title of provost, although in use at Worcester College, Oxford, was not usual in educational circles, American, English, or Scottish, but it was employed in Scotland for a civic official corresponding to the English and American mayor. Its use at Philadelphia must beyond question be attributed to Smith and to the College of Mirania, the head of which was called "*Provost* or *Principal*." Blank spaces were left in the charter for the names of the first provost and vice-provost. On February 22, 1755, Smith wrote to Richard Peters:

Mr Allen and you having signified to Mr Alison and me that the Trustees propose us the Honor of filling up the Blanks in the Charter with our Names, & desired us to confer together on the Subject, we have complied with that desire . . .

The result of this conference was that Smith was chosen to be provost and Alison vice-provost, largely because it was felt that Smith, being in charge of the teaching of the upper classes, should have the dignity and title correspondent thereto. Smith, however, was careful to stress that "I need not tell you that I think Mr Alison qualified for any Station in any College," and he requested the trustees to add "Rector of the Academy" to that gentleman's title, in order to emphasize that he had in no measure been demoted from his former position, but that a new dignity had been added to it. The whole letter breathed a spirit that promised well for the harmonious conduct of the new institution. The charter, with the names of Smith and Alison inscribed, was formally issued and recorded on June 16, 1755. The trustees had officially named Smith provost on March 7; on July 11, 1755, they set his salary at £200 a year.

Smith's reception at Philadelphia, as well as some of the difficulties (largely financial) under which he was laboring, was set forth in a letter to Thomas Penn on May 1, 1755:

. . . When I said Philadelphia seemed shy of Strangers, I did not mean to complain in my own Case. Those whom a

good Man would desire to be acquainted with have been so far
from being shy of me, that I have even been courted by them.
I have many more Acquaintances than I can possibly pay due
Civilities to, consistent with my Duty to the College, which
you may be sure neither Preaching nor Company shall divert
me from. I have not preached since Christmass, & cannot find
Time to compose any Thing this Way in such a Manner as I
would chuse to address the public. When my first Course of
Lectures is finished I shall have more Leisure, as all afterwards
will be little more than a Repetition of the same Subjects. And
when I can afford the Time, I am persuaded the Trustees
would not object to my profiting myself by preaching sometimes. As to what you hint about the Office of a Preacher being inconsistent with that of Head of a College, there might
be more Force in it, if the Trustees could afford an independent Salary; but as Matters stand I fear they will never find
Men of Learning and Character, as Masters, unless they permit them to better their Circumstances by any other Profession that is not inconsistent with the Duty of a Master. For
my Part as the Trustees have so far confided in me as to place
me in the Character of Provost or Head of their Seminary, you
may depend upon my doing every Thing in my Power for
its Reputation; & if I had not been fully resolved to do this,
I should not so easily have quitted my Expectations from other
Quarters . . .

The expectations to which Smith referred will readily be
understood to be those in New York and in England. Financial
difficulties were not limited to the new Provost. Then as now,
educational institutions were continually short of funds. A
means of raising money, no longer available, was utilized by
the Philadelphia trustees: seven different lotteries were held
for the benefit of the College and Academy before 1764.

It is difficult in discussing the work of a teacher and head of
an educational institution to distinguish between his relations
with the institution as such and his relations with his pupils.
If it was the provost of the College and Academy of Philadelphia who planned commencement exercises, plays, and similar affairs, it was William Smith the teacher who worked over
every detail with the students involved, rehearsing, revising,

and encouraging. Smith's relationship with most of the students who were in his charge is an inseparable part of his forty-year career as an educator. The more personal association between Smith and a small, closely knit group of his students, a group which he himself brought together and out of which came much of interest and importance to American life and letters, is reserved for another chapter.

Smith's pupils did not confine themselves to offering poetical tributes to his oratorical ability. Within a short time after the academy had been elevated into a college, several of them were able to give a more important testimony for their provost. Smith was active in public affairs, and some of his opponents had not hesitated to charge that he was using his position to indoctrinate his students with ideas prejudicial to freedom of thought and religion. The untruth of the charge is obvious at once to anyone who has read Smith's writings on education and apprehended the ideals which he set before himself, but it is equally obvious that a charge so made could have seriously affected both Smith and the college. The trustees realized this and appointed a special committee of their number to investigate the matter. In a report which was approved unanimously by the board, Smith was completely exonerated. One of the factors which influenced the committee was the following address made to it:

Gentlemen

Whereas, several unjust and malicious Insinuations have lately appeared in the public Papers and been spread through the City by the Heat of Party, against the Revd Mr William Smith Provost of this College, some of them designed to misrepresent his Conduct and injure his Credit with Respect to the Pupils under his Care; We whose Names are hereunto subscribed, being such of the Students of the Senior Philosophy Class as are now in Town, think it our Duty, in Justice to the Character of our respected Tutor, to certify to you, that for near the Space of two Years last, in which we have been under his immediate Care, he never did in any of his Lectures take Occasion to introduce any Thing relating to the Parties now subsisting in this Province, or tending to persuade us to adopt the Principles of one Side more than another. We further beg Leave to certify to you, that in the whole Course of his Lectures, on Ethics, Government, and Commerce, he never advanced any other Principles, than what were warranted by our standard Authors, Grotius, Puffendorf, Locke and Hutcheson: Writers whose Sentiments are equally opposite to those wild Notions of Liberty, that are inconsistent with all Government, and to those pernicious Schemes of Government, which are destructive of true Liberty: That he readily embraced every Opportunity of applying Morality to the sublime Truths of Religion and Christianity; on which Subjects he always dwelt with a peculiar and affecting Warmth, cautiously avoiding all Party-Distinctions and controverted Subjects; as a sufficient Proof of which we now lay our Notes of the Lectures, which he delivered upon the several Branches of Morality, before the Trustees; and any other persons willing to inspect the same, may also be favoured with them, upon Application to any of us:

> JACOB DUCHÉ junr (in his 19th year
> JAMES LATTA (in his 21. Year),
> FRANCIS HOPKINSON (in his 19 Year),
> HUGH WILLIAMSON (in his 21. Year.

Philadᵃ June 21. 1756.

The statements are unquestionably correct; surely no one could doubt that the author of *Mirania* "readily embraced every opportunity of applying Morality to the sublime Truths of Religion and Christianity." Aratus was more than the ideal schoolmaster of the hypothetical College of Mirania; he was the practical ideal Smith set for himself to follow in his own teaching.

On August 12, 1756, the *Pennsylvania Gazette* carried an impressive chart entitled "View of the Philosophy-Schools." This descriptive listing of the studies pursued in the College of Philadelphia was reprinted by William Smith in the October 1757 issue of the *American Magazine*, which Smith edited in 1757 and 1758. The reprinting was accompanied by a notable "Account of the College and Academy of Philadelphia," written by Smith himself and included in his *Works* immediately following the *College of Mirania*. The importance of the scheme of education described in the account is realized when one considers such a statement as that of Louis F. Snow in *The College Curriculum in the United States* (New York, 1907): "The scheme of study that is now the basis of all college curricula was initiated in America in the University of Pennsylvania, in 1756."

After a brief summary of the founding and history of the institution, Smith described its various branches. The lowest consisted of two charity schools. "In one of them forty girls are taught reading, writing, sewing, etc. In the other eighty boys are taught reading, writing and arithmetic, in order to fit them for the various sorts of business and mechanic arts."

The second branch "is properly an English academy, and consists of two parts: an English and writing school, and a school for the practical branches of mathematics, drawing, etc. In the former, besides writing, the pupils are taught the mother-tongue grammatically, together with a correct and just pronunciation." Smith took pains to emphasize that attention to public speaking was continued through the higher courses, particularly in the "philosophy schools, where the youth frequently deliver exercises of their own composition, at commencements, examinations, and other public occasions."

"The third and highest branch," Smith stated, "is the college . . . It consists of the Latin and Greek schools and three philosophy schools." Smith gave the list of books required to be read in the Greek and Latin schools, and added that "Some of the youth, it is found, go through these stages in three years, but most require four, and many five years, especially if they begin under nine or ten years of age." Entrance into the philosophy schools, each of which represented a separate year of study, depended upon a successful public examination in the books specified for the fourth "stage" of the Greek and Latin schools. From this, it will be seen that the Greek and Latin schools were really preparatory schools, and that the three philosophy schools corresponded to the present-day college.

"Freshmen or novitiates" in the philosophy schools had the privilege of wearing an undergraduate's gown and of entering upon the plan of studies scheduled in the "View of the Philosophy Schools."

Smith proceeded to defend and explain the curriculum, both in general and particular. The general comments are of more interest:

> Concerning the foregoing plan, it is to be remarked that life itself being too short to attain a perfect acquaintance with the whole circle of the sciences, nothing can be proposed by any scheme of collegiate education, but to lay such a general foundation in all the branches of literature as may enable the youth to perfect themselves in those particular parts to which their business or genius may afterwards lead them; and scarce anything has more obstructed the advancement of sound learning than a vain imagination, that a few years spent at college can render youth such absolute masters of science as to absolve them from all future study.
>
> Those concerned in the management of this seminary, as far as their influence extends, would wish to propagate a contrary doctrine; and though they flatter themselves that by a due execution of the foregoing plan they shall enrich their country with many minds that are liberally accomplished, and send out none that may justly be denominated barren or unimproved, yet they hope that the youth committed to their care will, neither at college nor afterwards, rest satisfied with such a general knowledge as is to be acquired from the public lectures and exercises. They rather trust that those whose taste is once formed for the acquisition of solid wisdom, will think it their duty, and most rational satisfaction, to accomplish themselves still farther by manly perseverance in private study and meditation.

Could every college graduate be given a copy of these words along with his diploma, they might easily prove of greater value to him than that document. Of course, Smith was not the first or the last to suggest that education does not end on commencement day, but his handling of the idea is still fresh and vital. What it must have been in 1757, when the idea itself was undoubtedly less widely acceptable, one can only conjecture. The same thought Smith had expressed rather less compactly and forcefully in *Mirania*. Here the expression strikes an inevitability that compels one to admit the presence of a master hand behind the pen. Perhaps not until the twentieth century and Henry Adams was there to be so cogent a phrasing of the conception that "at the utmost, the active-minded young man should ask of his teacher only mastery of his tools."

A list of approved writers, provided for the students as a guide to "private study and meditation," both during the course and in later life, was given in the last column of the "View of the Philosophy Schools."

A feature of Smith's plan was the order in which subjects were taught, an order which he believed logically suited to the "gradual opening of young minds." Composition, for example, was not studied until a sound knowledge of the best ancient and modern authors had been acquired. A knowledge of mathematics was not more necessary to an understanding of the natural sciences than was this to composition. "Thus," he wrote, "it is hoped that the student may be led through a scale of easy ascent, till finally rendered capable of thinking, writing, and acting well, which are the grand objects of a liberal education."

Circumstances, as Smith explained, had made it necessary to restrict the college to a three-year course. Otherwise one can read this account, compare it with the *College of Mirania*, and find little discrepancy between the ideal and the real. In both accounts, the reasons for doing things and the general thinking on education are of greater value than the specific outline of studies. It would not be fair or accurate, however, to dismiss without further comment the curriculum of the College of Philadelphia merely because the arts and sciences, including education, have advanced beyond it. That it was at the time a most advanced program of study can really be appreciated only by comparing it with other curricula of its own and even of later days. The eighteenth-century college in

America (and in England, for that matter) was, in general, a very narrowly conceived institution, the fundamental bases of which were the classical languages and other studies requisite to the making of clergymen. Smith was a distinct innovator when he adopted a curriculum designed not for training students to a single profession, but for the broader task of making good men and good citizens. His conception of a college and its functions was certainly different from that described by President Clap of Yale, in his *Religious Constitution of Colleges,* in 1754:

Colleges are *Religious Societies,* of a Superior Nature to all others. For whereas Parishes, are Societies, for training up the *Common People;* Colleges are Societies of Ministers, for training up persons for the Work of the *Ministry.*

William T. Foster, in discussing Smith's plan, remarked that its significance in the history of the college curriculum in America could be seen by comparing "the senior studies provided at Philadelphia in 1756 with the senior studies provided just a century later at Cambridge, Massachusetts." The comparison, it might be added, is all in Smith's favor.

The year 1757 was an eventful one for the College of Philadelphia. In the first month of the year, the students gave several performances of James Thomson's *Alfred: A Masque,* as revised for their use by their provost. The Historical Society of Pennsylvania owns a copy of *Alfred* containing a number of alterations, all in the handwriting of William Smith. The college version, quoted *in extenso* in an account of the performances published in four successive issues of the *Pennsylvania Gazette* (January 20 and 27, February 3 and 10, 1757), corresponds exactly to Smith's revision. The newspaper account is unsigned and at one time was generally attributed to Francis Hopkinson, on the strength of his signature to a poem appended to the account. The statement that "the Writer of this Account undertook to alter the Piece" points definitely to William Smith as its author, and corroboration is supplied by three entries on a list, now in the Smith Papers at the Historical

Society of Pennsylvania, which Smith made of his own writings. The entries read:

37 Alterations in Alfred
38 Prologue & Epilogue to D°
39 4 Papers in the Pennsylv^a Gazette Jan^r 20th & c on D°—

The introductory paragraph of the first installment of the account told much of interest:

To the Publishers of the Pennsylvania GAZETTE.
GENTLEMEN,
You will oblige many of your Readers, by publishing, at your Conveniency, the following Account of Alfred, *as it has been several Times represented, during the Christmas Holidays, in one of the Apartments of the College, as an Oratorial Exercise, by a Sett of young Gentlemen.*

It was explained that the study of oratory had been much encouraged in the college,

. . . the Youth having from Time to Time delivered proper Speeches, and acted Parts of our best dramatic Pieces, before large Audiences, with great Applause. This formed many excellent young Orators, whose Ambition to shine gradually encreased with the Encouragement they received; till at length they thought themselves capable of attempting a *whole dramatic Piece* as an *Oratorial Exercise*, and could no longer be satisfied with these lesser Excursions and humbler Efforts of Genius.

The nature of the changes which Smith made in *Alfred* is interesting in itself. Some of these changes were, of course, due to what may be called merely mechanical reasons. Women had to be eliminated from the cast, since the acting was to be done by the male sex exclusively (women were allowed to take "vocal parts," i.e., to sing in solo and chorus, usually off-stage). Other changes are more interesting and revealing. For instance, references to England and Denmark were often removed or altered to more generalized expressions, as in this speech in the first scene of Act I:

> Yet, my Corin,
> Resolve the stern decree, of that fierce tyrant,
> The *Danish* king: "Who harbours, or relieves
> "An English captain, dies the death of traitors:
> "But who their haunts discovers, shall be safe,
> "And high rewarded."

which became:

> Yet, brave Shepherd!
> Resolve the stern decree of that fierce Tyrant,
> Whose plundering Bands invade this prostrate Land—
> "The Foe who harbours, were it Son or Brother,
> Or Wife embosom'd—dies the Death of Traitors—
> But who their Haunts discovers, shall be safe
> And high rewarded."

Another example of this type of alteration occurs in a dialogue between Alfred and the Earl of Devon in the second scene of this act, in which

> Gracious Alfred,
> England's last hope, whose feeling goodness shews
> What angels are;

was changed to:

> My Gracious Liege,
> His Country's only hope, whose goodness shews
> What angels are;

This disinclination to use the name of England appears a bit strange at first; another instance of alteration may shed some light upon it. In a speech of Alfred himself,

> Hast thou Ought
> Of joyful to impart? or is the soul
> Of *England* dead indeed?

the word *England* is changed, significantly, to *Freedom*. Freedom and liberty were subjects much in Smith's mind and on his tongue. He apparently wished to stress loyalty to the abstract principle of freedom above loyalty to a definite place or person or thing. Another speech of Alfred, this one from the eighth scene of Act III, again shows this shift of emphasis, in the alteration from:

> To Him ascend all praise! whose will inspir'd
> Whose arm sustain'd this action, that restores
> My better name—and, O more glorious still,
> Of nobler, dearer consequence!—restores
> Lost *England* to her vigor, fame and freedom.

to:

> All Praise to him, whose will inspir'd,
> Whose arm sustain'd this action, that restores
> This ruin'd Country to her Fame & Freedom!

Although the original had mentioned the word, the stress thrown upon freedom is certainly much greater in Smith's alteration.

The performance was prefaced by a prologue and followed by an epilogue, both written for the occasion by Smith and to be found in the account in the *Pennsylvania Gazette*. The prologue is not especially remarkable, but the epilogue provides rather more interest, as it emphasized the application of *Alfred* to the circumstances of 1757:

> To rouse the slumb'ring *Virtue* of the FREE,
> And shew what *gen'rous* BRITONS still should be;
> To fire the Breast to Deeds of *publick Worth*,
> And call th' impatient Soul of *Glory* forth;
> To breathe *Humanity* into the Heart,
> And every nobler Feeling to impart:—
> For this, To-night, with trembling Hope and Fear,
> We humbly dar'd to greet your candid Ear;
> We bade *heroic Ages* roll anew,
> And call'd our *glorious* ALFRED back to View,
> In awful Pomp, the Godlike Chief appears
> From his deep Slumber of a thousand Years.
>
> .   .   .   .
>
> See! more than *Danish Rage*, with Bloody Hand,
> Spreads Death and Slaughter o'er this prostrate Land!
>
> .   .   .   .

For lo! to chear our Hopes and bring Relief,
Glad o'er the *Atlantic* comes the *gallant Chief;*
Before whose Arms our Foes have often fled,
And black *Rebellion* hid her gory Head.
Be you but BRITONS, as an ALFRED he;
And *War* and *Rapine* soon shall cease to be.

These words were spoken by Jacob Duché, Jr., who had taken the part of Alfred in the masque. The "more than Danish Rage" which was asserted to be at large in 1757 was, of course, a reference to Indian activities on the frontiers. The "gallant Chief" was most probably General Stanwix, who was to attempt to retrieve the settlements left deserted after Braddock's defeat.

At first thought, one may be somewhat surprised to find that a dramatic performance was given under the sponsorship of a college headed by a clergyman in America in 1757. Several qualifying factors should be considered. True, it was 1757 and it was America. But it was Philadelphia, more liberal in many matters than some places farther to the north, and already able to boast a theatrical tradition. In the second place, the clergyman concerned was a member of the Church of England, the clergy of which have rarely been noted for an over-developed asceticism. Especially in the eighteenth century was this true of the English clergy. Most important of all, the clergyman in question was William Smith, the author, it will be remembered, of the *College of Mirania*. One cannot escape the impression that Smith was an educator before he was anything else, and that even if he had had clerical scruples against plays, he would not have allowed them to stand in the way if he thought the production of plays was desirable training for his students. And he did think that. It is interesting to note that Smith may have brought something of a traditional interest in student-performed plays with him from Aberdeen, where as early as 1541 "playes" were among the reasons that led chroniclers to note that King James V and his Queen (Mary of Guise) were "well entertenit" on their visit to that seat of learning.

Significant as the production of *Alfred* was, a far more important event in Philadelphia was the first commencement of the college on May 17, 1757. Smith's charge to his pupils on that occasion was published, and in its preface were listed the names of those who took degrees. Paul Jackson, who delivered a salutatory address in Latin and is listed on the title-page as "Professor of Languages in the said College and Academy," received the degree of Master of Arts; Jacob Duché, Francis Hopkinson, Hugh Williamson, James Latta, Samuel Magaw, and John Morgan were made Bachelors of Arts; Josiah Martin and Solomon Southwicke were granted honorary B.A. degrees. Smith's address to his first graduates was full of sound good sense. As might have been expected, he exhorted them to "continue through life the votaries of Wisdom; and never drop your acquaintance with those sciences into which you have been initiated here." Perhaps Smith rose to greatest eloquence when he came to the very subject on which some of these same young men had testified as to his probity—their relationship to the body politic:

Should your *Country* call, or should you perceive the *restless Tools* of FACTION at Work in their dark Cabals, and "stealing upon the *secure Hour* of LIBERTY;" should you see the *Corruptors* or *Corrupted* imposing upon the Public with specious Names, undermining the *civil* and *religious* Principles of their Country, and gradually paving the Way to certain SLAVERY, by spreading *destructive Notions of Government* —then, Oh! then, be nobly rouzed! Be all Eye, and Ear, and Heart, and Voice, and Hand, in a Cause so glorious! *Cry aloud, and spare not,* fearless of Danger, regardless of Opposition, and little sollicitous about the Frowns of Power, or the Machinations of Villainy. Let the World know that LIBERTY *is your unconquerable Delight,* and that you are sworn Foes to every Species of Bondage, either of Body or of Mind!

These are Subjects for which you need not be ashamed to sacrifice your Ease and every other private Advantage— For certainly, if there be aught upon Earth suited to the native Greatness of the human Mind, and worthy of Contention, it must be to assert the Cause of *Religion and Truth;* to support the *fundamental Rights and Liberties of Mankind;* and to strive for the Constitution of your Country, and a "Government of *Laws,* not of *Men.*"

Aside from the remarkably prophetic nature of this statement to a group of young men to whom the matter was to become the most important of their lives, the high-mindedness and forceful eloquence of the passage must command admiration. To the youth of any generation, these commands would have been appropriate; to the graduates of the College of Philadelphia in 1757 they were very nearly inspired.

Smith also took advantage of the opportunity afforded by the commencement to deliver a second discourse, addressed less particularly to the graduates, in which he explained and defended the system under which these young men had been educated. It was a succinct recapitulation of much of Smith's educational philosophy and practice.

The year 1757, already so notable for Smith and the college, marked the beginning of a brief but distinguished enterprise. In November 1757 there was issued from the press of William Bradford of Philadelphia number one of volume one of the *American Magazine, or Monthly Chronicle for the British Colonies.* (The *or* was changed to *and* in subsequent issues.) The first number was that "for October, 1757," but it was advertised in Bradford's *Pennsylvania Journal* November 3, 1757, as to be published "ToMorrow." Although the title-page stated that the magazine was to be "continued by a Society of Gentlemen," Smith was evidently the moving force behind it. One might infer this from the tone of the political references and from the fact that publication ceased when Smith left Philadelphia for his trip to England in 1758. Fortunately, one is not thrown upon such indirect reasoning. Included in the *American Magazine* was a series of essays under the title of "The Hermit." In acknowledging his authorship of this series by reprinting it in his *Works,* Smith appended a postscript which clearly shows his relation to the magazine itself:

THE reader will easily see, that the HERMIT's labours terminate abruptly in his foregoing No. VIII. when he was just opening himself for their continuation, in subsequent numbers . . .

With the HERMIT's labours, the publication of the AMERICAN MAGAZINE, the vehicle of their conveyance, ceased also. The cause of this was some very arbitrary proceedings of the Assembly, or Legislature of Pennsylvania, of that day; which necessitated the author to undertake a voyage to Great-Britain . . .

His associates, therefore, in carrying on the MAGAZINE, (most of whom were among his ingenious young PUPILS, whose talents he wished to encourage and cultivate, both in sentiment and composition) declined the weight of continuing the work, in his absence, or without his aid and direction.

The encouragement of talent was undoubtedly one of the purposes in Smith's mind when he undertook the work of editing the new publication. Another is stated in the preface which appeared in the first issue:

It has long been matter of just complaint, among some of the best friends of our national commerce and safety, that the important concerns of these *Colonies* were but little studied and less understood in the mother-country, even by many of those, who have sustained the highest offices of trust and dignity in it.

One may be sure that Smith, while perfectly sincere in his wish to give the mother country more information about her colonies, would also see to it that the information was less partial to the Quakers and the Assembly than news from other quarters might be. The general design of the magazine was also announced in the preface:

This work will be carried on in six half sheets each month, as nearly as possible on the following plan; leaving to ourselves the liberty of improving or amending it, as occasion may require.

The *first* and *second* half sheets will contain an account of

EUROPEAN AFFAIRS, and particularly those of *Great-Britain* and her allies, with the most remarkable debates in parliament, controversies among the learned, and other material occurrences.

The *third* half sheet will be a PHILOSOPHICAL MISCELLANY, containing the newest discoveries and improvements in any of the branches of philosophy, natural history, agriculture, mathematics or the mechanic arts, made either by the *Literati* in other parts of the world, or by our ingenious correspondents in *America;* whose productions of this kind will always be received by us with singular pleasure, as it is one principal part of our design to propagate a love of knowledge in all parts of this young country.

Our *fourth* half sheet and part of the *fifth* are set aside for MONTHLY ESSAYS, in prose and verse. This, we hope, will not be the least valuable part of our work. Some persons of known abilities are engaged to furnish a series of papers for it on the most important subjects, and of different kinds, humorous, serious, critical, poetical, religious &c. And we shall think ourselves under particular obligations for every *essay* that may be communicated to us by others, so far as they tend to promote *peace and good government, industry* and *public spirit,* a *love of* LIBERTY and *our excellent constitution,* and above all a veneration of our holy undefiled CHRISTIANITY; for which particular subject, one paper will be set apart and kept sacred, during the whole continuance of this work. Any pieces that may be offered inconsistent with these good ends, will be steadily rejected, from whatsoever quarter they come. In this part of our work also, will be occasionally inserted such curious productions in prose or verse as have come abroad in *America* before the commencement of our magazine, and seem worthy of a longer duration than they would otherwise have in their former detached manner of publication.

The remainder of our fifth *sheet* will contain a history of the present war in *North-America,* and of every thing relating to, or connected with it. This history we shall begin as far back as the year 1749, and no further. . . .

The *sixth* half sheet will contain the particular monthly transactions in each colony, the account of new books both here and in *Great-Britain,* preferments, births, marriages, deaths, arrivals of ships, prices current, and other articles common in the last half sheet of magazines.

This plan was adhered to throughout the publication of the magazine, which had regular issues under dates from October 1757 through October 1758, and a supplement, largely given over to *An Account of the College and Academy of Philadelphia* and to an index. The "Philosophical Miscellany" often provided interesting material. James Logan's letter in which he established the fact that Thomas Godfrey, Sr., was the real inventor of Hadley's quadrant is a case in point. Smith himself contributed to this department, on one occasion printing a geometrical demonstration which he had worked out with his classes at the college. The "Monthly Essays," however, must have been of most general interest to readers in 1757 and 1758; it is certain that they are so today. The prose essays, as might have been expected, followed the series manner typical of the eighteenth century. Smith's "Hermit" series has been mentioned; others were "The Prattler," "The Antigallican," and "The Planter." He had a hand in these series, as stated in the 1802 prospectus of his *Works*. In his verse prologue to *Mirania*, Smith had seen other Newtons, Bacons, Lockes, Popes, and Spensers appearing in the new world; here, under his own ægis, were other Addisons, Steeles, Johnsons, and Goldsmiths.

It was in its poetical essays that the *American Magazine* was really distinguished. Perhaps its most noteworthy accomplishment in this field was the discovery of Thomas Godfrey, Jr., who submitted a pastoral poem, "The Invitation," which was published in the issue for January 1758, with this note:

This little poem was sent to us by an unknown hand, and, seems dated as an original. If it be so we think it does honour to our city; but of this we are not certain. All we can say is that we do not recollect to have seen it before.

The poem was not by any means great poetry, but it distinctly showed signs of talent. Its kind reception led to further poems from the same author, and these too found a place in the pages of later issues of the magazine. This discovery was apparently regarded by the editor as one of the achievements of his work, for an account of Godfrey was published before the year was out. Godfrey was one of the few contributors to have his name definitely connected with his contributions and the only one honored in so conspicuous a fashion.

The *American Magazine* also served as an outlet for much of the poetry of Francis Hopkinson, one of the members of Smith's first graduating class. Though he received no write-up like Godfrey's, his contributions are identifiable because they were later reprinted (with varying amounts of alteration, to be sure) in his collected works. The first number of the magazine carried his "ODE on MUSIC. *Written at* Philadelphia *by a young Gentleman of* 17, *on his beginning to learn the* Harpsichord." In the November issue he was represented by two poems, the titles of which need only to be mentioned to show under what influence they were written: "L'Allegro" and "Il Penseroso." The latter was *"Humbly inscribed to the Rev. Mr.* S——th" and contains flattering references to Smith's teaching. Several other poems of his certain authorship appeared, and some which he did not reprint may have been written by him. His biographer, G. E. Hastings, thinks it "highly probable" that he wrote the poem *"Upon Seeing the Portrait of Miss* **——** ** *by Mr.* West" in the February 1758 number. Whether or not he did, it is significant that this poem appeared. By printing it and other commendations of West, Smith earned for himself the credit of being the first person in America to put the name of Benjamin West into print. Jacob Duché and Nathaniel Evans and others of Smith's students probably contributed during the year of the magazine's existence, but it is no longer possible to identify their contributions.

The importance of the *American Magazine* to Smith and his group of pupils must be obvious. Apart from giving Smith an outlet for his own political and religious-philosophical writings, it afforded a publishing place for his most gifted pupil, Francis Hopkinson; Thomas Godfrey was moved to contribute and thus was introduced to the others and to the literary life; Benjamin West was praised in it for his painting. Surely, the *American Magazine* must have been, during the year it was published, as well as for some time before while it was a-borning, the nucleus about which gathered Smith and those of his friends, associates, and pupils who were interested in any kind of literary or artistic production. To the English-speaking world, and particularly to the world of colonial America and especially Pennsylvania, the magazine was also significant. Previous and some subsequent American magazines consisted chiefly of material copied from various English reviews. There was some reprinted material in Smith's magazine, but, as Frank Luther Mott has pointed out in *A History of American Magazines*, "there is more original material than had yet appeared in an American magazine." Mott also stated what one feels to be absolutely true, that the year's issue "bears comparison with any year's file of the *Gentleman's* or the *London Magazine*" and that it was the "most brilliant magazine issued up to that time" in America. Lyon N. Richardson, in *A History of Early American Magazines, 1741-1789*, was willing to go even further and call it "the most vital and original literary magazine published in America before the War of the Revolution"; he pointed out that "it was the only pre-Revolutionary magazine terminated for other reasons than inadequate support." When one considers that it was issued during one of the most eventful and exciting years of Smith's life, the year in which he and William Moore had their historic controversy with the Assembly of Pennsylvania, and in which he actually spent a considerable time in jail for contempt of that body, the force and vigor of his editorial labors appear all the more amazing and make it all the more regrettable that these labors were interrupted and that he never returned to them.

The commencement exercises offered both Smith and his students an incentive to literary activity. In 1761, for instance, there was performed "An Exercise, Containing A Dialogue and

Ode *Sacred to the Memory of His late Gracious Majesty,*
George II." The exercise was published in two different editions, one printed by Andrew Steuart and the other by
W. Dunlap. Dunlap's edition stated on the title-page that the
ode was "written and set to Music *By* Francis Hopkinson, *Esq.,*
M.A. *in said College.*" In Hopkinson's *Miscellaneous Essays,*
where the work is reprinted, the dialogue is definitely attributed to William Smith. This dialogue is fortunately short
enough for complete quotation and may serve as an example
of the dialogue-ode type of exercise, to which considerable
reference will be made. Eugenio and Amyntor are the speakers:

Eugenio.
What means that look of woe, that head reclin'd,
Those folded arms, with which I meet AMYNTOR?
That eye which wont, with love and sparkling joy,
To beam, munificent, on ev'ry friend—
Why bends it thus in sorrow to the ground,
As if no view could please but dust and earth?

Amyntor.
All things, EUGENIO, are but dust and earth!
Even kings themselves—those demi-gods enthron'd,
Rulers of empire, thunder-bolts of war,
At whose avenging nod the guilty tremble,
Nations are doom'd, and millions live or die—
Even kings themselves—are nought but dust and earth!

Eugenio.
Who knows not that AMYNTOR? but why damp
This festive day with such untimely lecture?

Amyntor
What festive day, can BRITAIN or her Sons
Now celebrate? the voice of joy is fled!
Let no rash hand, with myrtle or with bay,
Or other flaunting foliage of the grove,
Presume to deck these walls. Come baleful YEW,
And weeping cypress, from your midnight shades!
None other wreath but yours, from hill or dale,
Be pluckt to circle ACADEMIC brow.

See pale BRITTANIA on the wave-worn shore,
Incumbent o'er her massy trident, weeps;
And fond IERNE, sister of her grief,
Calls from her harp sad notes of DORIC strain—
From pole to pole, far as old ocean heaves
His troubled waves, and bears the BRITISH flag,
The voice of woe is heard. Even here, remote,
The awful genius of these barbarous woods,
That wont to roam from INDIAN height to height,
With nature's self, in frolic ever new,
Tears from his hoary head his feathery crown,
And breaks his arrows, and his quiver rends.

Eugenio.

In mystic words, and metaphoric strains,
Why would AMYNTOR strive to hide the cause
Of such unbounded sorrow!

Amyntor.

No, EUGENIO!

AMYNTOR would not hide, but speak the cause,
Could words be found to measure forth his grief,
And ease his labouring breast; the godlike GEORGE,
The friend of freedom, and the scourge of tyrants,
The FATHER OF HIS COUNTRY—sleeps in dust!
Of import dreadful, from BRITANNIA'S COAST,
Confirm'd and full, the mournful tidings come.

Eugenio.

ILLUSTRIOUS MONARCH! not the ROMAN boast,
The generous TITUS, joy of human kind;
Nor names of later date, WILLIAM and HENRY,
Or ALFRED's self, shall fill a brighter page
In FAME's eternal roll, than shall the name
Of gracious GEORGE! beneath his equal sway,
Oppression WAS NOT; JUSTICE poiz'd her scale;
No LAW was trampled, and no RIGHT deny'd;
The PEASANT flourish'd, and the MERCHANT smil'd.
And oh! my friend, to what amazing height
Of sudden grandeur, did his nursing care
Up-raise these COLONIES; beyond whate'er
Of ancient or of modern times is told.
Prepare we, then, due ELEGIES to frame,
Such as may well accord to heart of woe.

Amyntor.
That work is done. Behold the goodly choir,
With voice united to the deep-ton'd note
Of swelling organ, rise, in act, to sing
The consecrated lay. Hark! hark! they strike.

Then the ode was sung, and one more speech concluded the exercise:

Eugenio.
How soft the power of MUSIC to assuage
The pangs of grief! like balm of costly price
Pour'd o'er the streaming wound. Since, then, my friend,
Due tribute has been paid to royal worth
And royal dust; it boots us not to spend
Our fleeting hours in unavailing sorrow.
See! by the bounty of all-ruling heaven,
Another GEORGE to happy BRITONS given!
Gay youth and glory beam around his throne,
And glad BRITANNIA claims him as her own.
Let us embrace what heaven in kindness gives,
For GEORGE the SECOND, in the THIRD still lives.

Due allowance being made for the superfluities demanded by the occasion and for the poetic diction of the period, this is at least a good competent job of versifying. That the conception of the exercise was Smith's and that he suggested to Hopkinson the propriety of composing the memorial ode is beyond doubt. Hopkinson composed an ode for the commencement of the following year, but this time the accompanying dialogue was written by Jacob Duché. This effort was published by Dunlap under the title of "An Exercise, containing A Dialogue and Ode *On the Accession of His present gracious Majesty*, George III." The joint authorship is established by the reprinting of the exercise in Hopkinson's works with the explanation that Duché had written the dialogue.

It was Smith the educator of American youth whom his own university, Aberdeen, granted an honorary D.D. degree on March 10, 1759. The twenty-seventh of the same month, the University of Oxford conferred the same distinction on Smith, after a recommendation had been sent to it by the Archbishop of Canterbury and the Bishops of Durham, Salisbury, St. Asaph's, Gloucester, and Oxford. Smith had gone abroad for quite another purpose than the mere acquisition of degrees: he sought vindication in his controversy with the Assembly of Pennsylvania. The controversy will be discussed in a later chapter on public affairs. His presence in England, however, gave Smith the opportunity to make many friends who were to serve him and his college well when next he came to England. Smith also took the occasion to bring about an act which implemented the revenues of the college, while at the same time it reduced his own salary. The proprietary, Thomas Penn, had been making an annual donation of £50 toward the provost's salary since 1754; he had expressed an intention of abandoning this donation in favor of the permanent grant of his interest in certain lands. In 1759, Smith reminded Penn of this design, which was put into effect. The details Smith recorded in a letter to the trustees of the College and Academy. To the credit of the trustees, it must be added that two years later they restored the £50 to Smith's salary and made their action retroactive to the date when the Penn donation ceased.

The income from these lands was not, however, enough to relieve the financial strain under which the institution was laboring. On November 28, 1761, the trustees voted that a collection should be undertaken in England and that Smith be sent abroad for the purpose; they voted on December 17 to continue his salary during his absence. A letter of instructions from the trustees, signed by Richard Peters as their president, authorized Smith to proceed to Great Britain and Ireland. The idea of such a collection was Smith's, to judge from a remark in the trustees' letter: "You are sensible we have proceeded in this affair very much by your advice, and in expectation of the hearty concurrence of our Honorable Proprietors." One of the trustees, Benjamin Franklin, was in England at the time, and Smith was instructed to seek his advice and the advice of any other trustee who might be in England during his stay. He was also instructed to place the funds collected by him with the London banking firm of Barclay & Co. The trials and tribulations of the mission were many. Smith recounted some of them in letters to Richard Peters, and they were indeed more than enough to try the patience of any man, no matter how many times a saint.

The war between England and France having increased the danger of crossing the Atlantic, the trustees arranged a special credit of £100 for Smith's use and instructed Barclay's to pay the money only "if he should be taken by the enemy, and should find it necessary to draw on you in order to obtain a decent support or to procure his discharge and a conveyance to England."

Smith was fortunate enough to avoid the necessity of having to use this credit and arrived in England safely. He had barely started to solicit funds when he received the disheartening news that the College of New York was embarking on a similar venture and had sent James Jay (who was dubbed Sir James while about this business) as its agent. After a series of consultations, Smith and Jay decided to merge the appeals for the two schools. What had already been collected by each was to remain with each separately, but a royal brief was to be applied for, and all money collected under its authority to be divided equally. A royal brief was a permit granting certain privileges in the collection of funds for a charitable purpose; it not only authorized door-to-door solicitation throughout the whole kingdom, but also recommended the object for which money was sought to every church in the land and requested that special collections be taken and turned over to the holders of the brief. Through the influence of the Archbishop of Canterbury, such a document was obtained for the colleges of Philadelphia and New York at a meeting of the Privy Council on August 12, 1762, and the document was formally issued a week later. Compliance with various legal formalities, including the appointment of "brief layers" to see to the making of the copies required and to the affixing of the necessary government tax stamps, took so much time that Smith and Jay could not begin the active work of solicitation until September 29. For Smith, this meant not only making private application to persons he thought might contribute, but also preaching on behalf of the brief in churches throughout the kingdom. Special collections were taken on such occasions and added to the joint fund. It would be tedious and it is unnecessary to relate Smith's itinerary. It is enough to say that the mission was highly successful; in fact, Smith was doing so well that the trustees urged him to extend his visit beyond the period originally set. He remained in England over two years. In a letter to Mrs. Smith dated April 19, 1764, Smith gave an accounting of the funds which he had received. Philadelphia's half of the brief money was £4,800, its share of the private collections £1,136/10/6, and £310/10/— came from miscellaneous sources, including the proceeds of a benefit oratorio. Smith had collected £284/17/— before the New York appeal was joined to his. This sum, along with gifts of £500 from the Penns and £200 from the King, was not divided. Thus Philadelphia received a total of £7,231/17/6, a most respectable sum of money in 1764. Implicit in these dry figures is the fact that William Smith was an indefatigable worker and a very able one. That he could have raised so large a sum at a time when England was overrun with collections is a tribute to his personality and the effectiveness with which he presented his cause.

While in Dublin on this business, Smith was granted an *ad eundem* degree in divinity by Trinity College. It was perhaps due to the strain of overwork that he fell ill of a fever in Dublin; "four score" of doctor's visits were required, he wrote to Richard Peters.

By June 1764 Smith had returned to Philadelphia. With him he brought a letter which the Archbishop of Canterbury, Thomas and Richard Penn, and the Reverend Dr. Samuel Chandler (an eminent dissenting clergyman in England) had written to the trustees on April 9, 1764, congratulating them upon the success of Smith's collection and upon the freedom from religious or sectarian control which distinguished the college. They suggested that the trustees might well make a formal declaration of their intention to adhere to the same plan in the future. This was accordingly done by the trustees at a meeting on June 14:

The Trustees being ever desirous to promote the Peace and Prosperity of this Seminary, and to give Satisfaction to all its worthy Benefactors, have taken the above Letter into their serious Consideration, and perfectly approving the Sentiments therein contained, do order the same to be inserted in their Books, that it may remain perpetually *declaratory* of the present *wide* and excellent Plan of this Institution, which hath not only met with the Approbation of the great and worthy Personages above mentioned, but even the Royal Sanction of his Majesty himself. They further *declare* that they will keep this Plan closely in their View, and use their *utmost Endeavours* that the same *be not narrowed*, nor the Members of the Church of England or those dissenting from them (*in any future election to the principal Offices mentioned in the aforesaid Letter*) be put on *any worse Footing* in this Seminary than they were *at the Time of obtaining the Royal Brief*. They subscribe this with their Names and ordain that the same be read and subscribed by every new Trustee that shall hereafter be elected before he takes his Seat at the Board.

When Smith first appeared before the trustees upon his return from England, he was warmly thanked for the "great Zeal, Diligence, Ability and Address" he had shown on the mission. Two days later, at the meeting of June 14, 1764, he was voted an annuity of £100 as a reward for his personal services to the college by this trip to England. He was also named secretary of the board. Nearly a year later, on May 3, 1765, the trustees decided to allow him one guinea a day for traveling and other expenses he had had in England. Before leaving England, Smith had named several persons to act with power of attorney to receive any further brief money. On September 23, 1764, Thomas Penn, one of them, reported that another

£250 was on deposit at Barclay's. This firm, incidentally, took no commission for its services to the college.

Smith's abilities as a collector so impressed the trustees that on October 22, 1771, they were "unanimously of Opinion, that Dr Smith be desir'd to undertake a Journey to the Southern Colonies as far as South-Carolina, to sollicit Contributions for the Use of the College." About thirty students from South Carolina were enrolled in the college. Armed with £50 expense money, Smith sailed from New York on November 14, 1771, and arrived in Charleston on November 23, where he immediately put himself under a physician's care for a dangerous infection resulting from a fall on shipboard. Despite this handicap, his genius for raising money did not fail him. Within three months he had added £1,061/10/1 sterling to the funds of the college and was back in Philadelphia.

Smith and the trustees did not overlook Philadelphia in their search for funds, as one may see from reading a minute of the trustees' meeting of May 19, 1772:

Dr Smith reported that tho' upwards of £1200 were subscrib'd in Town for the College, yet there were still a great many well disposed Persons to be called upon who would contribute, if he could find Time to wait upon them. He is therefore desired, with the Assistance of the Gentlemen formerly appointed, to prosecute the Collection, & to get M^r McDowel to supply his Place such Forenoons as he may have Occasion to be absent on this Business.

The large sums of money which Smith raised for the College and Academy of Philadelphia would have entitled him to honorable memory had he never served the institution in any other way. Truly, as a later provost of the University of Pennsylvania, Charles J. Stillé, said of his predecessor, "If the founder of a charity be in fact, as well as in law, he who has contributed most largely himself, or who has induced others to contribute most largely to its original funds, then Dr. Smith was the true *Founder* of the University."

A letter from Smith was read at a special meeting of the trustees on February 22, 1774. Smith reminded the trustees that he had been enabled to add more than £14,000 to the capital of the institution. The purpose of the letter was not merely to remind the trustees of his services to them, of which they were fully aware. He went on to say:

When you consider the advanced Price of Necessaries, and the *growing* Expence of a growing Family, with the public Character which, for the Reputation of the Seminary, I must maintain,—I flatter myself, you will readily believe me when I declare that I cannot make the Sum of Three Hundred & fifty Pounds a Year, which I receive from you, answer my annual Expences, House-Rent &c, with all the Frugality which I can with Decency use.

The remedy Smith suggested was that a house should be built for his use on the college grounds. Not only would this partly mitigate his expenses and save him the trouble of making five or six round trips a day between his home and the college, but the institution would itself be served, since he would be able to keep a closer eye upon the students. The board unanimously agreed to erect a house at the corner of Fourth and Arch streets for the provost's use. A committee appointed to attend to the details reported back on March 15, 1774, and plans were then approved for a three-story house 40' by 34', with a one-story kitchen 21' by 18', all at a cost of £1,637. Part of this building, somewhat altered since 1774, is still standing on the southwest corner of Fourth and Arch streets, Philadelphia.

Settled in his new home, Smith continued to devote his energies to the affairs of the college. At the commencement of 1775, held on May 17, another of the familiar exercises was performed. A copy in the University of Pennsylvania Library bears this notation in the handwriting of Horace W. Smith: "This dialogue was prepared by William Smith D.D. I own the original M.S. H.W.S. 1871." Printed on the second page is an "N.B." by the author, explaining that:

The following Lines are chiefly collected from former Exercises of a like nature, and were hastily thrown together to supply the Place of another Exercise laid aside. But as they are suitable to the present Occasion, it is hoped they will be acceptable.

Probably the rejected exercise was laid aside because the Provost wished to honor the memory of Thomas Penn, word of whose death had just been received. Eugenio and Amyntor lamented his death in very nearly the same words with which they had mourned the passing of the second George fourteen years earlier. The chief change is that they were joined by a third speaker, Damon. A printed account of the commencement lists the three speakers of the dialogue as John Farrel, F. B. Sappington, and W. M. Smith. The last-named was the Provost's son, William Moore Smith, who also delivered an oration, "On the Fall of Empires."

The duties other than academic which devolved upon Smith were not all on a plane with his two-year fund-raising trip to England. Typical of the petty details thrust upon him is one indicated by an entry in the trustees' minutes for October 17, 1775, when Smith was instructed to advertise for a family to take charge of the college boarding house. Also typical is an entry for November 2, 1778:

Dr Smith is empowered to employ some Person to collect the old Rails scattered on the different Parts of the Norriton Plantation, and enclose the Meadows as soon as possible to prevent their being damaged further by Cattle and Swine. He is also to provide Boards and Slabs and get the Mason Work of the unfinished Part of the Mill-house secured from the Weather.

As the times in America became more troubled, as the year 1776 drew nearer, men and institutions both tended to be disrupted from their normal course. Provost Smith was interested in politics and was often called upon for sermons and addresses of a semi-political nature. Although these utterances were largely unexceptionable in sentiment, they still called attention to Smith and to his somewhat anomalous position as a clergyman of the Church of England in a day when any connection with England was beginning to be suspect. Smith's known friendship with the Penns was also a factor likely to attract attention to him and to the institution over which he presided. Even so, mere individual excess was probably responsible for the damage to property and grounds by soldiers quartered upon the college, against which the faculty protested in a letter to the Council of Safety on January 23, 1777. The withdrawal of students and the close approach of the theatre of war to Philadelphia also aided in making necessary the closing of the college on June 30, 1777. As soon as possible after the British had evacuated the city, the college was reopened, in January of 1779. The troubles of the college were now, far from being over, just about to begin in earnest.

While the state of Pennsylvania was engaged in adopting a new constitution in 1776, Smith had called a meeting at his home of "sundry gentlemen interested in the inviolability of religious and scientific corporations," as William White, one of them, described the gathering. Benjamin Franklin, president of the state constitutional convention, met with the group and "cheerfully promised to propose to the body an article drawn up by Dr Smith, securing all chartered rights." White noted that the article was adopted and became a part of the constitution. Although he did not specify which article it was, it is safe to assume that it was the forty-fifth, which, together with the forty-fourth, provided:

A school or schools shall be established in each county by the legislature for the convenient instruction of youth, with such salaries to the masters paid by the public as may enable them to instruct youth at low prices: And all useful learning shall be duly encouraged and promoted in one or more universities.

Laws for the encouragement of virtue, and prevention of vice and immorality, shall be made and constantly kept in force, and provision shall be made for their due execution: And all religious societies or bodies of men heretofore united or incorporated for the advancement of religion and learning, or for other pious and charitable purposes, shall be encouraged and protected in the enjoyment of the privileges, immunities and estates which they were accustomed to enjoy or could of right have enjoyed under the laws and former constitution of this state.

This clause should have been a safeguard to the college, as it was intended, but the course of politics, like that of true love in the old proverb, never runs smooth. The Assembly of Pennsylvania passed on November 27, 1779:

An Act

To confirm the estates and interests of the college, academy, and charitable school of the city of Philadelphia, and to amend and alter the charters thereof, conformably to the revolution and to the constitution and government of this commonwealth, and to erect the same into a university—27th November, 1779.

After a most pious first section, reciting the advantages to society of systems of education when properly conducted and the evil effects resulting from the ill conduct thereof, the act proceeded:

Sect. 2. *And whereas* the college, academy, and charitable school of the city of Philadelphia, were at first founded on a plan of free and unlimited catholicism; but it appears that the trustees thereof, by a vote or by-law of their board, bearing date the fourteenth day of June, in the year of our Lord one thousand seven hundred and sixty-four, have departed from the plan of the original founders, and narrowed the foundation of the said institution.

Sect. 3. *Be it therefore enacted, &c.*, That the charter of the said seminary, granted by the late proprietaries of Pennsylvania, bearing date the thirteenth day of July, in the year of our Lord one thousand seven hundred and fifty-three, whereby certain persons were incorporated by the name, style, and title of The Trustees of the Academy and Charitable School in the province of Pennsylvania, and the additional charter, granted by the same proprietaries, bearing date on the fourteenth day of May, in the year of our Lord one thousand seven hundred and fifty-five, by which the trustees of the same academy and charitable school were again incorporated, by the name, style, and title of The Trustees of the College, Academy, and Charitable School of the city of Philadelphia, in the province of Pennsylvania, together with all and singular the rights, powers, privileges, emoluments and advantages, and also all the estates, claims, and demands to the same corporation belonging discharged from the afore recited vote or by-law of the said trustees, confining and narrowing the true and original plan of the said institution, which vote or by-law, and all others, contrary to the true design and spirit of the said charter, are hereby declared to be void, be and they are in and by this act, ratified and confirmed to, and for the use and benefit of the same seminary for ever.

Stripped of legal verbiage, the act will be seen to have as its purpose the confirmation of the charter and estates of the College and Academy, but to another than the original board of trustees and their successors, "the said board and the faculty being hereby dissolved and vacated." Contrary to an opinion which seems still to be prevalent, the charter itself was not revoked. The control of the institution was vested in a new board of trustees, who were largely under the political domination of the state legislature. The real reasons for this action are not easy to discern. The "vote or by-law" of June 14, 1764, which was cited in the act as having narrowed the base of the college, was the very one which the trustees had recorded at the suggestion of the Archbishop of Canterbury, Thomas and Richard Penn, and Dr. Samuel Chandler, formally declaring the intention of maintaining freedom from religious or sectarian control (see p. 74); obviously the Assembly used this passage merely as a talking-point, since the minute certainly expressed no narrowing or limitation. Horace W. Smith suggested that personal animus on the part of President Reed of Pennsylvania toward William Smith and certain of the trustees was the fundamental reason. Although Horace Smith unquestionably exaggerated this particular angle, it is evident that

Pennsylvania politics, never perhaps noted for their purity or gentleness, were at the root of the matter.

With this act of the Assembly, the first part of William Smith's career as an educator in Philadelphia came to an end. Provost Charles J. Stillé justly remarked:

The History of the progress of the College of Philadelphia . . . during the first thirty years of its existence, (1749-1779,) is the history of the results of the extraordinary zeal, the unwearied devotion, and the wonderful skill, capacity and energy displayed in promoting its welfare by a single man—Rev. Dr. WILLIAM SMITH, the first Provost of the College.

The same capabilities Smith continued to expend on behalf of the college even after this "confirmation" of the charter had deprived him of the provostship. In season and out, he was untiring in his efforts to bring about what he considered justice.

The new trustees on December 16, 1779, appointed a committee to obtain the keys of the university from Smith; five days later the committee reported that Smith "had declined delivering them, as an account of the property formerly under his care had not yet been fully taken." Apparently the keys were given up without dispute as soon as the inventory was taken, but the provost's house was not relinquished so easily. On December 29, 1779, a committee was appointed to ask Dr. Smith when it would be convenient for him to vacate the house. It was not immediately convenient for Dr. Smith to vacate the house; one can be sure that he was emphatic in telling the committee so. In fact, he remained in it for nearly a year, and he finally gave it up only upon receiving a receipt for the keys which specified that "such delivery of Possession" should not destroy any legal claim he might conceive himself to have to the house. Smith's behavior may seem stubborn and spiteful. It was stubborn and, to some degree, spiteful. But it was the behavior of a man who had just seen the institution into which he had built his own ideals, for which he had labored twenty-five years, and most of the capital of which he had supplied by his efforts, suddenly taken out of his hands and the hands of those whom he considered its friends. He clung to whatever he could of its property, playing for time and hoping that somehow a change in the political scene might restore what had been lost.

Smith's financial condition did not permit him to remain idle. In 1780, therefore, he removed to Chestertown, in Kent County, Maryland, where he became rector of the parish church at a stipend of 600 bushels of wheat annually. To augment his living and to keep his hand in the work he knew and loved best, he accepted a few private pupils. His new "academy" was joined with the Kent County Free School that same year and Smith was put in charge. A most interesting phenomenon then took place. Within two years the school was granted a charter as Washington College, the name being chosen out of respect to George Washington. From *An Account of Washington College, in the State of Maryland*, which Smith published in 1784, one can see that the moving spirit in this erection of an academy into a college was the same that had been dominant when the Academy and Charitable School of Philadelphia became the College, Academy, and Charitable School of Philadelphia. A paragraph from the introduction will serve to show the author of *Mirania:*

In short, lasting provisions must be made by GOOD EDUCATION, for training up a succession of *Patriots*, *Lawgivers*, *Sages* and *Divines;* for LIBERTY will not deign to dwell, but where her fair companion KNOWLEDGE flourishes by her side; nor can GOVERNMENT be duly administered but where the principles of *Religion, Justice, Virtue, Sobriety*, and *Obedience* for CONSCIENCE-SAKE, are upheld.

The charter or "Act for founding a College at Chester" proves that Smith was still intent upon the college as an instrument for the making of better men and better citizens:

. . . And be it enacted, That the said Visitors and Governors . . . may take and receive any sum or sums of money

. . . and employ the same towards erecting, setting up and maintaining the said college, in such manner as they shall judge most necessary and convenient for the instruction, improvement and education of youth, in the vernacular and learned languages, and generally in any kind of literature, arts and sciences, which they shall think proper to be taught for training up good, useful and accomplished men, for the service of their country in church and state; and youth of all religious denominations and persuasions, shall be freely and liberally admitted to equal privileges and advantages of education, and to all the literary honors of the college.

A subscription was undertaken on behalf of the college, and by May 14, 1783, when the first commencement was held, about £10,300 of Maryland money had been collected. The list of subscribers was headed by General Washington; in his letter of August 18, 1782, permitting the use of his name to the college, he had given fifty guineas "as an *Earnest* of my wishes for the prosperity of this Seminary."

The first commencement was a College of Philadelphia commencement moved to Maryland. Smith's son Charles, who was one of the five to receive the B.A. degree, delivered the "English Valedictory Oration." He also recited the verses which his father had written, now some thirty years before, and had prefixed to the *College of Mirania*, and which had also been recited at the first commencement of the College of Philadelphia.

In the evening of the same day, Dr. YOUNG's TRAGEDY of the BROTHERS, notwithstanding the difficulty of the composition, was acted with the greatest applause before a vastly crouded and discerning audience, by the graduates and some others of the students. Messrs. *Charles Smith* and *John Scott*, who had before distinguished themselves in *Tamerlane* and *Bajazet*, as well as in some principal characters in other performances, during the last years of their education, concluded their scholastic labours in this way, by shining in the characters of the *Two Brothers!*

The next day, May 15, 1783, Governor Paca of Maryland laid the foundation stone of the new college. More **exercises** and ceremony attended this occasion. As a conclusion, a "pastoral dialogue" was spoken by three of the younger students, garbed in shepherds' costumes. Pastoral dialogues had been usual at Philadelphia under Smith's régime, and it is therefore not surprising that he transplanted the custom. Indeed, he did rather more than transplant the custom, for he actually transplanted, at least in part, a dialogue which had been composed at Philadelphia by Nathaniel Evans and used at the commencement there in 1763. This fact Smith acknowledged in a footnote appended to the verses as they appeared in the *Account of Washington College:*

> *This* Dialogue *was partly taken from one spoken on a similar Occasion, at the Conclusion of a former* PEACE.

Someone, probably Smith, made minor alterations in the borrowed lines, but the differences are too slight to justify their quotation and comparison.

Although old Ezra Stiles thought that the ceremonies at this commencement were something of a "bluster and parade" for the number of students involved, even he had to admit that "the College however will be a useful Institution." Ezra's information does not seem always to have been of the best, for he had recorded earlier in his diary, on April 7, 1781, that "Dr Smith late Provost of Philad^a College, has accepted an opulent Chh Living in Maryland & lately removed thither."

The published account of Washington College related that the institution was honored in May of 1784 by a visit from General Washington, who at that time subscribed his name to the list of visitors and governors. To commemorate the event,

> . . . the Students entertained the Public with the Tragedy of GUSTAVUS VASA, the great DELIVERER of SWEDEN from *Danish Oppression;* a Performance breathing, throughout the whole, the most animated Sentiments of *Liberty, Heroism* and *public Spirit.* It was received with the justest Approbation, and especially the following Lines of the *occasional Epilogue.* . . .

The epilogue, obviously written for the purpose of making clear the resemblance of Washington to Gustavus Vasa, and probably composed by Smith himself, closed with lines which 'drew Tears of Gratulation from every Eye, and repeated Bursts of Applause from every Heart":

> How late did fell Oppression, o'er this Land,
> With more than *Danish Fury* raise her Hand;
> When lo! a Hero of immortal Name
> From where *Potowmack* rolls his mighty Stream,
> Arose the Champion of his Country's Cause,
> The Friend of Mankind, Liberty and Laws;
> While, in the Conflict Heaven and Earth engag'd
> And gave us PEACE, where *War* and Rapine rag'd.

The second commencement was held on July 6, 1784. Three youths were granted baccalaureate degrees, and the master's degree was given to Joseph Coudon, long the chief master of the Kent County Free School, "on which this College is engrafted." The republication in the *Account of Washington College* of the "View of the Philosophy Schools," which had been printed in the "Account of the College and Academy of Philadelphia," shows that the system of education at Washington College was essentially the same as that which Smith had formulated for Philadelphia. He explained that the system

. . is now adopted for the Use of Washington College, with the Addition of such Books, Instruments, &c. as the many late Discoveries and Improvments in the Arts and Sciences render necessary.

The religious liberality which distinguished Washington College under Smith's guidance is well illustrated in this preface to the prayers of the college:

We shall therefore close the present Account with a Copy of the Morning and Evening Service which is at present appointed to be used, in their Turn of Prayer, by such of the Masters as are desirous of being assisted with a short *Form;* while every Master is left at his Pleasure to add to the same, or to *pray* without a *Form,* according to his *religious Persuasion,* and the liberal and *Catholic* Foundation of the Institution.

The prayers were composed or adapted by Smith. They breathe a spirit that is wiser, gentler, and more tolerant than that shown in the *Prayers, for the Use of the Philadelphia Academy*, in the preparation of which Smith had had a hand some thirty years earlier. The 1753 prayers, designed to be said by the students, were filled with petitions to be made duly respectful, and appreciative of their wonderful opportunities in attending the school. The masters were to say the Washington College prayers, and a more general and genuine humility was expressed, as in the "Prayer for Wisdom and Obedience":

O Thou, who art the Fountain of all Wisdom, be graciously pleased to inspire us, whose duty it is, to instruct them with such a Portion of thy divine Wisdom, as may enable us to discharge our great Trust with Fidelity and Success. May we ever bear in Mind, that the best Service we can render to Thee our God, or to our Fellow Creatures, is by our earnest and successful Endeavours to imbue the Minds of Youth with true and just Sentiments of Religion and Goodness.

The third commencement of Washington College was held on April 28, 1785, and was honored by the presence of the institution's patronym. Seven students received the B.A. degree, five were granted the M.A. rank, and nine reverend gentlemen were given the distinction of a D.D. degree. It is further testimony to the broadness of the foundation, founders, and first principal of Washington College that one of the clergymen so honored was the Reverend John Carroll, the eminent Roman Catholic prelate who became Archbishop of Baltimore.

During 1785 Smith had one brief contact with the University of the State of Pennsylvania. On July 13 of that year, the trustees resolved to allow Smith his arrears of salary up to November 27, 1779, the date on which the old faculty was legally dissolved, with interest added thereto, and to pay him a further quarter's salary. He was also to be paid with interest for the additional story which he had built on to the kitchen of the provost's house. At the same time, it was "moved and resolved" that Smith should be charged rent for the house from February 27, 1780, until he left it.

Smith's Maryland years were not devoted exclusively to the care of Washington College. He continued to hold his church living at Chestertown, and there is ample testimony that he was industrious in the discharge of his parochial duties. As will be seen later, this was one of the most active periods of his life in relation to the affairs of the church at large. Philadelphia and its college also occupied some of his time and thought. In 1788 Smith published *An Address to the General Assembly of Pennsylvania, In the case of the violated Charter, Of the College, Academy and Charitable School of Philadelphia, &c.* This thirty-page pamphlet was, for the most part, a straightforward and accurate account of the college, its history, its services, and the treatment accorded to it by the 1779 legislature of Pennsylvania. The pamphlet, and other efforts of Smith and the friends of the old college, bore fruit in the passage by the Assembly on March 6, 1789, of:

An Act

To repeal part of an act, entitled "An Act to confirm the estates and interests of the College, Academy, and Charitable School of the city of Philadelphia, and to amend and alter the Charters thereof, conformably to the revolution and to the constitution and government of this Commonwealth, and to erect the same into a University."

Bishop White said of this repeal that it would not have been effected, "notwithstanding the justice of the cause," but for Smith's "labours and perseverance." The act specifically provided that the trustees and members of the faculty, including the provost and vice-provost, should be reinstated and restored to their former rights. That portion of the earlier legislation which had set up a new board of trustees and put them in charge of an institution under the title of the University of the State of Pennsylvania was not repealed. Thus there were the two institutions, new and old, in simultaneous existence.

The act of March 6, 1789, was published contemporaneously as *An Act, To Restore the Charters and Property of the College, &C. of Philadelphia*. A copy of this leaflet in the Smith Papers at the Historical Society of Pennsylvania contains this manuscript note, in a handwriting that appears to be Smith's:

Memorandum—

On the morning of passing the foregoing Act, while the Members were collecting themselves, & before the *Speaker* Mr Peters took the Chair,—Dr *Hutcheson* came into the Committee Room, and offer'd to a Member, Thomas Fitzsimmons Esqr a Paper by way of *Rider* to the en*gross'd Bill*, requesting him to present the same to the house. Mr Fitzsimmons handed the same to Dr Smith, who hastily looking it over & finding its Purport was to indemnify what was called the *University* from any particular Account of their Expenditure of the College Stock & Property, during their *Usurpation* of eight Years & upwards, he return'd it to Mr Fitzsimmons, who went into the House, & Dr Hutcheson after him, the Speaker having taken the Chair, & Roll calling—

Dr Smith got a Slip of Paper, and wrote *extempore* as follow, viz

The RIDER

1

On Mischief bent, by *Ewing* sent,
   With *Rider* in his Hands,
Came Doctor Guts, with mighty Struts
   And thus of Smith demands—

2

"This *Rider*, Sir, to save all Stirr,
   "By Master Ewing's Will,
"I bring in Haste, pray get some Paste
   "And tack it to your Bill"—

3

Smith lifts his Eyes, "hoot Man he cries
   "Take back your stupid Stuff—
"Our Answer's brief—the crafty Thief
   "Has *ridden* lang enuff."—

N.B. This being privately thrown upon the Speaker's Table, who is a Man of infinite Humour, & loves a Joke, it was soon handed to some of the nearest Members, and spread thro' the House with a Laugh wch did more to smother the poor *Rider* in Cunabulis than many long Speeches a have done.

* The Doctor was bless'd with a goodly *Paunch*, but a good natur'd fellow, tho' a great Politician.

This bit of verse found its way into the *Pennsylvania Gazette* on March 12, 1789, but there the vowels of the various proper names were represented by discreet dashes. The Ewing referred to was, of course, the Reverend John Ewing, provost of the University of the State of Pennsylvania and a minister in the Presbyterian Church.

With the restoration of the college, William Smith moved his family back to the provost's house and took up his familiar round of educational duties in Philadelphia. Life at the college soon fell into the old pattern. At the first commencement after Smith's return there was given *An Exercise, Performed at the Public Commencement, in the College of Philadelphia, July 17, 1790. Containing an ODE, set to Music, sacred to the Memory of Dr. Franklin.* The title-page of this exercise, in the edition printed the same year by William Young in Philadelphia, stated:

This *Exercise* consists of lines, partly *original*, and partly selected or altered from former similar compositions in this College, as they were hastily thrown together, for the occasion of the present *Commencement;* it is hoped that they will be received with the usual indulgence of a candid public.

The most interesting borrowing was a satiric dialogue on commencement exercises, which took up the first three of nine printed pages. These lines were adapted, with only slight changes, from an oration in verse composed by Francis Hopkinson for the use of a young man at a commencement of the University of the State of Pennsylvania, but which the professors would not allow him to deliver. One can readily understand why; the satire is so pointed that its impertinence may well have outweighed its pertinence. It was an unusual professor, William Smith, and one with an abundant sense of humor, who used the lines as the prologue of a commencement exercise. The exercise continued with a eulogy upon Franklin, then the ode to Franklin's memory, and finally a dialogue on the progress of science and the blessings of peace. The concluding dialogue contained large borrowings from Smith's verse prologue to the *College of Mirania*, as well as some lines from the exercise which Nathaniel Evans and Paul Jackson had written for the commencement of 1763; this suggests that Smith compiled and arranged the 1790 exercise, aided by Francis Hopkinson, who not only contributed his rejected verses and probably himself made the changes in them, but who also very likely wrote the ode to Franklin.

It may be worth noting here that the College of Philadelphia awarded an honorary LL.D. degree to Hopkinson on December 15, 1790. Though it might be pleasant to imagine that this was a generous compensation for his contribution to the success of the commencement program earlier in the year, the real basis for the award was undoubtedly his legal attainments, since the degree was given on the occasion of the inaugural lecture of James Wilson as law professor in the college.

On the same date, December 15, 1790, William Smith delivered his last known charge to graduates of an institution under his care, this time to the graduates in medicine who were given degrees. He spoke feelingly and ably of the high calling for which the new physicians had prepared, and urged them to devote themselves zealously to the public good as well as to the advancement of medical knowledge. In his peroration the provost broadened his remarks to include the hope that at or near the seat of the national government a great national university might be erected, to which the graduates of colleges might come to pursue higher studies and especially to see at close hand the workings of the government. That the College of Philadelphia might become this institution was his obvious wish, and one that seemed possible of fulfillment, for the seat of the government was then in Philadelphia, and law and medical faculties were already attached to the college. Changes were soon to come to the College of Philadelphia, but not those which Smith envisioned.

The simultaneous existence of two institutions of higher learning was more than Philadelphia could support in 1790. This fact seems to have been independently and genuinely realized by the trustees of both the college and the university, for in the preamble to

AN ACT

To unite the University of the State of Pennsylvania, and the College, Academy, and Charitable School of Philadelphia, in the Commonwealth of Pennsylvania,

passed by the Assembly of Pennsylvania on September 30, 1791, it is expressly stated that

. . . the trustees of the university of the state of Pennsylvania, and the trustees of the college, academy, and charitable school of Philadelphia, in the commonwealth of Pennsylvania, by their several petitions have set forth, that they have agreed to certain terms of union of the said two institutions.

These terms included the election by each board of twelve of its members to be members of the board of trustees of the University of Pennsylvania, the governor of the state to be the twenty-fifth and presiding member. The new board thus set up held its first meeting on November 8, 1791. The terms of union provided for selecting the professors equally from the two schools. When the board came to name the arts faculty on April 9, 1792, it passed over Smith altogether, choosing among others the Reverend Dr. John Ewing as professor of natural philosophy and the Reverend Dr. John Andrews, a churchman, as professor of moral philosophy. Smith was naturally upset at his failure to be included in the new faculty. One week later he wrote to his old friend and student, William White, who was a member of the board:

Having been inform'd that the Trustees of the University are to meet this Evening, I must entreat You to lay my Request before them that I may be *duly* and *officially* notified whether by their present Arrangement they consider that, after all my Services, for near forty Years, in the Cause of Learning in Pennsylvania, I am now absolv'd from all future Duties and Connexion with the Seminary, in Consequence of, and agreeably to the Terms & Spirit of the *Act of Union.*

If this should be their Opinion, and that not voting *in*, is the same as actually voting *out*, and is to operate as a *Discharge*, even if more Professors were immediately necessary, it will be proper in the next place, for the Honor of the *Trustees*, as well as mine, and the Reputation which I have long had the Happiness to sustain as an Instructor of Youth, that such Discharge, if not accompanied with any direct Acknowlegement of my past Services, should at least bear no Marks of a Discharge for Incapacity, or Want of Will to be further useful in that Way to which my Life has been devoted, and at a Stage of it too, when I can seek for no other Employ. . . .

The trustees ignored this appeal and on April 26, 1792, proceeded to elect Dr. Ewing provost and Dr. Andrews vice-provost. On the same day, Smith wrote a letter to a committee which had been appointed by the board to consider his financial claims against the university, in which he emphasized his willingness—one might say his eagerness—to serve in any capacity at any time. It was not easy for Smith to reconcile himself to the fact that he was not to be on the new faculty. His letters to the trustees have been preserved and show that as late as April 2, 1793, he still hoped to be permitted to serve.

When he next wrote to the board, on December 3, 1793, Smith had apparently given up that hope, and his object now was to press his financial claims. The trustees had already agreed that "an Annuity of one hundred Pounds is due to Doctor Smith from the Time he ceased to be Provost of the late College, and to continue during his natural Life, in pursuance of an agreement made by the trustees of the late College," but Smith had other claims for back salary and arrears of his annuity. In particular he claimed £900 back annuity, with £432 accumulated interest on it, and some other amounts, including money advanced by him to purchase Rittenhouse's orrery for the college. These claims came up from time to time before the trustees and were referred to committees. It was not until

April 21, 1795, that the matter was finally settled by an agreement to pay £900 for all claims except the annuity, which Smith continued to draw. After this date, the name of William Smith virtually disappears from the records of the University of Pennsylvania.

By what chance or design it happened that Smith was not chosen to the new faculty it would now be almost impossible to say. Certainly some of the trustees were his friends and wanted him to continue, but there were others to whom he was personally objectionable. Even some of his friends may have felt that the unity of the new institution would be better assured if one who had been so prominent in the earlier dissensions were not to remain active after the breach had been healed. Smith had made most of his enemies not through his conduct of the college, but through his participation in politics, and some of the animosity he had aroused may have returned upon him here. His contentiousness, which was always part of his nature and which he allowed himself to express in several of his later letters to the trustees, did not help him. Whatever the cause, William Smith, for the first time since 1754, was no longer actively engaged in the work of educating American youth.

It must be apparent that Smith was a real force in education in this country at a time when the educator probably stood in an even more influential position than he does today. When a college education was more exclusively the privilege of a few, who largely constituted the governing class, the man who gave the college graduates their standards and their ideals was supremely important. That Smith realized the importance of this trust cannot be doubted. The product of education—"better men and better citizens"—was the fundamental note of his educational philosophy. As an educator and as a writer on education, he never allowed himself to become befogged by details. He kept in mind the primal idea that the worth of an educational institution was measured by the usefulness of its graduates to the world and to themselves. In a later day, it is somewhat fashionable to scoff at the "idealism" of our fore-fathers. William Smith, at least, joined that idealism with the hard-headed practicality which one associates with his race. The Scot may be a dreamer; he is very seldom a daydreamer.

Today, too, one hears much about the cultural necessity for education. Smith did not use the current terminology, but the idea itself permeates his writing. To give a man a taste for the best that has been thought and said in the world was Smith's ideal and practice long before Matthew Arnold came along to provide the pat phrase. One sometimes wonders whether Smith may not have been wiser and more far-sighted than some of our later educational theorizers who have put such great emphasis upon the twin idols of Utility and Culture. Smith realized—and it was important to do so in his time as it is in ours—that the educational system has failed of its op-portunities if its graduates are not better enabled than other men to understand the workings of the state in which they live. "Better citizens." The phrase could not be plainer. Smith did not hunt for big words to express himself on the subject of education; his writings and public utterances were simple, understandable, and conclusive.

Moreover, he put his preachings into practice. To recite the long list of distinguished men who received their training un-der Smith would serve no special purpose, since it might be objected that they would have become distinguished anyway. But a study of Smith's relations with a small group of his stu-dents will serve to reveal his methods as a teacher and his in-fluence as a man.

IV

SMITH AND HIS GROUP

THE almost simultaneous production, by three friends, of the first American musical composition, the first American drama to be professionally performed, and the first American painting of permanent worth is a phenomenon that invites inquiry. So far as the writer knows, the creation in a society of its first music, painting, and drama has never occurred elsewhere under similar circumstances. When one finds that the three friends—Francis Hopkinson, Thomas Godfrey, and Benjamin West—were associated in a small group under the leadership of an able critic and friend, one is compelled to recognize the singular importance of this group and its leader, William Smith. To appreciate fully their contributions, it is necessary to consider briefly the status of literature, music, and painting in Philadelphia before they began their work.

It was with reference to the contributors to Smith's *American Magazine* that the literary historian of Philadelphia, Ellis P. Oberholtzer, remarked: "It may be said unequivocally that Pennsylvania had no poets prior to the appearance on the scene of this interesting group." One can scarcely dispute his judgment. Samuel Keimer, whom Franklin found composing an elegy to Aquila Rose directly from the type case, and poor Rose himself, could hardly ask a better name than versifier. In other forms of letters the Philadelphia into which the young men of Smith's group were born was not much better off. Descriptions of the country and a few Quaker "theological" works were about all that could be claimed in prose for the English settlers, and the literature in German was too confined in circulation to be of general interest. In the field of translation, Philadelphia could really hold up her head, for James Logan's translations from the classics were not only the best of his work, but were of a quality that might stand comparison with any being done elsewhere. To be sure, a new era had begun by 1736, when Thomas

Godfrey, the oldest of the group, was born, for *Poor Richard's Almanac* was then in its third year and the name of Franklin was beginning to be reckoned with in the lighter forms of polite (and often indeed of highly impolite) literature.

American culture was, of course, transplanted from western Europe. In a sense, the drama was doubly transplanted, for both plays and players were imported. Companies of English actors performed the standard English repertory and translations of a few foreign plays, and by the time the first play written by a native American was produced, Philadelphia already had behind it an appreciable theatrical history. Certain elements of Philadelphia society would not have agreed that it was a respectable history, since they denied the right of anything theatrical to be called respectable. As a matter of fact, of the diversity of religious beliefs and believers which William Penn's tolerant "Charter of Privileges to Pennsylvania" had brought to the city, the only groups tolerant of the theatre were the Church of England and the Roman Catholic, and even among their members there was not complete harmony on the subject. It would be interesting to know whether it was a member of the Church of England or a Quaker wishing to use a good argument against the churchmen who wrote to the *Pennsylvania Journal* on March 19, 1754, citing the disapproval of plays expressed by eminent English divines, including Bishop Burnet and Archbishop Tillotson. The protest, whatever the source, was ineffective, for the theatrical season that year ran from April 15 until June 24.

The theatrical history of Philadelphia had begun even earlier than 1754, however. In August 1749 the Murray and Kean company played Addison's *Cato* in a reconstructed warehouse on Water Street. Their season had apparently opened the preceding January, since a protest against their performing had been made then. It was Lewis Hallam's company that visited Philadelphia during the spring of 1754, acting under a permit from Governor Robert Hunter Morris. In 1759, Hallam's widow, now Mrs. David Douglass, returned to the city with Douglass' company for a season that ran from June 25 to December 28. Douglass later returned to Philadelphia and built the South-wark, the first permanent theatre in America, which opened on November 12, 1766.

When Francis Hopkinson wrote his poem, "Ode on Music, written by a Youth of Seventeen on his learning to play the Harpsichord," the city of his birth could boast only a meager musical history. A "calendarium" of musical events in Philadel-phia from 1728 to 1759, compiled by O. G. Sonneck, the emi-nent student of early American music, shows that the first form in which music reached the city was as accompaniment to danc-ing. By 1730 a teacher of singing and spinet-playing had made her appearance. Other teachers followed, and soon many a gentleman scraped a fiddle or blew lightly into a flute by way of genteel accomplishment. A few churches had managed to acquire organs. Reprints of English psalm books and of such works as Watts's *Divine Songs* shared almost equal attention with secular music. There must have been occasional adapta-tions of music to the abilities or requirements of the performers. But as yet nothing had been attempted in original composition.

Little need be said about art in Philadelphia at the time Benjamin West first came to that city. One needs only to look at an advertisement of Matthew Clarkson in the *Pennsylvania Journal* for July 25, 1754, to see the popular taste of the day. "For ready money, or short credit" Clarkson offered "The four seasons, painted on glass, and in mezzotinto; the six sciences, painted on glass, and in ditto; the five senses, on glass, and in ditto . . . the jolly sailor, the twelve months, several History pieces, and sundry humorous pieces printed on glass . . . views about London, ditto in Rome, on the river Tyber, in Florence, in Holland, and on the Greenland whale-fishery." About the only painting being done in Philadelphia itself was the taking of portraits by itinerant painters, mostly Englishmen and Dutch-men.

Even so brief a survey must show that the young men of Smith's group had to look principally to themselves and their mentor for inspiration and encouragement. The group, it must be emphasized, had no formal organization, but consisted simply of five young men of talent whom Smith brought together for their mutual benefit. Three have already been named; the others were Jacob Duché and Nathaniel Evans. Within the limits of a chapter one can only indicate the part which Smith and the group association had in developing the creative impulse of each of the five; to do more would require a series of biographies.

An especially good example of Smith's ability to bring out latent talent may be seen in the fact that Francis Hopkinson and Jacob Duché each wrote his first poem after hearing Smith's funeral sermon for their classmate, William Thomas Martin, in 1754. Hopkinson and Duché were both members of established Philadelphia families and were both entered in the Academy of Philadelphia at its opening. Hopkinson, indeed, was the first pupil enrolled. The boys' poems were more remarkable for promise than for performance. In reading Duché's, Smith needed particularly to recall the rules he had set forth in *Mirania* for the guidance of those correcting the compositions of the young. It was perhaps in the hope of curbing somewhat the youth's over-exuberance that Smith took Duché under his wing and helped him revise a verse prologue which Duché was writing and was to recite at the first public exercises under Smith's direction at the academy on November 12, 1754. Hopkinson contributed to this occasion by delivering his oration, "On Education in General."

Not to be dated exactly, but obviously belonging to this early period, is Hopkinson's "Hermitage, a Poem, inscribed to Mr. Jacob Duché, Jun." The two young men had been fellow visitors to Hermitage, the Long Island home of the Martin family. The poem gains what interest it has from its mention of Smith's previous educational labors at the Hermitage and its romantic description of Duché himself as "Dear pensive youth." About the same time, Duché composed and sent to the Provost an "Ode to Rev Mr S——th," which Smith thought enough of to preserve among his papers. As the first stanza shows, the poem is a genuine testimony of Duché's affection for Smith:

> O thou! whose Precepts just & wise
> First taught my wakening Soul to rise
> At Wisdom's awful Voice,
> Still patient of her sacred Lore,
> Truth's winding Mazes to explore,
> And in the Search rejoice!

The closing weeks of 1756 must have been very busy for Duché, Hopkinson, and Smith, preparing as they were for the production at the college of Smith's version of the masque of *Alfred*, in which Duché played the title rôle. Duché was likewise chosen to recite an epilogue which the Provost had written. *Alfred* called forth original poems by both Hopkinson and Duché, poems very similar in nature. Duché's was addressed to Hopkinson's sister Elizabeth, paying her his compliments "on her excellent Performance of the vocal Parts in an Oratorial Exercise at the College of Philadelphia." It was to a Miss Lawrence that Hopkinson addressed his thanks "on her kind assistance in the vocal parts." Just exactly what part Hopkinson himself took in the masque is not known, but that he was active in it is unquestionable; else why should he have thanked Miss Lawrence for her assistance? The account in the *Pennsylvania Gazette* included the detail that:

. . . *Alfred* is further confirmed in his noble Purposes, by the following Song, sung by two invisible Spirits . . . which was altered from the Original, retaining only one or two Lines; and fitted to an excellent Piece of new Music by one of the Performers.

No better suggestion can be offered than O. G. Sonneck's that Hopkinson was the composer of this music. Certainly no other person who ever composed music is known to have been in any way associated with the production.

The year 1757 saw another event in which Smith, Duché, and Hopkinson were again intimately joined: the first commencement of the College of Philadelphia, at which the latter two received their bachelor's degrees. At the same time one of Smith's younger pupils was leaving his charge for a while. Nathaniel Evans, the youngest member of the group—he was born in 1742, Duché in 1738, Hopkinson in 1737—had been entered in the academy at its opening in 1751, but after six years was apprenticed by his father to a merchant. Evans apparently had not written any poetry while in the academy, but he began to do so during his apprenticeship. As Smith put it, "he devoted more of his time to the service of the Muses, than to the business of the Counting-House." In so small a school as the College and Academy of Philadelphia was at the time, Evans must surely have known the members of the class of 1757 and drawn some of his inspiration from them, as well as from Smith.

In November 1757 there appeared the first issue of Smith's *American Magazine*, founded partly for his pupils, "whose talents he wished to encourage and cultivate, both in sentiment and composition." It has already been observed that this magazine was of great service to the group, to which it served as both outlet and stimulus. The first issue and several later issues contained poems by Francis Hopkinson. The magazine also served as a vehicle for the publication of poems by Thomas Godfrey. Having a place to publish one's work must always please a poet and inspire him to write; so it was with Hopkinson and Godfrey.

Young Godfrey had apparently come under Smith's influence and into the group at some time prior to the publication of the *American Magazine*. Just what connection William Smith had with Godfrey's education is not certain. John Galt, the biographer of Benjamin West, published West's statement that Provost Smith had introduced him to "four young men, pupils of his own," of whom one was Godfrey. Godfrey's name, however, does not appear on any of the extant, though possibly incomplete, lists of students in the College and Academy of Philadelphia. Smith's express statement that Godfrey had only "a common education in his mother-tongue" suggests that he may have been a student in the Charity School, but lists of the charity pupils for the period before 1765 no longer exist.

The manner in which Smith learned of Godfrey's poetic talents is also in doubt. Galt may have been somewhat confused as to just what West told him. What he set down was this:

He [Godfrey] . . . had secretly written a poem, which he published anonymously in the Philadelphia newspaper, under the title of "The Temple of Fame." The attention which it attracted, and the encomiums which the Provost in particular bestowed on it, induced West, who was in the Poet's confidence, to mention to him who was the author. The information excited the alert benevolence of Smith's character, and he lost no time until he had procured the release of Godfrey from his indenture, and a respectable employment for him in the government of the state.

The chief difficulties in the way of accepting this statement at its face value are that no poem with such a title is to be found in Godfrey's collected poems, or in either the *Pennsylvania Gazette* or the *Pennsylvania Journal* between the years 1753 and 1758, and that no mention of this episode was made either by Smith in his account of Godfrey in the *American Magazine* or by Nathaniel Evans in his preface to Godfrey's *Juvenile Poems*. Unless a poem by the title of "The Temple of Fame" appeared in some unnoticed publication and its authorship was revealed by West to Smith, one must conclude that Galt was somehow in error. Of course, it is not necessary to assume that Smith knew of Godfrey's poetic ability when he introduced him to West, though he surely was aware of Godfrey's general capabilities and literary interests.

The first of Godfrey's poems to be printed (unless there was a "Temple of Fame") was "The Invitation," which appeared anonymously in the *American Magazine* for January 1758. The new poet again appeared in the August 1758 number of the magazine with "A *Pindaric Ode* On Friendship, By the Author of the Invitation," and in the September issue with "*A*

Pindaric ODE *on* WINE." Sometime before the publication of the September issue, Smith had discovered the identity of his contributor, for in that issue he published an account of Godfrey which is as interesting for its revelation of Smith's zest as a patron of the arts as for its telling of the story of Thomas Godfrey. Smith declared that "we reckon it one of the highest instances of good fortune that has befallen us, during the period of our Magazine, that we have had an opportunity of making known to the world so much merit," carefully adding, "When we say *Merit*, we mean in consideration of his circumstances and means of improvement."

Another perplexing question about the relationship between Smith and Godfrey is presented by Galt's statement that Smith obtained Godfrey's release from his indenture to a watchmaker and secured him "respectable employment . . . in the government of the state." On May 2, 1758, Godfrey was commissioned an ensign in the third battalion of the Pennsylvania Regiment. In view of the fact that Smith was then in the midst of his famous altercation with the Assembly of Pennsylvania, it seems somewhat unlikely that he could have secured a commission for Godfrey. He had friends in the executive branch of the government, but it is doubtful if the Governor would have cared to invite the ill-will of the Assembly by granting a favor to Smith. All that can be said with certainty is that Godfrey did receive the commission, and that Smith would have done everything in his power to aid a young poet of whose abilities he thought so highly.

Godfrey's four poems which appeared in the *American Magazine* were reprinted in the English *Grand Magazine of Universal Intelligence* for March 1759. This magazine was published by Ralph Griffiths, a friend and publisher of William Smith. C. Lennart Carlson, who first noted the republication, is unquestionably correct in suggesting that Smith was responsible for it.

The *American Magazine* had a further distinction in that it became the first publication to mention the name of Benjamin West and to call attention to his work when it printed in its February 1758 issue a poem signed "Lovelace" and entitled *"Upon seeing the Portrait of Miss **——** by Mr*. West." It has been suggested that Francis Hopkinson was "Lovelace," but no definitive answer to the question of authorship can be given. In his editorial introduction to the poem, Smith mentioned that "the lady who sat, the painter who guided the pencil, and the poet who so well describes the whole, are all natives of this place, and very young." A footnote proclaimed Smith's pleasure at making known to the world the name of "so extraordinary a genius as Mr. West" and stated his conviction that West would become "truly eminent in his profession" when he should have obtained more experience and the opportunity "of viewing the productions of able masters." Here was the first hint of a conviction that was already in Smith's mind, that the young painter must seek out better examples of art for his instruction than any he had seen before or could see in the new world.

Since the name of the young lady whose portrait occasioned this poetic outburst was not given, one wonders if it may not have been Miss Moore, who was soon to become Mrs. William Smith, and of whom West is known to have painted a portrait about this time, and if the poet was not complimenting the editor as well as the artist. This might help to account for the more than usually warm reception which the poem received from Smith. Assuming that the poet was Francis Hopkinson, the publication affords a splendid example of the way in which Smith encouraged his students, as well as of the camaraderie which they had established among themselves.

There is no serious doubt about the authorship of the *"Verses Inscribed to Mr*. WOLLASTON," to which the initials "F.H." were signed in the *American Magazine* for September 1758. It is of less importance that Francis Hopkinson inscribed some verses to an English portrait painter then in America, whose work exhibited no great merit but some skill, than that in those lines he took the opportunity to pay a compliment to his friend Benjamin West:

> Nor let the muse forget thy name O WEST,
> Lov'd youth, with virtue as by nature blest!
> If such the radiance of thy *early Morn*,
> What bright effulgence must thy *Noon* adorn?
> Hail sacred *Genius!* may'st thou ever tread,
> The pleasing paths your *Wollaston* has lead.
> Let his just precepts all your works refine,
> Copy each grace, and learn like him to shine,
> So shall some future muse her sweeter lays,
> Swell with your name, and give *you* all *his* praise.

The justice of these critical comments need not be called into question. After all, if young West could not see enough good painting in this country to form his taste as a painter, it would be ridiculous to assume that young Hopkinson could have seen enough to form his taste as an art critic.

William Smith, of course, was aware of the talents of Benjamin West long before "Lovelace" sent his poem to the *American Magazine*. West, born in 1738 in Chester County (now Delaware County), Pennsylvania, had grown up in a community where no opportunity for artistic development seemed to present itself. As an old man, he told his biographer, John Galt, how he had drawn his first picture, of an infant niece, in red and black ink at the age of six years. Members of a party of Indians showed him how to "prepare the red and yellow colours with which they painted their ornaments" and his mother presented him with a piece of indigo for blue. Thus did he acquire the use of the three primary colors. The fur of his father's pet cat provided his first brushes. The setting was complete for an Alger-like success story. In any third-rate novel, the boy could not have failed to become a painter of wide renown, to have the great of the world seek to have him paint them, and to be called by his first name by the king. West's career was to differ from this pattern of romantic fiction only in that it was fact.

In the near-wilderness that was his boyhood home, West's talents might easily have gone unheralded and unknown. Fortune assumed the guise of a Philadelphia Quaker merchant, one Mr. Pennington, who called upon his West relatives and was so much impressed by the sight of a boy just past seven making pictures that he sent him a box of paints and brushes, several pieces of canvas, and some engravings. The work done with these materials Mr. Pennington admired so greatly on a return visit that he asked permission to take Benjamin with him to Philadelphia on a visit. Through this visit and through other acquaintances which gradually came his way, West's horizons opened wider and wider. Recommended by a friend to a Lancaster acquaintance as a suitable artist for "taking" the portraits of his wife and himself, West found other commissions in Lancaster and there painted, at the suggestion of a local gunsmith, the death of Socrates.

The successful completion of this picture led to a great event in West's life. The painting was seen by William Smith, who happened to be in Lancaster at the time on business concerned with the proposed erection of a public grammar school. Smith, who, according to West's later statement, "was an excellent classical scholar, and combined with his knowledge and admiration of the merits of the antients that liberality of respect for the endeavours of modern talent, with which the same kind of feeling is but rarely found connected," was so taken by West's work that he proposed that the young artist, then eighteen, come to Philadelphia and pursue a general education under him, a proposal to which Benjamin's father readily agreed.

From the description which Galt gave of West's course of study, and from the available records, it seems evident that West was not a formally enrolled student in the College and Academy of Philadelphia, but that Smith directed his private studies:

There was something so judicious in the plan of study which Provost Smith had formed for his pupil, that it deserves to be particularly considered. He regarded him as destined to be a

Painter; and on this account did not impose upon him those grammatical exercises of language which are usually required from the young student of the classics, but directed his attention to those incidents which were likely to interest his fancy, and to furnish him at some future time with subjects for the easel. He carried him immediately to those passages of antient history which make the most lasting impression on the imagination of the regular-bred scholar, and described the picturesque circumstances of the transactions with a minuteness of detail that would have been superfluous to a general student.

Again one is afforded an example of William Smith's wisdom and liberality as a teacher. Realizing that West had too little formal schooling to attempt the regular course of study, Smith designed a program to fit his needs. The curriculum was not a sacred object to him. Here was a young man whom he had an opportunity to make into a better man and better citizen, but a man and citizen of a particular kind. The fetishes of educational theory were not allowed to stand in the way of the accomplishment of this purpose.

It was not long until Provost Smith had, to quote Galt, "introduced West, among other persons, to four young men, pupils of his own, whom he particularly recommended to his acquaintance as possessing endowments of mind greatly superior to the common standard of mankind." Galt erred somewhat in taking down the names of these four young men, but there will be little difficulty in recognizing "Francis Hopkins," Thomas Godfrey, "Reid," and "Jacob Duchey." "Reid" was undoubtedly Joseph Reed, who later became President Reed of Pennsylvania.

In his old age West spoke of the pleasant times which this group had enjoyed together as they fished along the banks of the Schuylkill and, more especially, as they rested under the shade of a clump of pine trees and listened to Godfrey recite his verses. It is to be regretted that West did not give Galt an account of the talk that went on. Knowing the young men from their works and realizing that they were students of William Smith, one can be fairly certain of some of the things that must have been said. The glories of the antique world, the rising glory of America, the future of the arts, the purpose of man and his life, the necessity of liberty, individual and social; all these and many other topics must have made the hours pass too quickly. West's recollections of his hours with Godfrey are strongly brought to mind in the lines of one of Godfrey's pastoral poems:

How oft together Schuylkil's verdant side
We've trac'd, or wanton'd in its cooling tide,
Or soft reclin'd, where spreading shades were wove,
With joyful accents fill'd the sounding grove.
Then all was gay, then sprightly mirth was found,
And nature bloom'd in vernal beauties round.

After spending some time under Smith's charge, West, in order to fill his pocketbook with larger fees and to broaden his outlook upon life, went to New York. As he told Galt, "The Society of New York was much less intelligent in matters of taste and knowledge than that of Philadelphia." Thinking the matter over in retrospect, West decided that "Dr. Smith, the Provost of the college, had largely contributed to elevate the taste, the sentiment and the topics of conversation in Philadelphia." West had been in New York eleven months when he received from Provost Smith a letter which changed the course of his life. Having learned that William Allen, a Philadelphia merchant, was sending his son abroad with a cargo of wheat and flour he was shipping to Italy, Smith saw an opportunity for his protégé to visit a country which had long been regarded as one of the art centers of the world. Allen acceded to Smith's request that West be allowed to make the crossing, and the young artist was soon off on his quest, reaching Rome on July 10, 1760. After this time West can no longer be considered an active member of Smith's group, but he was never to forget his old friends of Philadelphia.

Meanwhile, the other members of the group continued their activities. The year 1759 was particularly important to them, for in that year Francis Hopkinson wrote what is now believed to have been the first American musical composition and Thomas Godfrey finished his tragedy, *The Prince of Parthia*, which eight years later was to become the first American play to be professionally produced.

Francis Hopkinson's importance in the history of American music is indicated by a statement in Sonneck's capable monograph on Hopkinson:

Francis Hopkinson was the first native American composer of songs of whom we know, and his song "My Days Have Been So Wondrous Free" is the earliest secular American composition extant, dating back to 1759.

Hopkinson himself said, "I cannot, I believe, be refused the credit of being the first native of the United States who has produced a musical composition." His only possible rival is James Lyon, but the investigations of Sonneck and other scholars have clearly established Hopkinson's priority. One agrees completely with Sonneck's conclusion that "From all we know of Hopkinson's character, I doubt not that he investigated the correctness of his claim and found his earliest compositions to antedate those of James Lyon."

"My Days Have Been So Wondrous Free," a setting for Thomas Parnell's poem "Love and Innocence," is an unpretentious little song, with a grace and music-box-like charm of its own. It is one of six songs signed "F.H."—all undoubtedly Hopkinson's own compositions—in a manuscript volume (now in the Library of Congress) labeled "Francis Hopkinson his Book" and dated 1759; into this volume Hopkinson also copied selections from such composers as Handel and Purcell. One of the other original songs is of great interest, for the words of "Oh, Come To Masonborough's Grove" were written by Thomas Godfrey and refer to a locality in North Carolina, to which state he had first gone in the spring of 1759. The poem was not printed until 1765; Godfrey, knowing the musical interests of his friend Hopkinson, probably sent him a manuscript copy, either asking or hoping it would be set to music.

Godfrey had gone to North Carolina on being offered a position as a factor there; he remained about three years. The importance of the year 1759 and Godfrey's residence in North

Carolina is shown in a memoir which Nathaniel Evans later wrote of his friend:

At Carolina it was, that he finished the Dramatic Poem, called, *The Prince of Parthia*, as appears by a letter of his, to a Gentleman in this city; dated, as early as, November 17th, 1759; which was received after the manuscript of it. "By the last vessel from this place," says he, "I sent you the copy of a Tragedy I finished here, and desired your interest in bringing it on the stage; I have not yet heard of the vessel's arrival, and believe if she is safe, it will be too late for the Company now in Philadelphia."

Godfrey's letter was surely addressed to William Smith, and the Provost undoubtedly hastened with the manuscript to the company of actors then in Philadelphia. The theatrical season closed on December 28, 1759, however, and there was no possibility of getting up a new play in the time left.

After his graduation with the class of 1757, Jacob Duché had continued his studies under Smith, attending the Sunday evening meetings which Smith conducted for the benefit of students who intended to enter the ministry. Duché's inclination was confirmed by attendance at these sessions, and it was probably William Smith who recommended that he go to England for further and more intensive study. On February 7, 1758, Smith wrote a letter to the Bishop of London, presenting Duché. While he was abroad, Duché studied at Cambridge and obtained ordination as a deacon; upon his return to America he became one of the assistant ministers of Christ Church. He was also made professor of oratory in the College of Philadelphia, and in addition to his regular duties, acted as public orator for the college on ceremonial occasions.

With their classmates of 1757, Duché and Hopkinson were admitted to the M.A. degree at the 1760 commencement of the College of Philadelphia. In its account of the event the *Pennsylvania Gazette* reported:

One of the Students, who received his Master's Degree on this Occasion, conducted the Organ with that bold and masterly Hand, for which he is celebrated; and several of the Pieces were also his own Composition. In a Word, the whole gave great Satisfaction to Strangers as well as others; and certainly such Improvements in useful Science and polite Arts, in this part of the World, must give a very high Pleasure to every ingenious Mind.

There can be no doubt that it was Francis Hopkinson who played the organ—an organ which only the year before he had helped to buy when he wrote his "Prologue in praise of music," which was spoken at a benefit performance of *George Barnwell* by the Hallam company, the proceeds going "towards the Raising a Fund for purchasing an ORGAN to the COLLEGE HALL in this City, and instructing the Charity Children in PSALMODY." At the 1760 commencement Hopkinson also read "Charity, A Poem," which he had written as a tribute to the Charitable School. Soon the ties of friendship between him and Duché were strengthened by kinship, for on June 19, 1760, Duché was married to Elizabeth Hopkinson.

Hopkinson's talents were again employed on behalf of the college for the commencement of 1761, when he wrote the words and music of the ode in the dialogue-ode exercise then performed. Provost Smith wrote the dialogue. Duché, who had been elected a trustee of the College and Academy in 1761, collaborated with Hopkinson in the writing of "An Exercise, Containing A Dialogue and Ode *On the* Accession *of His present gracious Majesty*, George III," presented at the 1762 commencement. Hopkinson again wrote the ode and the music to which it was set; Duché's contribution was the dialogue. An advertisement in Dunlap's 1762 edition of this exercise announced that there was just published, "Neatly printed in a Quarto PAMPHLET, Price 1/6, SCIENCE A POEM BY FRANCIS HOPKINSON, Esq." This poem is especially interesting because in it Hopkinson reviewed his career in the pursuit of science, that is, as a student in the College of Philadelphia. Part of *Science* was very nearly a verse rendering of Smith's "Account of the College and Academy." One portion, indeed, was almost a direct versification of Smith's charge to Hopkinson and his classmates of 1757. The poem closed with lines celebrating the future glory of America under the reign of science, one of Smith's familiar themes.

Shortly after making his contribution to the commencement of 1762, Duché decided that he should return to England for full ordination. William Smith was in England at the time on his fund-raising mission and was able to use his influence to secure the ordination of his former student. On the same trip Smith met Benjamin West, who had spent three years in the study of his art in Italy and had come to England for a brief holiday before returning home. As it happened, the brief holiday was to extend for nearly sixty years and the rest of West's life. Smith also helped to promote the name of Thomas Godfrey, for that young man's poem "Victory" was published, surely upon the recommendation of Smith, in an English periodical, the *Library*, in 1762. During the same year Godfrey returned to Philadelphia from North Carolina on the death of his employer and published his poem "The Court of Fancy."

Another member of the group was also writing poetry at this time. The dialogue for the commencement of 1763, held in the Provost's absence, was written by Nathaniel Evans, who had returned to college after the expiration of his apprenticeship. Evans had seen his first published work, "A PANEGYRIC ODE, *On the late General* WOLFE, *on the Taking of* QUEBEC," appear in the *New American Magazine* for March 1760. His "Elegy to Theophilus Grew," professor of mathematics in the College of Philadelphia, was printed in the *Pennsylvania Gazette* for August 7, 1760, and on February 11, 1762, the same journal published the first of a series of three of Evans' poems, a "Rural Ode"; his "Ode to a Friend" and "Hymn to May" followed in March and June.

In 1763 Evans enjoyed the experience of having some verses dedicated to him, for Thomas Godfrey in that year wrote "A Cantata on Peace. 1763. To Mr. N.E." Godfrey's poem celebrated the conclusion of the French and Indian Wars. Evans was able to pay Godfrey in the same coin and on March 24, 1763, the *Pennsylvania Gazette* published his "*ODE:* Attempted in the Horatian Style. To the ingenious Mr. Th——s G–df—y." Only a few short months later the *Gazette* carried another poem by Evans relating to Godfrey, one which must have been written under the deepest stress: "Elegy to the Memory of Mr. Godfrey, 1763." In its issue for September 29, 1763, the *Gazette* had printed an "Extract of a Letter from a Gentleman in Wilmington, North-Carolina," which announced with great regret that Thomas Godfrey had died on August 3, 1763. The letter closed with a reference to Godfrey's works and to the expectation that a collected edition would soon be published.

The promised edition did not appear until 1765, when Henry Miller of Philadelphia published *Juvenile Poems on Various Subjects*. The poems were prefaced by Nathaniel Evans' account of his friend Godfrey and by elegies to Godfrey's memory written by Evans and another friend, John Green. As a postscript to the preface Evans published a letter addressed to him by William Smith. Smith's letter was devoted largely to answering, in the negative, the question put to him by Evans whether any attempt at correction or improvement of Godfrey's poems should be undertaken before their publication. Admitting that Godfrey's poems were not flawless, Smith nevertheless thought that they should be allowed to stand as they were.

Well over half the bulk of *Juvenile Poems* was devoted to the first printing of *The Prince of Parthia, A Tragedy*. Evans, in his introduction to the volume, had remarked that the play was "the first essay which our Province, or perhaps this Continent, has, as yet, publicly exhibited of Dramatic Composition." The historical importance of *The Prince of Parthia*, thus hinted at, became considerably greater about two years later. On April 23, 1767, the *Pennsylvania Journal* carried this advertisement:

By Authority.

NEVER PERFORMED BEFORE.

By the AMERICAN COMPANY,

At the N E W T H E A T R E, in *Southwark*, On *FRIDAY*, the *Twenty-Fourth* of *April*, will be presented, A TRAGEDY written by the late ingenious Mr. *Thomas Godfrey*, of this city, called the

PRINCE *of* PARTHIA.

The PRINCIPAL CHARACTERS by Mr. HALLAM, Mr. DOUGLASS, Mr. WALL, Mr. MORRIS, Mr. ALLYN, Mr. TOMLINSON, Mr. BROAD-BELT, Mr. GREVILLE, Mrs. DOUGLASS, Mrs. MORRIS, Miss WAINWRIGHT, and Miss CHEER.

To which will be added, A *Ballad Opera* called

The CONTRIVANCES.

To begin exactly at *Seven* o'clock.—*Vivant Rex & Regina.*

A similar advertisement in the *Pennsylvania Gazette* of the same day stressed that the play was "written in America."

As far as existing records can demonstrate, this performance marked the first time that the product of a native American's pen had been acted upon the professional stage. Colleges, including most prominently the College of Philadelphia, had staged commencement exercises written by faculty and students, and performed by students, but on April 24, 1767, with the first performance of Godfrey's play, another American tradition had been established and a native American had come to be recognized as a serious and worthy practitioner of another of the fine arts. No record of the performance has been preserved, but the Philadelphia newspapers of 1767 were not given to dramatic criticism; the information about plays which they afford comes largely from their advertisements and from occasional accounts of such special events as the opening and closing of the season. Had *The Prince of Parthia* not been performed as advertised, the withdrawal would have been a matter for comment, as, for example, was the case of *The Disappointment; or The Force of Credulity*, which was advertised in the *Pennsylvania Chronicle* on April 13, 1767, to be performed on the twentieth, while the *Gazette* and the *Journal* for April 16 announced that the performance would not be given, since the play was deemed "unfit for the stage."

The Prince of Parthia thus acquired an importance and an assurance of fame which might not otherwise have come to it. But Godfrey's play is worth attention for its intrinsic merits as well as its historical significance. Although it was not reprinted from 1765 until 1917, the play is readily accessible today, perhaps most conveniently in Arthur H. Quinn's *Representative American Plays*.

It is not surprising that Thomas Godfrey, friend and associate of William Smith and of those members of the group (Hopkinson, Duché, and Evans) who were active in the dramatic activities of the College of Philadelphia, should have written a play. That he should have written so creditable a play as *The Prince of Parthia* may legitimately cause wonder. Godfrey's native ability was implemented by his familiarity with the best traditions of English drama, and particularly with Shakespeare, a familiarity which must be regarded as due in large measure to William Smith, who most probably also introduced him to those Caroline lyrists who provided the inspiration for the best of his lyric poetry, and to Chaucer, the inspiration for his two longest non-dramatic pieces. Godfrey's career is in many ways as much a tribute to Smith as it is to Godfrey himself. Smith recognized the flame of talent in the watchmaker's apprentice and set him on the high road to literary achievement. The Provost, however, did not allow his interest in Godfrey to cloud his critical faculties; he closed his letter to Nathaniel Evans with a criticism that, if a little short of full justice, is nevertheless acute:

Upon the whole, I persuade myself that, the severest critic, looking over smaller matters, will allow these writings of Mr. Godfrey, to be aptly characteriz'd, in the following lines from the Court of Fancy—

> " Bold Fancy's hand th' amazing pile uprears,
> " In every part stupendous skill appears;
> " In beautiful disorder, yet compleat,
> " The structure shines irregularly great."

Besides editing Godfrey's poems, Nathaniel Evans contributed to another volume of poetry published in Philadelphia in 1765, a volume of Latin poetry by John Beveridge, professor of languages in the College and Academy. Evans' contribution was a faithful and graceful translation of one of the poems.

More important events were still in store for Evans in 1765. At the commencement of the College on May 30,

. . . on account of his great merit and promising genius, he was, by special Mandate *of the* Trustees, *upon the recommendation of the* Provost *and Faculty of Professors, complimented with a* Diploma *for the degree of* Master *of Arts; although he had not taken the previous degree of* Bachelor *of* Arts, *on account, of the interruption in his course of studies, during the term of his apprenticeship.*

On this occasion Evans addressed the trustees in a set of verses, which were later printed in his posthumous collection.

Like Duché, Evans had decided upon a career in the church. Shortly after receiving his degree, he sailed to England to seek ordination. Smith had already procured for him an invitation to occupy a mission in Gloucester County, New Jersey, and had even made the financial arrangements with the congregation as to the amount of Evans' salary. In a letter of introduction to the Bishop of London, Smith described Evans as "a gentleman of excellent Disposition, & singular Felicity of Parts." This letter and others which Smith wrote had the desired effect, and in the autumn of 1765 Evans was elevated to the priesthood and appointed missionary for the County of Gloucester in New Jersey by the Society for the Propagation of the Gospel in Foreign Parts. Evans proceeded to his charge and was soon sending back detailed accounts of his work to the society. It is likely that he often consulted and received advice from Smith regarding the conduct of his pastoral duties. The sincerity and honesty with which Evans set about his task are obvious. He was determined not to slacken his diligence in the good work while it was his lot to remain in the missionary parish. It was not his lot to remain there long. The *Pennsylvania Chronicle* for November 2, 1767, carried a notice informing its readers that Nathaniel Evans had died on the preceding Thursday, October 29.

The exercise which the College of Philadelphia presented at its commencement of November 17, 1767, included a tribute to the memory of Nathaniel Evans. Under the name of "Strephon," Evans was mourned by Pollio, Eudosius, and Amyntor, in a typical pastoral dialogue. A few months later, William Smith and Richard Peters joined in an action that they must have regarded as a tribute to their young friend when they wrote letters supporting the claim of Nathaniel's father for compensation from the Society for the Propagation of the Gospel. It was in all probability because of their recommendations that Edward Evans was awarded a gratuity of twenty pounds.

Smith's interest in Nathaniel Evans did not cease with this action. In January 1770 the *Pennsylvania Gazette* published proposals for a volume of Evans' collected poems; the prospectus was signed by Smith. When Smith wrote to Richard Peters on December 2, 1771, from Charleston, South Carolina, whence he had gone on college business, he mentioned that he had been detained off New York for six days by adverse winds and had "spent all that Time in looking over & copying some Scraps and Fragments of Evans's Poems to send by the Pilotboat to Mr Duche." Jacob Duché's part in the project, if only as a messenger taking copy to the printer, emphasizes again the manner in which the lives of the members of Smith's group were interwoven. Finally, on August 17, 1772, the *Pennsylvania Packet* advertised that "This Day is Published and to be Sold by John Dunlap" the *Poems on Several Occasions* of Nathaniel Evans. Smith had written a brief account of Evans as a preface to the volume. The consideration of twenty pounds which Dunlap paid him for the privilege of printing the book Smith generously turned over to an organization for the relief of the widows and children of Anglican clergymen in America.

The volume contained one piece not previously mentioned which showed Evans' attachment to the college and its provost. "An Oration on Science" is noted as having been "spoken at a Performance of Solemn Music and Oratory, in the Hall of the College of Philadelphia." By science the orator meant education, and education as William Smith conceived it . Another poem deserves mention, because it entitles Evans to a certain amount of fame quite apart from its own merits. "A Sea Piece" is the first known poem on the subject of the sea by a native American. The impulse for it was most probably Evans' voyage to England, but his appreciation of his own voyage must have been heightened by what he had heard Smith tell of his trips across the Atlantic. This poem gives credit for another American "first" to Smith's group.

Nathaniel Evans' early death did not deprive the world of a great poet. Yet had he lived longer, Evans would undoubtedly have written better poetry than anything he left behind. He was a poet of labor and revision, not of inspiration and genius. That his rather slender talents produced what they did is an evidence of the stimulating effect of contact with William Smith and the group.

With Godfrey and Evans dead and with Benjamin West settled in England, the original group may be said to have been broken up by 1767. The barest summary of the subsequent careers of Hopkinson, Duché, and West will suffice to show their place in American history and to show that the influence of Smith and the group association was not completely lost.

It is convenient to take 1766 as marking the end of the early phase of Francis Hopkinson's career, for he then took a trip to England and was abroad for more than a year. Of the poems which were published in Hopkinson's *Miscellaneous Essays* in 1792, thirty-nine seem to have been written before his trip abroad; of these, nineteen are associated in some way with the college, the Provost, or members of the group. But this numerical proportion gives a false impression, for the nineteen poems thus associated include by far his best work up to that time. The same general proportion is true of his early musical activities. Obviously the most outstanding influence on Hopkinson in this period was William Smith, his preceptor, editor, collaborator, and friend. It is important to realize that Hopkinson was able to publish those of his poems and prose pieces which appeared in print before 1766 almost exclusively through the agency of Smith. When one also considers Smith's direct influence upon him in such poems as *Science*, it becomes clear that although Francis Hopkinson would have written under any circumstances, his development would surely have been slower and his achievement less notable without William Smith. He profited greatly, too, from contacts within the group, especially from the interplay and exchange of ideas between himself and Jacob Duché.

Hopkinson's trip abroad, which in one sense marked the end of his connection with the group, renewed his friendship with Benjamin West. When Hopkinson wrote to his mother in August 1766, he was able to tell her that "Mr West received me with the utmost Cordiality; I am indeed as agreeably situated as my Heart could wish." On September 23, 1766, after telling his mother about a day's outing he had had at Greenwich with the Wests and Dr. Franklin, Francis added: "Mr West & Mr West entertain me with the utmost Hospitality—their House is my Home in London, where I live quite agreeably." Although it is impossible to verify the tradition that Hopkinson studied painting under West at this time, he must have spent many hours with West in his studio, watching him at work, and occasionally trying his own hand with the brush or pencil. "Genius," one of the poems Hopkinson wrote while abroad, contained a further tribute to West, a tribute in more specific terms than he had used previously, for here he mentioned the "quick Conception," the "great Design," the "skilful Hand," and the "flowing Line."

It would be impossible, if desirable, to review briefly and satisfactorily the career that followed Francis Hopkinson's return to America. A signer of the Declaration of Independence, a judge of the Federal and State bench, a holder of responsible offices under the Continental Congress, Hopkinson also went on to greater literary and musical achievement. His humorous pieces in both verse and prose were effective satire against the British before the Revolution and mighty weapons of derision against them during the struggle. His pen was also well employed in the great controversy over the adoption of the Constitution. Only his untimely death in 1791 prevented his exceptionally versatile talents from being put to even greater service.

After his ordination Jacob Duché turned most of his attention to his clerical career, which culminated in 1775 in his appointment as rector of Christ Church and St. Peter's in Philadelphia. In 1774 Duché published a volume entitled: *Observations on a Variety of Subjects, Literary, Moral and Religious; In a Series of original Letters, Written by a Gentleman of Foreign Extraction, who resided some Time in Philadelphia. Revised by a Friend, to whose Hands the Manuscript was committed for Publication.* Another edition specified on its titlepage that the gentleman of foreign extraction was one Tamoc Caspipina. The letters in both editions were signed with this mouth-filling name. Caspipina's identity is made clear when it is recalled that from 1759 to 1775 Duché held the position of *T*he *A*ssistant *M*inister *O*f Christ Church *A*nd *S*aint *P*eter's *I*n Philadelphia *I*n *N*orth *A*merica. The first letter (supposedly addressed to a nobleman at Oxford) contained a description of the College and Academy of Philadelphia. The fifth and thirteenth letters included the first publication of three of Francis Hopkinson's poems. Duché mentioned in his thirteenth letter that he was sending his correspondent copies of the poetical works of Thomas Godfrey and Nathaniel Evans, both of whom he recommended.

During the Revolutionary War, Duché adopted a defeatist attitude and was indiscreet enough to suggest in a letter to George Washington that the General should deal for peace with or without the consent of Congress. Because of the publicity which the letter received, Duché felt impelled to retire to London while the British were still in occupation of Philadelphia. He was not able to return to his native city until a few years before his death in 1798. Duché's career was one of great promise, but circumstances and his own character prevented him from achieving what perhaps his talents might have led him to accomplish. His literary endeavors, not outstanding in an absolute sense, have historical interest as a reflection of the period and influences which brought them forth.

After Francis Hopkinson's return to America in 1767, it was not until Jacob Duché came to London during the Revolutionary War that West again saw one of his friends of the group. Duché used engravings by Sharp from paintings by West for the frontispieces of the two volumes of his *Discourses on Various Subjects,* which he published in London in 1779. His son, Thomas Spence, studied painting under West and attained a certain degree of proficiency before his career was cut short by an early death.

Indeed, to all who came to him from America, and particularly to aspiring artists, West was always cordial. Matthew Pratt was but the first of a long line of American painters who found in West's London studies not only instruction in art, but friendship and often a home as well. Gilbert Stuart, John Trumbull, Charles Wilson Peale, Joseph Wright, William Dunlap, Samuel F. B. Morse, Washington Allston, and many another were proud to regard West as their master. This "tribe of Ben" constitutes one of West's important contributions to American art. It was a fortunate thing that West was truly eclectic, that he had no desire to found a school whose members should paint exactly alike. He tried to show his pupils that the important thing was to do well whatever they did. This genuine tolerance on his part was unusually important, since his pupils were to become the painting masters of the new world. Freedom was the American political tradition; thanks to Benjamin West, it became the American artistic tradition. If American art perhaps lost for a while some of the scope which West's pupils had imparted to it, the reasons are primarily to be found in the social *milieu* which surrounded the artists. When William Smith arranged to have a twenty-one-year-old youth from Chester County go to Italy for a look at the paintings of the masters, he took the first step toward insuring that American art should possess that most precious of all the gifts of the gods, the liberty of the creative spirit.

Any attempt to recapitulate the relations of the members of this group with each other and with William Smith would be to repeat a large part of what has already been said. Under the guidance of a great teacher, the group was unique for the birth within it of American drama, painting, and music. Such a phenomenon could not have happened without favoring circumstances. Smith's labors in the College and Academy had increased in Philadelphia the number of persons capable of appreciating "the finer things of life." An intellectual atmosphere and a receptive audience had been provided. Upon students of talent and ability, Smith brought all his influence to bear, urging them to create, publishing a magazine to give them a further incentive, and bringing them into close fellowship with one another. The friendly competition of a group of persons of nearly the same age, with common goals and aspirations, eager to be of all possible help to one another, cannot be overestimated.

There was published in Philadelphia in 1786 a pamphlet entitled *A Plan for the Establishment of Public Schools and the Diffusion of Knowledge in Pennsylvania*. In a copy of this work in the Historical Society of Pennsylvania, a hand nearly contemporary with 1786 has written "By W. Smith D.D." The work, however, seems to have been composed by Benjamin Rush. The style is not Smith's, but one does have a faint regret that at least the following sentence was not written by William Smith, so well does it apply to his group:

Passing by, in this place, the advantages to the community from the early attachment of youth to the laws and constitution of their country, I shall only remark, that young men who have trodden the paths of science together, or have joined in the same sports, whether of swimming, scating, fishing, or hunting, generally feel, thro' life, such ties to each other, as add greatly to the obligations of mutual benevolence.

Certainly the members of Smith's group passed hours of pleasant recreation fishing in the then clear waters of the Schuylkill on lazy summer afternoons, skating on the river on brisk winter mornings, tramping through the Wissahickon Valley on hazy fall days, continually aware of a feeling of camaraderie, of "us against the world." It cannot be doubted that many a time the fishing or hunting gave way to long talks in which the daydreams and ambitions of each were related to a sympathetic audience. Young Tom Godfrey told of how he longed to see actors on a real stage performing a play which he himself had written; Francis Hopkinson offered to write incidental music and the accompaniments for the songs which his friend intended to include; young West declared that he would immortalize the performance by painting its most dramatic moment. Jacob Duché was still torn between a desire to write poetry and become famous that way, and an ardent wish to achieve fame as a pulpit orator. In his imagination, multitudes were swayed by the sound of his voice; sinners left their evil paths to follow him, and everyone acclaimed him for his goodness and greatness. Younger than the rest of his fellows, Nat Evans listened to their words and dreamed of the day when he, too, should write poetry that men would read and remember. He might not be so bright and clever as his companions, but one thing he did know—he could work as hard as anyone else.

Often the discussion must have turned to the latest lecture of the Provost, and they would speak appreciatively of his interest in their hopes. Sometimes they would meet him by the banks of the river and they would all stop for a long talk about everything under the sun, and a few things beyond it. For, important as their mutual contact was, the guiding and disciplining hand of this group, especially in its early days, was that of William Smith.

Smith's energies were continually exerted in urging his young friends to create and in helping them to improve their work. Yet, to the group as to all his students, he emphasized that the arts were not an end in themselves, but only a means toward

the higher end of making better men. The member of the group
who most nearly lived according to Provost Smith's charge to
his first graduates put the essence of that admonition into one
of his early poems. Though less able than some of his later work,
the poem is animated by a transparent sincerity and affection.
"Once more," Francis Hopkinson wrote in *Science,*

> Once more my heart beats quick with anxious fear:
> Once more methinks the solemn charge I hear—
> " Go forth my sons, our first, our early pride,
> " Thro' life's dark maze be virtue still your guide;
> " Without *religion, learning* is but vain,
> " And fruitless toil philosophy to gain:
> " 'Tis not sufficient that what's right you know,
> " Your conduct ever should that knowledge show:
> " Should injur'd freedom for assistance cry,
> " Nor eye, nor ear, nor hand, nor heart deny;
> " With pious zeal up raise her drooping head!
> " There's nought but *vice* and *tyranny* to dread."

V

PUBLIC AFFAIRS

In ORDER to form an accurate opinion of any man, it is necessary to consider his contacts with the questions of moment in his time. This is doubly true of William Smith, so decidedly were his character and temperament revealed by his relations to public affairs. A man of his boundless energy and strong opinions could hardly have been expected to confine himself to his academic duties, particularly in a place where matters of public policy were the subject of almost continual controversy.

From the day of assuming his duties at Philadelphia, William Smith was in a delicate position. He was a clergyman of the Church of England in a community the political control of which lay largely in the hands of an opposing faction, dominated by members of the Society of Friends. During the early years of Smith's residence, the Pennsylvania borders suffered from French and Indian attacks, and Smith felt strongly that the Quaker doctrine of non-resistance hampered adequate preparations for defense. Added to this difference of opinion were others of a more complex nature, including the relationship of the Penn proprietaries to the government of Pennsylvania, the taxing of Penn lands, and the grants of money by the Penns. To enter fully into these questions would require many volumes; to say which side was in the right on each question would be beyond the range of one so far removed from the events. Smith, in his official capacity, had to steer a course that would be of greatest benefit to the institution under his care. The one inescapable conclusion that comes out of the welter of testimony, documentary and hearsay, surrounding the disputes in which Smith had a part is that he was sincere and honest in his determination always to promote what seemed the best interests of the College of Philadelphia. Not less in its way than his love for the college was his profound love of liberty. A Scotsman is likely to be an independent sort of person, jealous of his rights and privileges, though willing enough to see other persons confirmed in theirs. It is only human to give primary importance to one's own concerns, and Smith was both Scottish and human. He was himself what he charged his first graduates to be, a "sworn Foe to every Species of Bondage, either of Body or of Mind," but he was first of all a foe to any threat to the liberty of those institutions and causes which were closest to him.

Even before coming to America, young Smith had his first taste of public affairs when he went to London as the representative of the Scottish schoolmasters. The experience of waiting upon committees of Parliament gave him insight into the vast amount of red tape and delay which could and usually did surround an appeal to the fountain of honor and power. In New York, Smith joined whole-heartedly and forcefully with the church party in the agitation over the erection of a college.

Smith's interest in the public affairs of Pennsylvania may be said to have begun before the date of his actual settlement there. In December 1753, while he was in England for ordination, Smith presented a memorial to the Society for the Propagation of the Gospel in Foreign Parts, setting forth a plan for educating the Germans in Pennsylvania. This plan shows not only that Smith was keenly aware of the dangers inherent to a state from an unassimilated group within its borders, but also that he was equally aware that education of the young was the only means by which such a group could be attached to the whole beyond the possibility of disaffection. Smith also took occasion to pay a compliment to the Academy of Philadelphia, for in speaking of the desirability of employing only teachers educated in America, he noted that "it is a happy circumstance, in Pennsylvania in particular, that there is a flourishing Seminary, where such men may be educated." To further this project a society was formed in London, and the Reverend Dr. Samuel Chandler was made its secretary. On March 15, 1754, Dr. Chandler addressed a letter to James Hamilton, Lieutenant Governor of Pennsylvania, William Allen, Chief Justice of

Pennsylvania, Richard Peters, Secretary of Pennsylvania, Benjamin Franklin, Conrad Weiser, and Smith, asking these gentlemen to accept nominations as trustees to carry on the work of the society. This letter Smith carried with him when he returned to Philadelphia, and on May 30, 1754, he had the pleasure of writing back to Chandler that all the nominees had accepted their appointments.

Smith was much occupied with this scheme during the next few years, especially during 1754 and 1755, when his correspondence was heavily concerned with it. The scheme encountered opposition, most of which came from Christopher Sauer and other German sources and seems to have been founded upon a general mistrust of the English and a fear of losing the old German ways. In order to explain their purposes, the trustees decided to publish an account of the scheme, which Smith accordingly prepared and read at a meeting of the trustees on December 10, 1754. This account was published early in 1755 in three editions, one each in English and German, and one in both languages. The title is of some interest, since it completely explains the contents: *A Brief History of the Rise and Progress of the Charitable Scheme, Carrying on by a Society of Noblemen and Gentlemen in London, For the Relief and Instruction of poor Germans, and their Descendents, settled in Pennsylvania, and the adjacent British Colonies in North-America.*

Although it may be seen from the names of the trustees that the society had influential backers on this side of the Atlantic, and although its English backers included some imposing and important names and titles, the plan never met with much success. This appears to have been in no sense due to a lack of attention by its proponents, but rather to the nature of the situation with which they were attempting to deal. The various denominational schools were apparently more influential among the Germans than those established by the society's trustees, possibly because the former were more nearly under the control of the Germans and were entirely free from any suspicion of ulterior motive. After an enthusiastic beginning, the society found the execution of the scheme progressively more difficult. On December 19, 1769, the trustees of the College and Academy of Philadelphia received a letter from Dr. Chandler in London, stating that the remainder of the funds on hand for the use of the German schools would be turned over to the trustees for the use of the Charitable School. A sum of £ 88/12/4 was thus available. All outstanding accounts of the German schools were made payable to the trustees for the same use, but there is no record that any more money was ever received.

Early in his residence in Philadelphia, Smith began to busy himself in affairs that were more distinctly political. In 1755 there appeared two editions (a third was issued in 1756) of:

A Brief State of the Province of Pennsylvania, in which The Conduct of their Assemblies for several Years past is impartially examined, and the true Cause of the continual Encroachments of the *French* displayed, more especially the secret Design of their late unwarrantable Invasion and Settlement upon the River *Ohio*. To which is annexed, An easy Plan for restoring Quiet in the public Measures of that Province, and defeating the ambitious Views of the *French* in time to come. In a letter from a Gentleman who has resided many Years in *Pennsylvania* to his Friend in *London*.

Smith's authorship of this work can be proved from internal and external evidence, but the absolute proof is its inclusion on a list of his writings in his own hand. Since the forty-five-page pamphlet was printed in London and was ostensibly a letter addressed to a gentleman in that city, some purely factual and statistical information about Pennsylvania was given; most of the paper, however, was an attack on the reputed failure of the Quakers to provide proper protection for the province. It was admitted that at first the Quakers, in whom "the Powers of Government rested for the most Part," had exercised their power "with great Mildness and Prudence" and had not yet "conceived any Thoughts of turning *Religion* into a *political Scheme of Power*." This idyllic situation, Smith claimed, did not last long; conditions had changed so greatly by the time of his writing that

Our Assemblies apprehend, that as soon as they agree to give sufficient Sums for the regular Defence of the Country, it would strike at the Root of all their Power, as *Quakers*, by making a *Militia-Law* needful, in Time of Danger. Such a Law, they presume, would alter the whole Face of Affairs, by creating a vast Number of new Relations, Dependencies, and Subordinations in the Government. The *Militia*, they suppose, would all vote for Members of Assembly, and being dependent on their Officers, would probably be influenced by them. The Officers, again, as they imagine, would be influenced by the Government; and thus the *Quakers* fear they would soon be out-voted in most Places. For this Cause, they will suffer the Country to fall into the last Extremity, hoping that when it is so, our Neighbours will, for their own Sakes, defend it, without obliging them to pass a Law, which, they fear, would so soon strip them of their darling Power. But this Backwardness of theirs has quite a contrary Effect; for the neighbouring Colonies, seeing this Colony, that is immediately attacked, doing nothing, refuse to exert themselves for a People, who are able, but unwilling, to defend themselves.

The five-point plan proposed for the remedy of the situation may be summarized briefly:

1. Members of the Assembly to take an oath of allegiance to the King and perhaps make a declaration that they will not refuse to defend their country against his Majesty's enemies.

2. Germans to be denied the right of voting until they have a sufficient knowledge of the English language and constitution.

3. School teachers and Protestant ministers to be sent among the Germans.

4. All bonds, wills, contracts, etc. to be void unless in English.

5. No newspaper, almanac, or periodical to be printed in a foreign language, or, if this be thought too severe, not unless also accompanied by an English version "in one Column of the same Page or Pages."

Some of the violence of this pamphlet may perhaps be excused on the score that it was written in the heat of political conflict. Smith spoke, as he later admitted, rather too sharply against the "Popish" influences on the frontiers. Like many Americans of the day, he associated the Catholicism of the French with their practice of using Indians against the British settlements. From the vantage point of time, it is easy to condemn this attitude and to scoff at its logic. That such was the logic of the day will not condone Smith's words, but it does help to explain them. In a letter which he wrote to Thomas Penn on May 1, 1755, Smith stated what might have been expected: "The Pamphlet has made a prodigious Noise in this City." Speculation as to its authorship was rife, and rewards were even offered for disclosure of the writer's identity. Smith reported that "Every Person capable of writing has been suspected, & I have the Honor to be one of those against whom strong Suspicions are levelled." It was the fighter as well as the canny Scott who responded: "I told them that they never would know, for I thought that whoever had the Spirit to write such a piece, would have the Wisdom to do it beyond the Reach of Discovery." Smith told Penn that the appeal to the public by means of a pamphlet had been against his better judgment, "but when I found it resolved upon, I could not let the Cause suffer for want of a well laid Scheme for it in London."

When Smith next wrote to Penn, he sent him a copy of a sermon which he had preached in Christ Church on June 24, 1755, under the title of "An Earnest Exhortation to Religion, Brotherly Love, and Public Spirit, in the present dangerous State of Affairs." "As it was delivered to a vast Audience," Smith explained to Penn, "and I knew would be ordered to the Press, I gave it a Turn towards public Affairs; & I flatter myself, from the Reception it met with, you will find the concluding Address truly animated with a Love to the Public." The sermon was preached before the Masons of Philadelphia, and Smith took as his text 1 Peter 2:17, in which three commands were given: "Love the brotherhood; Fear God; Honour the King." It was the third of these commands that inspired Smith to his highest eloquence and gave the sermon its most direct "Turn towards public Affairs":

Thirdly, we are commanded to *honour* the king; that is, all those in general, who are lawfully vested with authority for the public good. . . . Government, . . . in some form or other, must be the will and appointment of God. But government, without honouring and regarding law governors, is impracticable. Hence, whatever the form may be, provided it is founded on consent, and a view to the public good, the submission of individuals must be a most sacred duty.

Nay, though wicked men bear sway, as cannot fail sometimes to happen, yet still it must be a duty to honour them on account of their station, because through them we honour that constitution we have chosen to live under. This is clear from the apostle's injunction to the Christians, not to molest the government under which they were born, but to honor the king, who was then Nero, the most cruel of men, and their bitter persecutor. The reason is obvious. The Christians were but a few, and the constitution much older than their new sect, as it was then called. To redress grievances, and reform the state, was the business of the majority, who alone had power to make innovations; and any attempt in the Christians, however just, might have been construed into sedition, and would probably have been productive of more evil than good.

But it would be absurd to argue from thence, as some have done, that the apostle meant to enjoin a *continued* submission to violence; and that a whole people injured might, in no case, recognize their trampled majesty.

The doctrine of non-resistance is now sufficiently exploded; and may it be forever treated with that sovereign contempt, which it deserves among a wise and virtuous people. God gave us freedom as our birth-right; and in his own government of the world he never violates that freedom, nor can those be his viceregents who do. To say they are, is blaspheming his holy name, and giving the lie to his righteous authority. The *love of mankind*, and the *fear of God*, those very principles from which we trace the divine original of just government, would lead us, by all probable means, to resist every tyrant to destruction, who should attempt to enslave the free-born soul, and oppose the righteous will of God, by defeating the happiness of man!

This, however, is to be a last resource; and none but the majority of a whole people, both in wisdom and force, can determine in what cases resistance is necessary.

Both in substance and in style, this is a remarkable passage, especially for a man not quite twenty-eight years of age. That the words were those of a genuine lover of liberty and a genuine liberal is beyond all question. Smith was enlisted in the unending fight against the enslavement of the free-born soul and the consequent defeat of the happiness of man. In his mind the struggle assumed a more religious setting than it has in other and differently trained minds. But Smith's was an early statement of what has become one of the great traditions of the best American thought: the inherent and inalienable right of the individual to his own liberty. It is this liberty that God himself, so Smith declared in an inspired moment, never violates in His government of the world. From this fundamental conception, the development of Smith's ideas on civil liberty followed naturally. Confident in the ultimate triumph of liberty, he felt that revolution was seldom a necessary political weapon; a majority of both the wisdom and the force of a whole people had to determine when it was necessary as a last resource. The far-seeing and statesman-like qualities of this passage reveal a mind of a high order at work on a problem that it seemed instinctively to feel was to be of the greatest importance in its time.

Writing once more to Thomas Penn, Smith on November 27, 1755, again took a poke at the Quakers:

. . . You will see by the enclosed Representation, Remonstrance &c (which as well as the Petition to the King were drawn up by Me) that the Assembly have been *pelted* into a military Law, such as it is. I assure you they are broke to pieces & never attempt to justify their Conduct on the Principles of Reason. . . .

Seeing, then, their [the Quakers'] Principles & Attachment to their own Party, can never be thoroughly changed, I hope you will support every Step that shall be taken for their Exclusion from Assembly. For they will never act like other People for Defence & the good of the Country in general, however they may patch up Matters at the last Extremity to keep their Power & serve their own Party.

. . . what I can do shall always be at your Service, while I am convinced of your Attachment to the Welfare of the Province, & the Preservation of the just Rights of Government, against a levelling & licentious Race of Republicans. . . .

The last sentence, rightly understood, is an index to Smith's attitude toward the proprietors. He was not servile to them—or, indeed, to anyone; but as long as he was convinced that the Penns were upholding the best interests of the province, he would be their faithful ally. His epithet "Republicans," though it calls attention to a strain of conservatism that ran through his political thinking, must be interpreted in its historical context. Like most political epithets, it was neither thoughtful nor accurate; it was simply the most damning thing a loyal but hotheaded subject of the King could think of to say about his political foes.

The petition to the King, which Smith mentioned in his letter to Penn as having been drawn up by himself, was impressively labeled "The Petition of Sundry of your Majesty's dutiful and loyal Subjects the Inhabitants of the Province of Pennsylvania in Behalf of themselves and others." In it, the petitioners recited the woeful state of affairs in Pennsylvania, stressing the Indian raids on outposts and the lack of proper defenses. Although in so dignified a piece of writing as an appeal to the throne rather more restrained language had to be used than in a "letter addressed to a friend in London," the opportunity to complain against the Quakers was not lost. The fifth article accordingly informed the King:

That from long Experience We have no Hopes of Seeing the aforesaid Grievances redressed here, while a great Majority of Men whose avowed Principles are against bearing Arms, find means continually to thrust themselves into the Assembly of this Province, who have been frequently called upon to put the Province in a Posture of Defence, both by Messages from their Governors and Petitions from great Numbers of their Constituents in different Counties, but they have always evaded the Point and Spun out the time by unseasonable Disputes, altho' nothing be required, for this purpose, but the bare

Sanction of a Law to collect and conduct our natural Strength as a Colony.

The prayer to the King requested that he, with Parliament, take steps to put the province of Pennsylvania in a proper state of defense, without taking away any of its liberties. William Smith's name was one of many signed to the document.

Naturally such expressions as Smith's, particularly in his pamphlet, did not go unchallenged. In order to hold up his end of the controversy, Smith published a sequel to the *Brief State*, under the title:

A Brief View of the Conduct of Pennsylvania, For the Year 1755; So Far as it affected the General Service of the British Colonies, particularly the Expedition under the late General Braddock. With an Account of the shocking Inhumanities, committed by Incursions of the *Indians* upon the Province in *October* and *November;* which occasioned a Body of the Inhabitants to come down, while the Assembly were sitting, and to insist upon an immediate Suspension of all Disputes, and the Passing of a Law for the Defence of the Country. Interspers'd with several interesting Anecdotes and original Papers, relating to the Politics and Principles of the People called *Quakers:* Being a Sequel to a late well-known Pamphlet, Intitled A Brief State of *Pennsylvania.*

This pamphlet of eighty-eight pages was printed by Ralph Griffiths in London in 1756. Some of Smith's general remarks have more interest and pertinence today than his statements directed exclusively to the quarrel then at hand. One passage shows that he had found out for himself what anyone who writes on political subjects discovers at some time or other:

There is not a more unpromising Subject, on which to write, than the Times we live in. If we are obliged to blame the Administration, and *probe* into the Bosom of a prosperous Villainy, it is like waking a Nest of Hornets, who will be sure to sting and pursue, if they can, to Destruction. 'Tis the same, if Truth requires us to pay a candid Applause to Virtue in Power: It equally rouses the Resentment of every little Pretender who is out of *Power:* In either Case, to touch upon living Characters, is to embark on a Sea of Troubles.

Smith had come to this unpleasant bit of wisdom by the simple process of blaming the Assembly for its administration of Pennsylvania and defending the Penns in their exercise of their power.

Most of the *Brief View*, however, was concerned with more specific matters than the paragraph quoted. The Braddock campaign had aroused much feeling in Pennsylvania, and Smith devoted several pages to it. It is interesting that he spoke very highly of the part which Benjamin Franklin had in the hiring of wagons for Braddock. Franklin, it will be recalled, had been instrumental in convincing the British of the necessity of gaining public good will by hiring wagons instead of impressing them into service. Against the Quakers, Smith was as determined as ever. One must continually bear in mind that the Quakers of 1755 were not only a religious sect but a powerful political body. Smith attacked them not for their religion but for what seemed to him their inability to discharge properly the responsibilities of government. Insisting that he bore no ill will toward them as men, he made it clear that as "Rulers, Assembly-Men, and Politicians" they were anathema to him and, in his opinion, enemies to their country and even violators of their own traditions:

For, if they were really that meek and *primitive* People they pretend to be, would they delight to embroil themselves in Government, at a Time when they are avowedly unfit for it, and thereby fill their Country with Discord, Confusion, and Misery?

Smith's pamphlet was one of the means by which the Pennsylvania protest against the Quakers reached English ears. To the average Englishman the spectacle of an assembly refusing to provide proper defense measures was extremely surprising and disgusting; his disgust tended to work itself out upon both English and American Quakers. Early in 1756 a bill was drafted for introduction into Parliament which would have dissolved the Pennsylvania Assembly and disqualified Quakers by requiring an oath of all members. The "Meeting for Sufferings" of British Quakers, learning of this proposal, assured the Government that the Friends would retire from the Assembly. With this assurance, action upon the bill was delayed. Messengers were sent to Philadelphia to convince the Pennsylvania Friends of the wisdom and necessity of retiring from the Assembly. Accordingly, in June 1756, six Quakers, headed by James Pemberton, resigned from the Assembly, telling their fellow-members that

. . . as many of our Constituents seem of Opinion that the present Situation of Public Affairs call upon us for Services in a military Way, which, from a Conviction of Judgment, after mature Deliberation, we cannot comply with, we conclude it most conducive to the Peace of our own Minds, and the Reputation of our religious Profession, to permit in our Resolutions of resigning our Seats, which we accordingly now do; and request these our Reasons may be entered on the Minutes of the House.

On October 16, 1756, two days after the first meeting of the new Assembly just elected, four more Quakers withdrew from the Assembly. Although it would probably not be correct to say that William Smith was chiefly responsible for these withdrawals, yet there can be little doubt that his efforts were among the most energetic aimed in this direction and that the results must have seemed to him to constitute a victory for his point of view.

Quite to be expected was the opposition which met Smith's publications. Answering pamphlets issued from London presses; Philadelphia newspapers became the scene of charges and countercharges. On March 25, 1756, a gentleman who took refuge in the pseudonym of "Humphry Scourge" published in the *Pennsylvania Journal* a long letter of "Mild Advice to a certain Parson." Although Smith was not named, there can be no doubt that the advice was meant for him. The truth of some of the accusations against him can, however, be questioned. The charge of contentiousness is at least partly true, but that Smith was seeking favor with the Penns in order to be made

"BISHOP of *America*" is hardly credible. A letter in the *Journal* on May 6, 1756, defended Smith, again without naming him. On June 10, 1756, Smith himself, in an affidavit published in the same paper, brought into the open a matter which had been smoldering underground for some little time. He expressly denied having told one Daniel Roberdeau that he had no real sentiments in the quarrel between the Assembly and the proprietors, and that he had merely "dressed the sentiments" of one side and would have done the same for the opponents, had they not already had men capable of doing their writing. The absurdity of the charge is manifest. Smith's public statements are proof enough of the intensity of his views; his private letters show the sincerity with which he held them. Nevertheless, Roberdeau answered with affidavits supporting his character and his story. Without realizing for what purpose their names were to be used, a number of members of Christ Church were persuaded to sign an affidavit stating that they had long known Roberdeau and thought him a person of probity. When it was published, most of the signers joined in an apology to Smith and a declaration of confidence in him.

One of the statements which "Humphry Scourge" made about Smith bears examination, since it expresses what a modern reader may also feel: "I perceive thee art extreamly busy in many Matters, some of them not pertaining to the Duty of thy Calling." It is natural to question whether Smith's aggressive participation in politics was entirely becoming to a clergyman, even when due allowance is made for different standards of opinion regarding clerical conduct which may have grown up since 1755. Partly, it may be, with a view to justifying himself, Smith permitted the Reverend Thomas Barton to publish, prefatory to Barton's sermon *Unanimity and Public Spirit*, a letter he had written to Barton "concerning the Office and Duties of a *Protestant Ministry*, especially in times of public Calamity and Danger." Smith recognized that a distinction could be made between the clergyman's participation in public affairs as a minister and his participation as a common citizen. It was with special regard to the former that he advised his colleague:

I would not, however, be understood from any Thing I have said, to think it expedient for Ministers of the Gospel to interfere any farther in civil Concerns, than is just necessary to support the *Spirit of Liberty*, with which our holy *Religion* is so inseparably connected; for such a Conduct might engage us in Broils, ruffle our Tempers, and unfit us for the more solemn Part of our Duty. Nor do I think we ought to dwell any farther on the *Errors* of others, than just to enable those to shun them, with whom we are connected; lest instead of the Spirit of true Holiness, a Spirit of Vain-glory and hypocritical Pride should be propagated. 'Tis true, as I have already shewn, that in our Situation we can never be too much on our Guard against the alarming Growth of a *slavish* and *corrupt* Religion among us; but we should remember withal that we may be in as much Danger, on the other Hand, from *Infidelity*, or an entire Want of all Religion. Hence, then, tho' on proper Occasions we are to rise, with a noble Contention of Soul, both against VICE and ERROR; yet still our Favourite Subjects ought to be on the brighter Side of Things,—namely, to recommend the *Love* of GOD and our *Neighbours*, together with the Practice of every *social* and *divine* Virtue.

It would not have been altogether inappropriate for some kind spirit to have whispered *de te fabula narratur* into Smith's ear when he wrote about broils and tempers. This passage shows nevertheless that Smith did not approve of unnecessary entrance into a quarrel; he would have claimed in good faith that his opposition to the Quakers was absolutely necessary. Unfortunately almost every person who becomes engaged in a quarrel, particularly one in which politics is concerned, feels all too strongly the merits of the cause which he is upholding and all too weakly the values of his opponent's. Smith did not realize that he had fallen into the same trap that has caught almost every controversialist since Eden.

In his letter to Thomas Barton, Smith further defended the right of the clergyman to speak on public affairs and, indeed, erected that right into a duty:

BUT what is it that GOD reuires us to *know* and to *do* as the Means of Happiness? Is it not to *know* and *do* HOMAGE to HIM as our *supreme Good*, and to *know* and *do* our DUTY to OTHERS in the several *Relations* he has appointed us to sustain? Shall those, then, who are called to *instruct* Mankind be told after this, that Things belonging to *civil* Happiness fall not within their Sphere? Has not GOD himself joined the TABLE of *social* DUTIES, to that of *religious* ones? Has he not, in his benevolent Constitution of Things, made *temporal* Wisdom and Happiness introductory to that which is *eternal?* And shall we perversly put asunder what GOD hath so kindly joined? Or is it not evidently our Duty, as *Teachers*, to explain to others their great *Interests*, not only as they are *Creatures* of GOD, but also as they are *Members* of a particular COMMUNITY?

No one who has read thus far can doubt that Smith discharged this duty or, if one prefers, took advantage of this opportunity.

Smith had the opportunity to speak publicly on questions of the moment when, on May 21, 1756, a day of public fasting appointed by the government of Pennsylvania, he preached an appropriate sermon in Christ Church, Philadelphia. Most of his attention was devoted to a comparison of the difficulties of the Jews, as described by Jeremiah, with the difficulties which were then afflicting Pennsylvania. The remedy he proposed was the removal of the sins which had called down the wrath of God. It was largely a "repent ye, repent ye" sermon, but even here Smith's fundamental religious and political philosophy shines through:

If we search the annals of mankind through, we shall find that no people was ever truly great or prosperous, but by supporting a sense of Liberty, and upholding the majesty of virtue. Government cannot be maintained on any other principles than justice, truth, and sobriety. Vice is a standing rebellion against God and government, and a total subversion of all order and faith, and peace, and society among men.

On April 5, 1757, Smith preached to the forces commanded by General Stanwix a sermon under the title of "The Christian Soldier's Duty, The Lawfulness and Dignity of his Office, and the Importance of the Protestant Cause in the British Colonies."

The sermon, in addition to justifying the soldier's calling, particularly justified the campaign which the troops he addressed were about to undertake.

The various quarrels and disturbances which had been blowing around William Smith culminated in a violent storm in 1758 and 1759. The first interesting fact about this affair is that Smith became involved in it only secondarily. William Moore, a justice of the peace in Chester County, Pennsylvania, who, like Smith, had incurred the displeasure of the Assembly, was in August 1757 ordered by the Assembly to appear before it to answer charges of improper conduct of his office, preferred against him in petitions to the Assembly by various persons in Chester County. The charges against Moore were mostly of a petty nature, though some were more serious. He was said to have fostered suits before him so that he might collect fees and to have used the prestige of his office to browbeat some of his less knowing neighbors into entering business transactions advantageous to himself. Moore, in a formal reply, not only denied the charges, but also the right of the Assembly to try him for them, since they were all of a nature that permitted regular proceedings in law to be taken against him. The Assembly, however, saw fit to act upon the testimony of the petitioners and proceeded to ask the Governor for Moore's removal from office. Its petition to the Governor was printed in the *Pennsylvania Gazette* for September 28, 1757, although Moore's statement was not printed. Some of the accusations were grievous enough, if true, to have justified the Governor in removing Moore from office. Governor Denny, however, was perfectly correct in his insistence upon examining both Moore and his accusers personally before removing him. Denny set January 9, 1758, as a date for the hearing, but the Assembly's arrest of Moore on January 6, 1758, effectively prevented that hearing from taking place. A hearing was finally held on August 24 and 25, 1758, before the Governor and Council, who agreed that Moore had purged himself of every one of the charges and "appeared to them to be perfectly innocent." This hearing was limited to charges of malfeasance of office, an investigation by the Governor of those charges which dealt with actions punishable at law being considered unnecessary, since other remedies existed for aggrieved parties in such cases. There is no indication that any supposedly injured party ever attempted to bring court action against Moore. The Assembly naturally felt resentful that the Governor did not accede to its request to remove Moore, and many unpleasant remarks were passed on both sides.

After the Assembly of 1757 had been dissolved and had therefore ceased to have legal existence, Moore addressed a letter of protest against its actions directly to the Governor. Moore's letter charged that the whole affair had arisen because he had drawn up and signed, with thirty-five other inhabitants of Chester County, a petition praying that the Assembly "would not keep up unnecessary Disputes with the Governor, nor, by Reason of their religious Scruples, longer neglect the Defence of the Province." He claimed that this action had so angered the Assembly that it had determined to procure his downfall by any means whatever. The means adopted, he asserted, was the collecting of petitions against him "by one of the Members, or rather Tools, of the late Assembly, thro' the most unjustifiable Practices, many of them, at a Tavern, and a Time when the Petitioners were render'd incapable of reading or knowing what they signed." "The Humble Address of William Moore, Esq." has been aptly characterized by William Renwick Riddell, in the *Pennsylvania Magazine of History and Biography* (LII, 254), who said that "a more serious charge in more virulent language was never made against any body of men." The address was printed in the *Pennsylvania Gazette* for December 1, 1757, only after the publisher had consulted with the speaker and several members of the old Assembly and received their permission. It was likewise printed in the supplement to the *Pennsylvania Journal* on the same day. Wishing to have his side of the story presented to the Germans of Pennsylvania, Moore turned to the German paper of which William Smith, by reason of his connection with the scheme for educating the Germans, was a trustee. Neither Moore nor Smith could see any harm in publishing what both the English papers had printed. Smith accordingly gave a copy of Moore's letter to the translator for the German paper and recommended its publication. This was his sole part in the affair. When the new Assembly met in January 1758, one of its first acts was to order the arrest of Moore and Smith for libel. A statement of the sergeant-at-arms shows that Smith was taken into custody on January 6, 1758, and kept in custody for nineteen days.

This was not the first time that Smith had been haled before the bar of the Assembly. In July 1756 he had been asked to identify as his a letter signed "W. Smith" which had appeared in the London *Evening Advertiser* for April 17 to 20, 1756, and which the Assembly felt "contains divers wicked Calumnies against Numbers of sober and valuable Inhabitants of this Province, and likewise most infamous, libellous, false and scandalous Assertions against the two Branches of the Legislature of this Province." Smith's answers the House adjudged "trifling and evasive," as indeed they were, but nevertheless "*Resolved*, That as this House have Matters of considerable Moment before them at this Time, and can stay but a little While together, that all further Proceedings in Relation to the said *Smith*, be postponed to a more convenient Opportunity." The opportunity was at hand in January 1758, and to the charges then held against Smith one may be sure that the Assembly mentally added those of eighteen months before.

Moore's case was heard first. He was swiftly sentenced for his refusal to admit the Assembly's right to try him, for his conduct of his office, and for his libel against the former Assembly. When Smith came before the bar of the House on the afternoon of January 17, 1758,

Mr. *Ross*, Counsel for the said *Smith*, then begged Leave to be allowed, in the Course of his Defence for the Prisoner, to enquire chiefly into the three following Points, *viz. First*, What Authority has this House to take up Persons for writing and publishing *Libels* against a former Assembly? *Secondly*, How far the Paper Mr. *Smith* is charged with being an Abettor of, is a Libel?—And, *Thirdly*, Whether the said *Smith* can be proved to be an Abettor and Promoter of the same?—As to the two first Heads, Mr. Speaker acquainted the Counsel, they were not at Liberty to enquire into, or controvert, them, because inconsistent with, and contrary to, certain Resolves, which the House had previously entered into.

The Assembly had resolved in the morning of the same day that Smith could not bring the first two points into question. The hearing of evidence proceeded, and although the publishers of the *Gazette* and the *Journal* both testified that they had previously published Moore's letter, Smith was in due course convicted on January 24, 1758, of "promoting and publishing a false, scandalous, virulent and seditious libel against the late House of Assembly of this Province, and highly derogatory of and destructive to the rights of this House and the privileges of Assembly." Upon Smith's refusal to apologize, he was ordered committed to jail until he should "make satisfaction to this House." The warrant for his commitment was dated January 25, 1758.

The Assembly refused to accept an appeal to the King which Smith offered; it even refused to allow Smith's offer and its refusal to be entered on its minutes. Further, it ordered the sheriff to disregard any writ of habeas corpus or any other writ which would free Smith from jail, and promised to support the sheriff in his obedience to its order. Smith nevertheless addressed a letter to the speaker of the House, informing him that he was still determined to appeal his case to the King in Council. He sought the aid of the Chief Justice and the Governor of Pennsylvania, but neither felt able to oppose the action of the Assembly. A direct appeal to the crown was the only course now open to Smith, apart from making satisfaction to the Assembly.

One may wonder that Smith did not avail himself of the easy way out of his difficulties and "make satisfaction" to the House in the terms which its speaker had suggested. When convicted, he refused to do so, stating, according to the minutes of the House, that "he could not in Conscience make any Acknowledgements, or profess Sorrow and Contrition to the House for his Conduct; and, striking his Hand upon his Breast, assured them, no Punishment they could inflict, would be half so terrible to him, as the suffering his Tongue to give his Heart the Lie." Undoubtedly this was true. Smith's tremendous pride would not let him humble himself before those whom he considered his persecutors. At the same time, he probably realized that his foes had at last overstepped the bounds of law and that by persisting in his course he could bring them to terms—his own terms. His heart must have leaped up when he learned of the Assembly's order to the sheriff, for it gave him the clinching argument upon which to perfect his appeal. The sheriff was, after all, an officer of the crown, and the writ of habeas corpus was a crown writ. In directing a crown officer to disobey a crown writ, the Assembly had gone far beyond its authority and had taken an action which could not be regarded except unfavorably in England.

Few college students have had the privilege of attending classes in moral philosophy in the county jail. But mere prison bars could not keep William Smith from meeting his classes. On February 4, 1758, the trustees of the College of Philadelphia agreed to the following resolution:

The Assembly of the Province having taken Mr Smith into Custody the Trustees considered how the Inconvenience from thence arising to the College might be best remedied, and Mr Smith ha..ing expressed a Desire to continue his Lectures to the Classes, which had formerly attended them, the Students also inclining rather to proceed in their Studies under his Care They ordered that the Said Classes should attend him for that Purpose at the usual Hours in the Place of his present Confinement.

When the Assembly adjourned on April 8, 1758, Smith was freed by the Supreme Court of Pennsylvania. The House reconvened on April 18, and eight days later ordered that new

warrants be issued for Smith and Moore. Apparently neither of
the gentlemen was apprehended before the House adjourned on
May 3. When the fall sessions began, the House once more
ordered their apprehension. The sergeant-at-arms arrested
Smith on September 27, 1758, and kept him in custody for two
days, until the final dissolution of the Assembly on September
30 made Smith a free man again.

The county jail, during Smith's occupancy, became the scene
not only of college classes but also of romance. Smith's fellow
prisoner William Moore had a daughter Rebecca. Realizing that
the predicament of young Mr. Smith was in large part due to
his having aided her father, she did not hesitate to bestow upon
him her warmest sympathy and her most charming smile. Smith
soon came to have so high a regard for the ministrations of this
young lady (whose dutiful visits to her father may have proceeded from more than mere duty) that he could not conceive
of going on without them. Love moved in its mysterious way,
and he who a few months earlier had been writing fiery political pamphlets was now writing on such tender subjects as "An
Elegy to Amanda," "On Amanda's Fan," "On Amanda's Birth
Day. A Song," and "To Amanda—Extempore—On being unable to write upon divine Subjects." The degree to which Smith
was upset by the advent of Rebecca into his life is easily judged
by the last-named of these pieces:

> What means this Change, that revels in my Breast;
> Fills all my Soul, and robs me of my Rest?
> Oft-wrapt in Transport, from my earliest Youth,
> My Pen I've grasp'd, smit with the Love of Truth!
> Quick as my Thoughts, the willing Numbers came—
> How should they stay? My Maker was the Theme!
> But now, nor Thoughts nor Numbers wait my Nod;
> Amanda comes between me & my God!
> Amanda!—By that Virtue you adore—
> Me to my God, and to myself restore!

A note which Smith added later explains that Amanda was "The
Lady to whom I was soon after happily married." On June 3,
1758, at Moore's residence, Moore Hall, the rector of St.

David's, Radnor, performed the marriage ceremony for William Smith and Rebecca Moore.

Even marriage could not keep Smith's mind off public affairs altogether, for in the same month of June 1758, he published "An Earnest Address to the Colonies." Written at the request of Brigadier General Forbes, who was levying forces for the expedition against Fort Duquesne, the pamphlet urged the people to rally to the defense of the province:

Rise then, my countrymen! as you value the blessing you enjoy, and dread the evils that hang over you, rise and shew yourselves worthy of the name of Britons! rise to secure to your posterity, peace, freedom, and a pure religion! rise to chastize a perfidious nation for their breach of treaties, their detestable cruelties, and their horrid murders! remember the cries of your captivated brethren, your orphan children, your helpless widows, and thousands of beggar'd families! Think of Monongahela, Fort-William Henry, and those scenes of savage death, where the mangled limbs of your fellow citizens lie strewed upon the plain; calling upon you to retrieve the honor of the British name!

Thus animated and roused, and thus putting your confidence, where alone it can be put, let us go forth in humble boldness; and the Lord do what seemeth him good!

From the "Philadelphia County Gaol" on February 6, 1758, Smith had addressed his appeal "To the King's most Excell^t Majesty, in Council." After going through the usual channels, the appeal came to rest with the Attorney-General and the Solicitor-General, to whom it was referred for legal opinion. On May 25, 1758, James Hamilton, Smith's counsel in England, wrote to his client that the infirm and overworked Attorney-General had gone to the country for the Easter holidays to improve his health; he had taken Smith's papers with him, but unfortunately he had been indisposed and unable to work since his arrival in the country. When an opinion might be forthcoming, Hamilton could not guess.

Months went by and nothing more was done. It became evident to Smith that the only way to obtain action on his appeal was for him to go to England. He accordingly sailed in the closing month of 1758. Ocean travel was a hazardous thing at best in those days, but a winter crossing in war-time was especially unpleasant and dangerous. Mrs. Smith was not in a physical condition to undertake such a voyage. On June 1, 1759, while his father was still in England, William Moore Smith, first son of William and Rebecca Smith, was born. Many an anxious moment must have been Smith's as he thought about his wife's health and wondered how long it would be before he would see her again. He had the satisfaction of knowing that his mission in England, if successful, would make her doubly happy, since her father as well as her husband would be vindicated.

When the new Assembly of Pennsylvania asked its sergeant-at-arms on February 27, 1759, why he had not obeyed its order to arrest Smith, he explained that he had "endeavoured to take the said *William Smith* into Custody, but had been prevented, by his having lately embarked for *England*."

It has been mentioned that the Assembly's actions had been of a sort that could not fail to meet disapproval in England. This was in Smith's favor, as was the fact that the Penns, who were opposing the Assembly in other matters, were only too glad to extend their influence to help Smith. The influential clergy of the Church of England were likewise disposed to assist one of its ministers who had been jailed by the hostile Assembly. But in spite of this backing, Smith found that the mills of justice, though he hoped they would grind exceeding fine, certainly ground exceeding slow. The Smith Papers at the Historical Society of Pennsylvania contain copies of many of the documents presented by Smith during the course of his hearings before committees of the Privy Council. Precedents going back to 1690 were cited to show the limitations upon the right of legislative bodies to punish libel upon previous bodies. Page after page of foolscap was consumed in the beautiful round hand of the legal copyists; one can almost see the lawyers' fees rising with each page.

While Smith's appeal was going through the slow processes of the law, he himself was neither idle nor neglected. On March 10, 1759, Aberdeen honored him with its D.D. degree, and Oxford followed suit on March 27. Smith was collecting and preparing a number of his earlier writings for reprinting. He wrote to the Archbishop of Canterbury on May 21, 1759, describing his proposed publication and asking the prelate's permission to dedicate the work to him. The Archbishop, replying on the same day, regretted that he must refuse the desired permission, but only because "I have long ago resolved against consenting to let any person whatsoever publish a Dedication to me." The work must have been well through the press when Smith wrote to the Archbishop about it, for on June 5, 1759, he was able to send him a copy of *Discourses on Several Public Occasions During the War in America*. In the accompanying letter Smith conveyed the glad news that the Solicitor-General and the Attorney-General, the chief law officers of the crown, had finally made their report on his case; it was, Smith told his Grace, "as favorable as my Heart could wish it."

One more step remained: the report of the law officers had to be confirmed by the Privy Council. This was usually a routine procedure, but Smith was fearful lest some final slip occur. The routine, however, was undisturbed, and on June 26, 1759, "The Lords of his Majesty's most honourable privy Council" formally delivered an order vindicating Smith and severely rebuking the Assembly of Pennsylvania. The Governor of Pennsylvania was instructed to signify "his Majesty's High Displeasure" at the unwarrantable behavior of the Assembly and to use utmost care and all the means in his power to prevent further transgressions. Governor Hamilton sent a message to the Assembly on February 13, 1760, fulfilling the obligations imposed upon him by the Order-in-Council, and the affair was closed. The law officers had held that Moore's letter was a libel, but a libel only upon an Assembly which had ceased to exist before its publication, and that no subsequent Assembly had the right to try an action upon it. The Assembly's direction to the sheriff to disregard a writ of habeas corpus was censured in the strongest possible terms. Smith's motive in prosecuting the appeal was largely a desire for personal vindication. Yet he was fully conscious that the success of his appeal would also be a vindication of those constitutional liberties that Englishmen regard as their immemorial rights.

If the particular case of William Smith versus the Assembly of Pennsylvania was settled, the animosities and ill feelings that it had stirred up were long to persist. The least pleasant aspect of Smith's visit to England is that it seems to have marked the beginning of a certain degree of hostility between him and Benjamin Franklin. The two men had been on opposite sides of the political fence almost ever since Smith had come to Philadelphia, but until this time their relations had been at least amicable, if less cordial than at first. Even in 1755 and 1756, when Smith was publishing the *Brief State* and *Brief View*, he remained on friendly terms with Franklin. His letters to Thomas Penn often told of his discussions with Franklin and of their agreement to disagree. But in 1759 Franklin was in London as the official agent of the Assembly of Pennsylvania, and in that capacity had as his duty the opposing of Smith's efforts to obtain redress of his grievances through an Order-in-Council. Smith felt (as he showed in his letter to the Archbishop of Canterbury on June 5, 1759) that Franklin continued his opposition after he must have known that it was useless, merely to cause more delay for Smith and to put him to greater expense. Whether or not this assertion was correct, it is no longer possible to say; but it is true that Franklin and the attorneys for the Assembly persisted in what they must have realized was a losing cause.

He would be a brave man who would contend that Franklin was animated entirely by a love of truth in the reply he made to a London bookseller who had inquired about Smith. Franklin told David Hall (of the partnership of B. Franklin and D. Hall) about the incident in a letter from London on April 8, 1759:

Parson Smith has been applying to Osborne for a large Cargo of Books, acquainting him that he could be of vast Service in selling great Quantities for him, as there was only one Hall at Philad^a who demanded excessive Prices; and if another Shop was but open'd where People could be supply'd reasonably, all the Custom would run to it. I know not whether he was to sell them himself or employ some other. He gave Osborne a Catalogue. Osborne came to me and ask'd me if I knew him, and that he should be safe in trusting him. I told him I believ'd my Townsmen who were Smith's Creditors would be glad to see him come back with a Cargo of any kind, as they might have some Chance of being paid out of it; And so I could not in Conscience dissuade him from trusting him. "Oh, says he, is that the Case; then he shall have no Books of me I assure you: He persuaded me to trust him 10 £'s worth of Books, and take his Note payable in Six Months. But I will have the Money immediately or the Books again."

Obviously Osborne went to the one man in London least likely at that moment to give a friendly account of Smith. Besides the political differences between Franklin and Smith, the threat of commercial rivalry may, in this instance, have entered into Franklin's attitude. But politics was at the bottom of their differences and had led, as it will, to personal ill feeling. Franklin had been instrumental in bringing Smith to Philadelphia; naturally he was not pleased when the young Scotsman turned out to be the most effective fighter in the opposing political party.

The Smith of Burlington manuscripts in the Library Company of Philadelphia contain several letters from William Logan of Philadelphia to John Smith of Burlington, New Jersey, which tend to confirm Franklin's insinuations about Smith's credit. On June 18, 1770, Logan wrote:

Parson Smith was with me to take thy house where Doctor Graeme lived, is willing to give £ 55 ^{pr}Year & take it on a Lease, but Expects thou will put it in Repair which I think will near, if not quite, sink one Years rent to make it and its premises decently tenantable— I told him I would write to thee to know thy mind, which I now do agreeable to my Promise, but at the same [time] I must do the Justice to tell thee that he is accounted So very bad a Pay Master that it may be difficult for thee to get thy Rent from him— If his Character be true—

However bad a "Pay Master" Smith may have been, it is undeniable that he had less with which to pay than many another man in his position. "I declare," he once wrote to Richard Peters, "I cannot cloth my Children & go to Market with what I have from the College. Finley at Jersey & Cooper at York, whose Services have not been equal to mine, have much larger Salaries than mine, besides Houses & c——."

The most unfortunate result of the disagreement of these two men was that Franklin, in his attempts to discredit Smith, did not hesitate to attack the institution which Smith headed and of which he was himself a trustee. When Smith went abroad in 1762 to collect funds for the College of Philadelphia, his instructions from the trustees advised him to get in touch with Franklin, who was then in England, and to ask his counsel on how to proceed. On March 22, 1762, Smith wrote back to Richard Peters, the chairman of the trustees, that "Mr Franklin has readily offered his Assistance in every Thing, but he talks of embarking in about six Weeks Via Virginia." Perhaps it would have been better all around if Franklin had kept to that intention; the quality of the assistance he rendered is shown in Smith's later letters from London. To Richard Peters on August 14, 1762, Smith wrote:

. . . Dr Franklin is gone from hence to embark at Portsmouth, but in what Temper I cannot say. He & I were not in the best Terms, nor the worst. He heard when down at Oxford, of a Letter I had sent three years ago there to prevent his having a Degree, which he took in great Dudgeon; tho' as we stood then, & his doing all he could to support the Assembly in oppression & prevent my obtaining Redress, he could not expect that I could say any Thing in his Favor. At Mr Strahan's Desire, we met at his House & had the Matter of the Letter over; b[ut] explaining did not mend the Matter much on either Side. However we parted tolera [ms. torn] he offered to take Care of any Thing I had to send to Philada and I troubled h[im] with two Books & a Letter to Mr Coleman, & a Letter to my Family directed to Ph. Bond. If he says Nothing about the Oxford Letter, I would not have you say any Thing. But in Case he should, I propose as soon as I have Leisure to send you a Copy of it & all that passed upon it. Among other Things, when he seemed to hint that I had been ungrateful to him, I put him in Mind of his Conduct to Mr Allen, & told him that Govr Dunwiddie [*sic*] had just mentioned to me in the Park that he (viz D^r F) denied having any Obligations to Mr Allen for the Post Master's Office; that this seemed strange when we knew the way he applied to Mr Allen for his Interest, viz proposing first one Man & then another to be recommended, till at last Mr Allen found out his meaning & offered to recommend Franklin himself, which he did in a Letter to Mr Allen of Bath wch several People had seen. Mr Franklin says he never denied this Obligation, & 20 others here say he has— So I know not how it is. But in any Case, you will wait to see what Part he takes in our Academy. If disposed to befriend it, you will not refuse his Aid; tho I think you should have more than one or two Marks of his Regard to it; before you admit him to take any Lead among you. Your Constitution I hope will be adhered to, & particularly you will keep the Church & all religious Societies scrupulously on our *Catholic Charter* footing, as all are friends to us, & know perfectly how we are constituted. Let no Disrespect be shew[n] to the Church, where we have so many warm Friends here. Let no particular Master have any particular Perquisite or Government in our New Buildings, but the Faculty in general; who may take their Turn in visiting the Rooms at Night. But I must put this Subject off to another Time; & as I do not mean this for any public Use, but only for yourself or such as you may chuse to shew it to, you'll forgive the Freedom of it & the Incorrectness.

If this letter betrays considerable pettiness on the part of both men, it also shows that Smith had the interests of the college fundamentally at heart. This is more than can be said of Franklin at the time, as may be seen from others of Smith's letters to Richard Peters, one of which follows:

London 7^{ber} 14th 1762.

Dear Sir

Since Mr Duchè left me, an eminent Dissenter called on me and let me know that Dr Franklin took uncommon Pains to misrepresent our Academy before he went away to sundry of their People; saying that it was a narrow bigotted Institution, got into the Hands of Proprietary Party as an Engine of Government; that the Dissenters had no Chance in it (tho' God know all the Masters but myself are of that Persuasion) with many Things grievously reflecting on the principal Persons concerned in it; that the Country & Province would readily support it if it was not for these Things; that we have no Occasion to beg; & that my Zeal proceeds from a fear of its sinking & losing my Livelyhood— But alas! who can believe this—I am sure I could get £ 150 p^r Annum many Ways, if that was all my View— But I have a better Design before me than any Thing that concerns myself—

His Virulence on this Subject betrayed itself and disgusted the Gentleman, who had promised me 40 Guineas to the Design. He accordingly took the first opportunity of seeing me, & I satisfied him by many Circumstances; and especially by shewing him a Letter from Dr Alison which began as follows— "Dear Sir—I rec^d your Letter directed to the Care of Mr Sted- "man, for which I am obliged to you. I heartily pray God for "your Success. The Standing or Falling of this Useful Insti- "tution, in a great measure, depends on your Interest & In- "dustry, which I know will not be wanting."—

The Gen^t who knew Alisons Character took this Extract, declared himself perfectly satisfied, gave me Leave to use his Name, & will give me all this vouched under his Hand to carry back with me, & has a bad opinion of Franklin, as I am sure I cannot but have, as he always pretended to me that he spoke well of the Design. You may most infallibly depend on this, & I thought it my Duty to let you know, & I hope you will let the Governor, Mr Allen, Dr Alison Mr Stedman & such others as you think proper know— For the old Rancor is still brooding at the Heart of this Man. He has not however been able to do any Hurt to my Business, & it now stands so well that I am under no Pain about him. You will only take Care on your Side of the Water. Mr Penn has still further Intentions of serving us, & every Regard is due to him, consistent with our general Plan of Liberty; & he would be the last Man to wish any Thing else.

W.S.

To be understood completely, this letter must be considered along with another from Smith to Peters, which does not bear the date of its composition, but which Peters marked "rec'd 2ⁿ 8ᵇᵉʳ 1762":

. . . I fear I was too hasty in believing Franklin's Professions for our College. Soon after I wrote you last, I had Occasion to be with one Mʳ Hanna, a very benevolent & wealthy Gentleman of Barbadoes, into whose Hand I put one of the Cases for our College. Calling some time afterwards, he told me he had enquired about the College of some Gentlemen from Philadᵃ & was informed it was "an Instrument of Dissension"— I replied that I believed that Intelligence must have been thro' a very partial Channel; that I thought the Names of the Gentlemen concerned in it might shew that it was a misrepresentation, & if it could be viewed in that Light, with any Shadow of Justice, I should be ashamed to apply to any Gentleman in its behalf; & begg'd he would take his Account from some other Persons, I then named. He said he could not take that Trouble, & then gave me £ 25 intimating that it was not near so much as he intended, & that he did not give it freely. I begg'd him to keep his Money till I could remove his Scruples; but he declined it, saying there was scarce one Day in ten that his bad Health would allow him to see Company. I soon found that Mʳ Hanna had his Information from an intimate Friend of his Mʳ T. Allen, who had it from young Franklin, who is continually after Miss Downs, Allen's Sister in Law. . . . I was, however determined that I would conclude nothing concerning the old Gentleman from this, till I had some opportunity of Judging by his own Conduct. This I soon obtained. For, on applying to Mʳ Sergant, as a Gentleman who had large Dealings with Philadᵃ he told me he would consult his Friend Dʳ Franklin to know what was proper to be done, being very ready to encourage every public Design in that City. Waiting upon him soon afterwards, he told me that he had taken the Advice he mentioned; that in respect to contributing money, he thought it would never do to trouble People here; that we ought to apply to our own Legislature for Support; that he would not give any Thing that Way; but that he would give two Gold medals annually £ 5 Value, to some of the best Scholars, & had given his Directions about the Matter to Dʳ Franklin. I told him that I was concerned on another Plan for the Increase of our Funds, which Dʳ Franklin might have told him if he would, the Assembly had declined doing any Thing for from the very Beginning But that we must accept the

Favors of Gentlemen in their own Way; & if that of Medals was his, it was very well; we were obliged to him.

You know it is my Business to be civil, even where refused. However I think this Plan of Mr Sargent's rather a Scheme for serving himself than us, & shall have no further dependence on Dr Franklin's Assistance, but do my best in my own Way. It was very wrong that no letter was got from Mr Chambers to Mr Sargent, as you promised. It would certainly have got us £ 100. I beg you will apply to him yet, or to Mr Francis, in which Ph. Bond will join you. A Letter from Francis to Sargent would be of infinite Use, & all other Letters you can think of. I beg I may not be left so bare of Credentials & Recommendations.

Whether or not Franklin was himself all things to all men, he seems to have represented the College of Philadelphia as all things to all men in a distinctly unfavorable way. How it could happen that "Dissenters had no chance" in an institution which was "an Instrument of Dissension" would have been difficult even for Poor Richard to explain.

From this time the paths into which chance and circumstances directed the lives of Franklin and Smith made their encounters less frequent and less intimate, a not altogether undesirable situation where two such strong-minded men were concerned.

Years later, when the College of Philadelphia was restored to its pre-Revolutionary status, Smith, as secretary of the old board of trustees, called the first trustees' meeting, which was held on March 9, 1789, at Franklin's home. The minutes of this meeting, in Smith's handwriting, contain this entry:

The Body being now duly organized & assembled, proceeded in the first Place to the Election of a President, and the venerable Dr Benjamin Franklin the Father and one of the first Founders of the Institution, was unanimously elected.

It is to Smith's credit that, shortly after Franklin's death, he accepted the invitation of the American Philosophical Society to deliver a eulogy. Smith spoke on March 1, 1791, before an audience that included the President and Congress of the United States and the Legislature of Pennsylvania. With clarity and precision he considered Franklin in three capacities: as a citizen of Pennsylvania, as a citizen of America, and as a citizen of the world. His own former opposition to Franklin and Franklin's to him he mentioned honestly under the first of the three heads:

The unhappy divisions and disputes which commenced in the Provincial Politics of Pennsylvania, in the year 1754, obliged him soon afterwards to chuse his party. He managed his weapons like a veteran combatant; nor was he opposed with unequal strength or skill. The debates of that day have been read and admired as among the most masterly compositions of the kind, which our language affords; but it is happy for us, at the present day, that the subject of them is no·longer interesting; and if it were, who now addresses you was too much an actor in the scene to be fit for the discussion of it.

Smith devoted only one paragraph to his second classification, on the ground that Franklin's services to America were too well known to need detailed mention. Under the third head he spoke at some length of Franklin's scientific work. The final section was devoted to Franklin's belief in immortality, a belief which Smith held a man must have to be great. After quoting from a letter of condolence written by Franklin to his niece at the time of his brother's death, the last paragraph of which read:

"Our *Friend* and *We* are invited abroad on a party of pleasure, *that is to last forever*. His *Chair* was first ready, and he is gone before us. We could not all conveniently start together; and why should you and I be grieved at this, since we are soon to follow, and *we know where to find him*,"

Smith went on to close in a burst of oratory:

Yes, thou dear departed Friend and Fellow-Citizen! Thou, too, art gone before us—thy Chair, thy celestial Car, was first ready! We must soon follow, and we know where to find Thee! May we seek to follow thee by lives of Virtue and Benevolence like thine—then shall we surely find thee—and part with thee no more, forever! Let all thy Fellow-Citizens; let all thy Compatriots; let every Class of Men with whom thou wert associated here on Earth—in devising plans of government, in framing and executing good laws, in disseminating useful knowledge, in alleviating human misery, and in promoting the happiness of Mankind—let them consider thee as their *Guardian-Genius*, still present and presiding amongst them; and what they conceive thou would'st advise to be DONE, let them advise and DO likewise—and they shall not greatly deviate from the Path of *Virtue* and *Glory!*

Certainly Smith had made much more than an *amende honorable* for anything he might have said of Franklin thirty years earlier. Horace W. Smith, in his biography of his great-grandfather, told what he called an *anecdote de famille*, in which Smith's daughter Rebecca was supposed to have charged him after the delivery of this eulogy with not having "believed more than one-tenth part of what you said of old Ben Lightning-rod." The only recorded response of William Smith was a hearty laugh.

It is extremely difficult to appraise accurately motives and actions in a period so long past. Franklin's obvious lack of sympathy for Smith's efforts to raise money in 1762 must be understood as proceeding not only from their personal and political quarrels, but also from a fundamental disagreement over matters of policy regarding the Academy and College of Philadelphia. As one may see from a reading of Franklin's "Observations relative to the intentions of the original founders of the Academy in Philadelphia," written in June 1789, Franklin felt that the English school in the academy had been unfairly treated and preference given to the Latin school. Franklin and Smith were both strong willed and each had a definite idea of how the academy should be run. In the early struggles of the institution, Franklin had been one of its staunchest friends. Later, when he looked at his child and could not recognize his mark upon it, he naturally felt somewhat piqued. Other matters had increasingly absorbed his attention, and the deviation of the school from his plans for it accentuated his loss of interest. Franklin's misunderstandings with Smith are deeply regrettable, since these two great men, acting in harmony, could have accomplished much more than either of them was able to do singly for the College and Academy of Philadelphia.

Smith's interest in science, particularly astronomy and mathematics, occasionally impinged upon his interest in public affairs. In a letter to Thomas Penn on October 22, 1760, he revealed a little disappointment because he had not been appointed one of the commissioners to draw the Delaware-Pennsylvania boundary line; nevertheless he offered his services in any capacity and made some pertinent suggestions about the matter. Two years later, while in London, he wrote to the Secretary of the Society for the Propagation of the Gospel on March 11, 1762, saying that he would attend a committee meeting if possible, but that "I am engag'd the same forenoon, together with some other Mathematicians, at the Instance & in the Presence of Lord Baltimore & Mr Penn, to be at Mr Sissons, to view & give our Opinion of a new Instrument making by Sisson to run the long-disputed West-Line between Pennsylvania & Maryland."

Further evidence of Smith's scientific interests, although less directly connected with public affairs, may be seen in the first volume of the *Transactions of the American Philosophical Society*, in which Smith appeared as the author (or joint author) of four articles:

"Terrestial Measurement between the Observatories of Norriton and Philadelphia, with the difference of latitude and longitude thence deduced."
"Transit of Mercury as Observed at Norriton."
"Report of the Committee on the Transit of Venus, June 3, 1769."
"Sun's Parallax as found by the Transit of Venus, 1769."

It may be worth notice that the transit of Mercury referred to occurred on November 2, 1776, a time when a man in America might well have been excused from his duties to absolute science.

Reference to the year 1776 naturally brings to attention and into focus the most important events which took place in

America during the lifetime of William Smith: events in which he had a part and, one feels constrained to add, an honorable part. Before a particular account can be given of Smith's course during the American Revolution and the preceding years, a few general considerations must be regarded. Not only had Smith been born and educated in Great Britain, but he had been ordained a priest of the Church of England. In the ordination service, which could only have been one of the most solemn occasions of his early life, he had sworn allegiance to the crown. The King was not alone his temporal sovereign; he was also his spiritual superior-in-chief, the "supreme governor" of the church and so established by its canons. Even at this day, every English coin informs whoever can read its cryptic abbreviations that he who is *Omn. Brit. Rex* and *Ind. Imp.* is also *Fid. Def.* (or sometimes simply *F.D.*). Defenders of the Faith were the second and third Georges to William Smith. In absolute theory, at least, disobedience to them was quite as heretical as a denial of revelation itself. The time was to come when Smith and other men had to distinguish between obedience to George the temporal ruler and spiritual submission to George the Defender of the Faith. Still later, legal measures would be taken to dissolve the spiritual submission. Until such measures were taken, however, and until men could distinguish in their own minds between the dual functions of the crown, there was bound to be anguish of spirit and torment of mind among those of the clergy of the Church of England in America who were conscientious about the fulfillment of their vows and at the same time sympathized with the colonists for resisting the autocratic policies of the home government. That William Smith was such a man can, it is thought, be shown out of his own mouth. It must be recognized that Smith had many other ties binding him to the mother country. He had been successful in raising funds there for his beloved college, and in doing so he had made valuable friends for that institution. He himself had many British friends in all stations of life. And he believed genuinely in the principles of the British constitution and in its ability, when properly administered, to provide the best of all possible governments. This was an attitude entirely natural to one with Smith's background and experience; perhaps it was even the truth. The mismanagement of that constitution had never given it a real chance to prove its worth, although one is probably justified in suggesting that a form of government which was capable of such mismanagement must have had something fundamentally wrong with it. In any event, the question was soon enough settled in a way that left no room for further theoretical discussion.

The prelude to the American Revolution began in earnest about ten years before the Declaration of Independence. Likewise, Smith's concern over the relations between the colonies and Great Britain began about the same time. On December 18, 1765, he wrote a letter about the Stamp Act to Dr. Tucker, Dean of Gloucester, who had spoken in favor of the act and had chided the colonies for their attitude. Smith advised the distinguished prelate that he had previously chosen silence as his part in the unhappy state of affairs, but now felt compelled to ask the Dean to use his influence to help restore mutual trust and consideration. Smith could not refrain from telling Dr. Tucker that any act of Parliament which, like the Stamp Act, took money from America by other means than the vote of the colonial legislatures would be looked upon as contrary to the charters and as violating the inherent rights of Englishmen, and could be executed only by force. Although the letter was moderate in statement, it inflamed the Dean, who referred to it in the presence of Francis Hopkinson, then in England, as "impudent." Having heard of the incident in a letter from Hopkinson, Smith sent his old pupil a copy of the original letter, so that "if the Dean should again call it *impudent*, it may be in your Power to shew that it deserves no such Name." Smith thought the letter "as prudent & well-guarded as any Things ever I wrote; which was very lucky, considering the Times & Circumstances. Indeed, I do not care if all the World saw it."

Except for one brief reference, there is no record for the next few years of what Smith was saying about the future of the colonies. In an oration before the American Philosophical Society on January 22, 1773, he looked forward to "that glorious Period . . . when the Regions on this Side of the *Atlantic*, as well as those on the other, shall enjoy their *Day* of Freedom, Light and polished Life!"

The time was soon approaching, however, when Smith was to have an active rôle. On May 19, 1774, a letter from the people of Boston was brought to Philadelphia by no less a person than Paul Revere. This letter asked the advice of Philadelphia as to what action Boston should take on the act of Parliament closing its port. At a meeting the next day a committee of correspondence was chosen, one of the members of which was "William Smith, D.D." The following resolution was adopted:

That the Committee shall write to the People of Boston assuring them that we truly feel for their unhappy situation; that we consider them as suffering in the general cause. That we recommend to them Firmness, Prudence and Moderation; that we shall continue to evince our Firmness to the cause of *American Liberty*.

It was decided to transmit this resolution to the other colonies and to apply to the Governor for a session of the provincial Assembly. The committee of correspondence met on May 21 and agreed upon a letter to be sent to Boston. The style of this letter, as well as the fact that Smith preserved a copy among his papers, strongly suggests that Smith drafted it. After assuring the Bostonians of sympathy, the letter continued:

But what farther advice to offer you on this sad occasion is a matter of the greatest difficulty. . . . If satisfying the East India Company for the damage they have sustained would put an end to this unhappy controversy and leave us on the footing of constitutional liberty for the future, it is presumed that neither you nor we could continue a moment in doubt what part to act; for it is not the value of the tax, *but the indefeasible right of giving and granting our own money* (A RIGHT FROM WHICH WE CAN NEVER RECEDE), that is now the matter in consideration. By what means the truly desirable circumstance of a reconciliation and future harmony with our mother country on constitutional grounds may be obtained is indeed a weighty question. Whether by the methods you propose, of a general *non-importation and non-exportation* agreement, or by a *general congress* of deputies from the different colonies, clearly to state what we conceive to be our rights, and to make a claim or petition of them to his Majesty in firm but decent and dutiful terms (so as that we may know by what line to conduct ourselves in the future), are now the great points to be determined. The latter method we have reason to think would be most agreeable to the people of this province, and is the first step that ought to be taken. The former may be reserved as our last resource, should the other fail, which we trust will not be the case, as many wise and good men in the mother country begin to see the necessity of a good understanding with the colonies upon the general plan of liberty as well as commerce.

When several resolutions (presumably prepared by the committee of which Smith was a member) were offered for vote at a public meeting on June 28, 1774, Smith made a speech stressing the gravity of the occasion and the need for cool and deliberate consideration. Three sentences from it deserve to be heard, not only because of their relevancy in 1774 but because of their enduring worth:

There ought to be no party, no contention here, but who shall be firmest and foremost in the common cause of America. Every man's sentiments should be freely heard, and without prejudice. While we contend for liberty with others, let us not refuse liberty to each other.

After serving on this committee, Smith sent an account of his activity to the Bishop of London, defending his conduct and expressing a hope for peaceful settlement of the disputes between Great Britain and the colonies. He had the honesty to add that he fully sympathized with Boston in its plight. "This great Continent," he predicted—and the words have a portentous ring today—"is design'd by Providence, to be the last Seat of Liberty and Knowledge, and I believe, no human purpose, or human Power, shall be able, finally to defeat this gracious Intention of heaven." This is hardly the truckling speech of one who was "looking up to government for an American episcopate, and a pair of lawn sleeves," as Smith was described to John Adams by an unnamed "gentleman who returned into town with Mr. Paine and me in our coach." It would be interesting to know the name of the gentleman.

The reconciliation for which Smith hoped did not come about; rather than mending, things became worse. His state of mind was reflected in the exercise which he prepared for the 1775 commencement of the College of Philadelphia. The first third of the dialogue was given over to a lament for the death of Thomas Penn. To Damon's inquiry if it were not possible to indulge in "the wonted strain of joy" after due tribute had been paid, Amyntor answered:

> Ah! Damon, no.
> Yet other causes damp this festal day—
> When *peace* is fled—when sacred *freedom* mourns,
> And her fair sister *commerce*, by her side
> *Sits bound in fetters*—when untwisted lies
> The golden chord of mutual trust and love
> That should unite the *parent* and the *child*,
> And slaughter'd brethren strew th' ensanguin'd plain—
> Say, can the sympathizing muse forget
> To share her country's pangs? Can she delight
> In frolic strain, or flaunt in gaudy dress,
> When *sable* garb may best beseem her state.

Eventually, one of the characters prophesied, freedom would "again erect her head" and rule in the western world. Pitt, Rockingham, Richmond, Cambden, and Burke were named in a tribute to "the splendid list of Britain's sons who dignify our cause."

A little over a month after the performance of this exercise, Smith preached one of the great sermons of his life. The officers of the third battalion of volunteer militia of the city of Philadelphia and district of Southwark had requested that Smith preach a sermon to them; accordingly, on June 23, 1775, Smith addressed them in Christ Church, Philadelphia. Two days later they held a meeting and resolved that Smith be thanked for his "excellent Sermon, preach'd at their Request the 23d Instant;

and that he be requested to furnish a Copy of the same for Publication; as, in their opinion, it will promote the Cause of Liberty and Virtue." The resolution was signed by John Cadwalader, colonel of the battalion.

If one were to pick the high point of Smith's life, it might be the day he ascended the pulpit of Christ Church to deliver this sermon. Smith had just entered his forty-ninth year. The bumptious self-confidence of his youth had mellowed into a becoming assurance and poise which gave him an air of authority. He stood at the very zenith of his intellectual powers. Contemporary accounts describe him as a speaker of much earnestness and few gestures. He was tall and rugged; John Adams had found him "rather awkward," but it is difficult to believe that this description could be applied to him in the pulpit once he had warmed to his subject. When he spoke, his hearers knew at once that they were listening to one born north of the Tweed, for there still clung to his tongue a definite trace of the Scottish burr.

In the preface to the first edition of this sermon, Smith reiterated his joint attachment to both the mother country and the colonies and his belief that their best interests were not essentially different, but he insisted upon justice being done to the colonies:

Animated with the purest zeal for the mutual interests of Great-Britain and the colonies; ardently panting for the return of those Halcyon-days of harmony, during which both countries so long flourished together, as the glory and wonder of the world; he thought it his duty, with the utmost impartiality, to attempt a state of the unhappy controversy that now rends the empire in pieces; and to shew, if peradventure he might be permitted to vouch for his fellow citizens, so far as he has been conversant among them, that the idea of an independence upon the Parent-country, or the least licentious opposition to its just interests, is utterly foreign to their thoughts; that they contend only for the sanctity of charters and laws, together with the right of granting their own money; and that our rightful Sovereign has no where more loyal subjects, or more zealously attached to those principles of government, under which his family inherits the Throne. . . .

Enough has surely been attempted, by way of experiment, to be convinced that the people of this country know their rights, and will not consent to a *passive* surrender of them— It is, now at least, time to pursue another mode, and to listen to some plan for averting the dreadful calamities which must attend a hostile prosecution of this unnatural contest. The author's wishes for the accomplishment of such a plan, have been so frequently expressed, as to subject him perhaps to suspicions which he would not wish to merit, either here or elsewhere. But still, if he could see it take place, upon a just and permanent foundation, he would be content, if it were required, to sing his "*nunc dimittis,*" and to take a final leave of earthly concerns.

It has become trite to remark that if a scheme such as the present British Commonwealth of Nations had been in existence in 1776, there might not have been a Revolutionary War. One does not feel that it is claiming too much for Smith to say that his suggestions, had they been put into practice, would have resulted in something closely resembling the present Commonwealth. What Smith seemed to want (without knowing the pat words we have for it today) was Dominion status for the colonies.

The text of the sermon was taken from Joshua XXII :22:

The Lord God of Gods—the Lord God of Gods—He knoweth, and Israel he shall know—if it be in Rebellion, or if in Transgression against the Lord— Save us not this day.

This, Smith explained, was the cry of a people divided from their parent land; fortunately the tribes of Reuben and Gad and the half tribe of Manassaeh were able to compose their differences with Israel. Smith made the application clearer:

The whole History of the Bible cannot furnish a passage more instructive than this, to the members of a great empire, whose dreadful misfortune it is to have the evil Demon of civil or religious *discord* gone forth among them. And would to God, that the application I am now to make of it could be delivered in accents louder than Thunder, till they have pierced the ear of every Briton; and especially their ears who have meditated war and destruction against their brother-tribes of Reuben and Gad, in this our *American Gilead*. And let me add—would to God too that we, who this day consider ourselves in the place of those tribes, may, like them, be still able to lay our hands on our hearts in a solemn appeal to the God of Gods, for the rectitude of our intentions toward the *whole* commonwealth of our British Israel. For, call'd to this sacred place, on this great occasion, I know it is your wish that I should stand superior to all *partial motives*, and be found alike unbiass'd by favor or by fear. And happy it is that the parallel, now to be drawn, requires not the least sacrifice either of truth or virtue?

Like the tribes of Reuben and Gad, we have chosen our inheritance, in a land separated from that of our fathers and brethren, not indeed by a small River, but an immense Ocean. This inheritance we likewise hold by a plain *original contract*, entitling us to all the natural and improveable advantages of our situation, and to a community of privileges with our brethren, in every civil and religious respect; except in this, that the throne or seat of Empire, that great altar at which the men of this world bow, was to remain among them.

The parallel was pushed even further, for, like the Gileadite tribes, the Americans had raised new altars (that is, new constitutions) on the model of the British constitution, and had intended them for the worship of the same sovereign and as a proof of their being sprung from the same race as their brothers at home.

But it is said that we have of late departed from our former line of duty, and *refused* our homage at the great *altar* of British empire. And to this it has been replied, that the very *refusal* is the strongest evidence of our veneration for the *altar* itself. Nay, it is contended by those charged with this breach of devotion, that when in the shape of unconstitutional exactions, violated rights and mutilated charters, they were called to worship *idols*, instead of the true *divinity*, it was in a transport of holy jealousy, that they dashed them to pieces, or whelm'd them to the bottom of the ocean.

From this point on, Smith spoke more directly of current problems and made less effort to draw parallels with biblical history. He made a simple and affecting appeal for consideration of the difficulty in which one of his station was placed: "I am sure you will indulge the passing tear, which a preacher of the Gospel of Love must now shed over the scenes that lie before us." Reverting for a moment to his text, Smith regretted that Great Britain had not appointed a Phinehas to inquire into the American situation, and pointed out that no essential benefit to the empire was to be gained by the present policy. If it were, the colonies would submit to the general good.

But for Dignity and Supremacy! What are they when set in opposition to common utility, common justice, and the whole faith and spirit of the Constitution? True Dignity is to govern Freemen, not Slaves; and true Supremacy is to excel in Doing Good.

It is time, and indeed more than time, for a great and enlightened people to make *names* bend to *things*, and *ideal honor* to *practical safety?* Precedents and indefinite claims are surely things too nugatory to convulse a mighty empire. Is there no wisdom, no great and liberal plan of policy to re-unite its members? . . . To devise such a plan, and to behold British Colonies spreading over this immense Continent, rejoicing in the common rights of Freemen, and imitating the Parent State in every excellence—is more glory than to hold lawless dominion over all the nations on the face of the earth!

This was now a visionary dream, Smith admitted; hence he would not weary his audience with "fruitless lamentations concerning things that might be done."

The question now is—since they are not done, must we tamely surrender any part of our birthright, or of that great charter of privileges, which we not only claim by inheritance, but by the express terms of our colonization? I say, *God forbid!*

Smith made it clear that the members and clergy of the Church of England in America, although they felt it their duty to seek reconciliation as long as was honorably possible, realized that civil and religious rights were inevitably bound together, and that they therefore could not have any interest separate from that of the country at large. "Religion and liberty must flourish or fall together in America. We pray that both may be perpetual." Declaring that "continued submission to violence is no tenet of our church," Smith reminded his hearers that the greatest divines of the Church of England had been friends of liberty and "jealous of the national rights." In forceful language he repeated, even more clearly and with less qualification, what he had said in substance twenty years before almost to the day in the same church:

The doctrine of absolute Non-resistance has been fully exploded among every virtuous people. The free-born soul revolts against it, and must have been long debased, and have drank in the last dregs of corruption, before it can brook the idea "that a whole people injured may, in no case, recognise "their trampled Majesty." But to draw the line, and say where submission ends and resistance begins, is not the province of the ministers of Christ, who has given no rule in this matter, but left it to the feelings and consciences of the injured. For when pressures and sufferings come, when the weight of power grows intolerable, a people will fly to the constitution for shelter; and, if able, will resume that power which they never surrendered, except so far as it might be exercised for the common safety. Pulpit-casuistry is too feeble to direct or controul here. God, in his own government of the world, never violates freedom; and his scriptures themselves would be disregarded, or considered as perverted, if brought to belie his voice, speaking in the hearts of men.

He continued in an inspired and surely inspiring vein:

The application of these principles, my brethren, is now easy and must be left to your own consciences and feelings. You are now engaged in one of the grandest struggles, to which freemen can be called. You are contending for what you conceive to be your constitutional rights, and for a final settlement of the terms upon which this country may be perpetually united to the Parent State.

Look back, therefore, with reverence look back, to the times of ancient virtue and renown. Look back to the mighty purposes which your fathers had in view, when they traversed a vast ocean, and planted this land. Recall to your minds their labours, their toils, their perseverance, and let their divine spirit animate you in all your actions.

Look forward also to distant posterity. Figure to yourselves millions and millions to spring from your loins, who may be born *freemen* or *slaves*, as Heaven shall now approve or reject your councils. Think that on you it may depend, whether this great country, in ages hence, shall be filled and adorned with a virtuous and enlightened people; enjoying Liberty and all its concomitant blessings, together with the Religion of Jesus, as it flows uncorrupted from his holy Oracles; or covered with a race of men more contemptible than the savages that roam the wilderness, because they once knew the "things which be-"longed to their happiness and peace, but suffered them to be "hid from their eyes."

It is difficult to realize that the last two paragraphs of this passage come from a sermon on the situation of American affairs in 1775, so well do they apply to a later world in which men are in perhaps greater danger of suffering to be hid from their eyes the things which belong to their happiness and peace.

The cause of virtue and freedom, which Smith asserted was the cause of God upon earth, had, he said, raised up heroes in ancient times and should animate the conduct of men of his day. In a passage as inspiriting now as it must have been when first spoken, Smith made this magnificent declaration of his faith in America:

For my part, I have long been possessed with a strong and even enthusiastic persuasion, that Heaven has great and gracious purposes towards this continent, which no human power or human device shall be finally able to frustrate. Illiberal or mistaken plans of policy may distress us for a while, and perhaps sorely check our growth; but if we maintain our own virtue; if we cultivate the spirit of Liberty among our children; if we guard against the snares of luxury, venality and corruption; the Genius of America will still rise triumphant, and that with a power at last too mighty for opposition. This country *will be free*—nay, for ages to come, a chosen seat of *Freedom, Arts, and heavenly Knowlege;* which are now either drooping or dead in most countries of the old world.

It is important to notice that in conclusion Smith insisted:

. . . by every method in your power, and in every possible case, support the Laws of your country. In a contest for liberty, think what a crime it would be, to suffer one *Freeman* to be insulted, or wantonly injured in his liberty, so far as by your means it may be prevented.

It is no abuse of the word to call this sermon statesmanlike. But at bottom it was, and properly, the philosopher and clergyman who spoke.

If this sermon was too well tempered to satisfy the extreme elements on either side of the controversy (and that in itself may be counted a merit rather than a defect), it was in no way a mere piece of fence-straddling. Nor was there in it any lack of courage or conviction. In June 1775, many men still believed —or at least hoped—that matters could be mended without an open break. Smith, one feels, hoped rather than believed. His words leave no doubt in the mind of a present-day reader that liberty was his first consideration and that revolution, if necessary to secure liberty, was justified. It was inevitable that the sermon should arouse comment. Smith prefixed to it in the 1803 edition of his *Works* a brief account of its reception, particularly in England. The sermon was widely reprinted there, the Chamberlain of London having ten thousand copies printed "at his expense, in so cheap a form as to be sold at two-pence each." In one copy, probably of this or a similar edition, the price "2d. 50 for 5s." indicates that the sermon was sold in quantities. Sabin's *Dictionary of Books Relating to America* lists two Philadelphia, one New York, one Wilmington, three London, three Bristol, one Belfast, and two Dublin editions of the published sermon. As might have been expected, the opinions of the reviewers as to the merits of Smith's sermon divided exactly according to their own political views. The Whigs thought that it was fine, the Tories, abominable. The comment of the *London Magazine* for August 1775 seems an admirably clear and accurate statement of Smith's real attitude:

Dr. Smith, though an Episcopal Clergyman, appears to be as zealous a friend to the Liberties of America, and as warm against the measures of administration, *as any* person whatsoever.

Among those who opposed Smith in print was John Wesley. Wesley, who was also, of course, an Anglican clergyman, appended his criticism to his *A Calm Address to Our American Colonies*, noting that Smith's sermon "has been much admired, but proceeds all along upon wrong suppositions." Wesley's contention was not that the colonists had not been denied certain rights, but that these rights were not the rights of Englishmen. Since he himself, having no freehold in England, had no vote for "parliament-men," Wesley supposed that he had no representation in Parliament and was therefore taxed without representation. Why then should the colonists complain, he wondered. This rather peculiar twist of reasoning is typical of Wesley's argument, which he thus concluded:

Ten times over, in different words, you "profess yourselves to be contending for liberty." But it is a vain, empty profession; unless you mean by that threadbare word, a liberty from obeying your rightful sovereign, and from keeping the fundamental laws of your country. And this undoubtedly it is, which the confederated colonies are now contending for.

The preface to this sermon in Smith's *Works* also relates that Governor Tryon of New York wrote Smith that he had, thinking it his duty, sent a copy to the Bishop of London. Smith was able to reply that he had already sent a copy himself. He had enclosed it in a letter to the Bishop dated July 8, 1775, in which he also enclosed a letter signed jointly by the Episcopal clergy of Philadelphia. The Smith Papers at the Historical Society of Pennsylvania contain two copies of this letter from the clergy, one evidently the copy kept by Smith at the time of its composition and the other copied later into a blankbook in which he once started to enter a detailed record of his publications and letters referring to the American Revolution. In this book Smith expressly stated that he drew up the letter. Suggestions and alterations were probably made by others of the group which signed it, but even without the direct evidence of

Smith's statement one could not mistake the style. The original letter sent to the Bishop of London does not at present seem to be in the manuscripts at Fulham Palace. The copy quoted here (and this letter can be given only in full) is taken from the files of the Society for the Propagation of the Gospel, to the secretary of which, Dr. Hind, Smith sent it, to be given to the Bishop of London should the copy sent directly to him miscarry:

The Lord Bishop of London—

My Lord—

We now sit down under deep Affliction of mind to address your Lordship upon a Subject, in which the very Existence of our Church in America seems to be interested. It has long been our fervent Prayer to Almighty God, that the unhappy Controversy between the Parent-Country and these Colonies, might be terminated upon Principles honorable & advantageous to both, without proceeding to the Extremities of civil War, & the horrors of Bloodshed. We have long lamented that such a Spirit of Wisdom and love could not mutually prevail, as might devise some liberal Plan for this benevolent Purpose; and we have spared no Means in our Power for advancing such a Spirit so far as our Private Influence and Advice could extend. But as to public Advice we have hitherto thought it our Duty to keep our Pulpits wholly clear from every thing bordering on this Contest, and to pursue that Line of Reason and Moderation which became our Characters; equally avoiding whatever might irritate the Tempers of the People, or create a Suspicion that we were opposed to the Interest of the Country in which we live.

But the Time is now come, My Lord, when even our Silence would be misconstrued, & when we are called upon to take a more public Part. The Continental Congress have recommended the 20th of next Month as a day of Fasting, Prayer and Humiliation, thro all the Colonies. Our Congregations too of all Ranks have associated themselves, determined never to submit to the Parliamentary Claim of taxing them at Pleasure, and the Blood already spilt in maintaining this Claim, is unhappily alienating the Affections of Many from the Parent Country, and cementing them closer in the most fixed Purpose of a Resistance, dreadful even in Contemplation.

Under these Circumstances, our People call upon us, and

think they have a Right, to our Advice in the most public Manner from the Pulpit. Should we refuse, our Principles would be misrepresented, and even our religious Usefulness destroyed among our People. And our complying may perhaps be interpreted to our Disadvantage in the Parent Country. Under these Difficulties (which have encreased by the Necessity some of our Brethren have apprehended themselves under of quitting their Charges) and being at a great distance from the advice of our Superiors, we had only our own Consciences and each other to consult and have accordingly determined on that Part which the general good seamed [sic] to require. We were the more willing to comply with the request of our fellow Citizens, as we were sure their Respect for us was so great, that they did not even wish anything from us inconsistent with our Characters, as Ministers of the Gospel of Peace—

Military Associations are no new Things in this Province where we never had any regular Militia Law. They subsisted during the different Alarms in the last War, and they now subsist under the special Countenance of our own Assemblies, professing the most steady Loyalty to his Majesty, together with an earnest Desire of reestablishing our former harmony with the Mother Country, and submitting in all Things agreeable to the ancient Modes of Government among us.

Viewing Matters in this Light, and considering not only that they were Members of our own Congregations who called upon us, but that Sermons have heretofore been preached to such Bodies, we thought it advisable to take our Turn with the Ministers of other Denominations; and a Sermon was accordingly preached by Dr Smith the 17th Instant, in which he thought it necessary to obviate any misrepresentations that might be made of the Principles of our Church.

Mr Duche is likewise to preach on the 7th July, upon a similar Invitation; and all our Clergy thro'out the Colonies, we believe, will preach on the Day recommended by the Continental Congress for a fast: And God knows that, exclusive of such a Recommendation, there never was a Time when Prayer and Humiliation were more incumbent upon us.

Tho it has of late been difficult for us to advise, or even correspond as usual, with our Brethren, the Clergy of New York, we find that they have likewise in their Turn officiated to their Provincial Congress now sitting there, as Mr Duche did both this Year and the last, at the opening of the Continental Congress.

Upon this fair & candid State of Things, we hope your Lordship will think our Conduct has been such as became us; and we pray that we may be considered as among his majesty's most dutiful & loyal Subjects in this & every other Transaction of our Lives. Would to God that we could become Mediators for the Settlement of the unnatural Controversy that now distracts a once happy Empire. All that we can do is to pray for such a Settlement, and to pursue those Principles of Moderation and Reason which your Lordship has always recommended to us. We have neither Interest nor Consequence sufficient to take any Lead in the Affairs of this great Country. The People will feel & judge for themselves in Matters affecting their own Civil happiness; and were we capable of any Attempt, which might have the Appearance of drawing them to what they think would be a slavish Resignation of their Rights, it would be destructive to ourselves, as well as the Church of which we are Ministers. And it is but Justice to our Superiors, & your Lordship in particular, to declare that such a Conduct has never been required of us. Indeed, could it possibly be required, we are not backward to say that our Consciences would not permit us to injure the Rights of this Country. We are to leave our Families in it, and cannot but consider its Inhabitants entitled, as well as their Brethren in England, to the Right of *granting their own Money*; and that every Attempt to deprive them of this Right, will either be found abortive in the End, or attended with Evils which would infinitely outweigh all the Benefit to be obtained by it.

Such being our Persuasion, we must again declare it to be our constant Prayer, in which we are sure your Lordship joins, that the hearts of good and benevolent Men in both Countries may be directed towards a Plan of Reconciliation, worthy of being offered by a great Nation that have long been the Patrons of Freedom throughout the World, and not unworthy of being Accepted by a People sprung from them, and by Birth claiming a Participation of their Rights.

Our late worthy Governor, the Honble Richard Penn Esqr does us the favor to be the Bearer hereof, and has been pleased to say he will deliver it to your Lordship in Person. To him therefore we beg Leave to refer your Lordship, for the Truth of the Facts above set forth. At the ensuing Meeting of our Corporation for the Relief of Widows & c^a which will be the 1st Week in October next, we shall have an Opportunity of seeing a Number of our Brethren together, and consulting more generally with them upon the present state of our Affairs, and shall be happy on all Occasions in the Continuance of your Lordship's paternal Advice and Protection.

                          Signed   RICHARD PETERS
June 30th. 1775   WILLIAM SMITH
                                    JACOB DUCHE
A true Copy   THOMAS COOMBE
        Wm Smith   WILLIAM STRINGER
                                    WILLIAM WHITE

When it is remembered that these men were writing to the English bishop and member of the House of Lords who was their direct superior in the Church of England, the bishop under whose license they performed their ministerial functions in the colonies, their courage seems the more remarkable. Smith's covering letter to the Bishop on July 8, 1775, added a few personal details, but the general substance and tone are essentially the same as in the joint letter. He told both the Bishop and Dr. Hind, to whom he wrote on July 10, that no man had labored more earnestly than he had "to avert the dreadful Calamities in which both Countries are now involved." In mentioning his sermon, Smith observed to Dr. Hind:

It was my Desire that there might not be one intemperate Expression in it, or one Sentiment that does not tend to a happy Reconciliation, upon any Plan that does not require an absolute Submission which would deprive us of every Right by which Britons ought to be distinguished.

The twentieth of July, 1775, as Smith told the Bishop of London, had been recommended by the Continental Congress as a day of fasting throughout the colonies. Smith on that day preached a sermon at All Saints Church, Philadelphia. The tone was quite different from that of his sermon of the month before; this performance was pitched in a minor key, grave and foreboding, showing more than ever Smith's awareness of the terrible nature of the impending struggle:

From the first origin of this unhappy strife, it has been my unfeigned Wish and Prayer, that, in the dreadful conflict, wherein this country seems about to engage with the great Nation from which we sprung, a deep and solemn pause might be made, on both sides, for serious meditation; and that all of us, in the first place, might turn our thoughts to God and his Providence; consider the gracious purposes for which he seems to have planted us in this Land; search our own hearts narrowly, and discover how far we conspire with, or counteract his Will and Ways, in the dissemination of human Wisdom, and human Happiness!

Smith's religious philosophy, however, prevailed to some extent over the gloom of the hour. He reminded his congregation that he wanted to bring them comfort rather than to increase their afflictions, to bring them rather to a "consideration of what God hath promised to the Virtuous, than of what He hath denounced against the Wicked, both through Time and in Eternity." He emphasized the necessity of spiritual reformation among the people of the colonies.

In this view of things, and on this solemn occasion, let me therefore sum up all I have to say by entreating you, in the name of God and by the love you profess for your country, to regulate all your conduct by the principles of Truth, Justice and Righteousness. Keep in view the divine Work in which you are called to be Instruments, so far as we seem capable to comprehend the Promises and Revelations of the Almighty. Strive in the first place to preserve your spiritual Liberty, and to resist the Dominion of Sin, adorning your profession by the Purity of your Lives; and then you may hope for a blessing in every effort for the support of your civil Liberty— Let no Acts of Violence, Rashness, Intemperance, or Undutifulness to the country from whence we spring, ever disgrace our cause. And be assured, as I said before, that he is truly the greatest Patriot, and the best man, who, in all his ways, supports the majesty of Religion, reverences the laws of his country, and keeps a conscience void of offence towards God and towards man.

On August 28, 1775, Smith wrote again to Dr. Hind concerning the conditions of the times:

. . . The Americans continue firm in the Measures they have adopted for opposing Parliamentary Taxation and the Colony of Georgia has now joined the other Twelve Colonies. Administration can expect Nothing by Hopes of Disunion Here— Would to God that a Suspension of Hostilities & Negociation could take Place, before either Side have proceeded too far in Measures so ruinous to both— For this I pray, & for this I labor daily; & in such a Way perhaps, as may subject me to the Blame of the Violent of both Sides— But I look far beyond the present heated Times— I know the Dignity of the Parent State may be well supported without invading any Essential Right of the Colonies, & till a Plan for this Purpose is devised & executed we can never more expect a Return of our former Harmony. It was with a View to propagate these Principles that my Sermon was drawn up, as I mentioned in my last. Whether it may be considered in that Light on your Side of the Atlantic I know not— But God knows my Love is strong & my Zeal ardent for the Prosperity of both Countries.

According to Christopher Marshall's *Remembrancer*, Smith was reported to have spoken disrespectfully of the Continental Congress and its proceedings, but when a committee of the Philadelphia Council of Safety met on January 6, 1776, it was unable to find evidence against Smith, "So y^t no hold Could at present be taken of him." Although a further investigation was ordered, nothing seems to have come of it.

The Congress must have considered the report to be without foundation, for on January 25, 1776, it passed a resolution inviting Smith to deliver an oration commemorating General Montgomery and the men who had fallen with him before Quebec in the campaign of the preceding December. When Smith addressed the Congress on February 19, he devoted most of his attention to a review of Montgomery's career and to a eulogy of the bravery and exploits of those who fought and died in the campaign. His few remarks on the general situation were consistent with what he had said at other times. He defended the action at Lexington as having been dictated by self-preservation, "the first great law of Nature as well as Society." In a familiar vein is the following paragraph:

God forbid that any of the profession to which I belong, should ever forget their peculiar character, exercise a turbulent spirit, or prostitute their voice to enflame men's minds to the purposes of wild ambition, or mutual destruction. I am happy in knowing that nothing of this kind is wished from me; nay that the delegated voice of the continent, as well as of this particular province, supports me in praying for a *restoration* "of "the former harmony between Great Britain and these Colo-"nies upon so firm a basis as to perpetuate its blessings, unin-"terrupted by any future dissentions, to succeeding generations "in both countries."

In the published oration, Smith appended a footnote to this paragraph because it had been "either misrepresented or mis-understood by some." The quotation was taken from the latest petition which Congress had sent to the crown, and Smith explained that until Congress had itself declared that it had changed its opinion, he could not fairly suggest that it had. If the petition no longer expressed the sentiments of many members of Congress, it still represented a hope which Smith was reluctant to abandon. But he took pains to point out that he was more the friend of liberty than of mere union with Great Britain:

But suppose these terms cannot be obtained? Why then there will be no need of further arguments, much less of aggrava-tions. Timid as my heart perhaps is, and ill-tuned as my ear may be to the din of arms and the clangor of the trumpet, yet, in that case, sounds which are a thousand times more harsh—"even the croaking of the frogs in the uncultivated "fen," or the howling of wild beasts on the mountain top, where Liberty dwells, would be "preferable to the nightingale's "song" in *vales of slavery*, or the melting notes of Corelli in *cities clanking their chains!*

When the readers of the *Pennsylvania Gazette* opened the issue of March 13, 1776, they found the first page and part of the fourth page occupied by Letters One and Two of a series addressed by "Cato" "To the People of Pennsylvania" and be-ginning "My dear Countrymen." The third letter followed on March 20, the fourth on March 27, the fifth on April 3, the sixth and seventh on April 10, and the eighth on April 24. "Cato" was William Smith. The authorship is established by the fact that the letters were later listed in the prospectus for Smith's collected works. These letters expressed Smith's well-known views on the subject of the relation of the colonies and Great Britain. The occasional shrillness of the style may be the sign of a certain desperation. Smith's genuine attachment to liberty cannot be doubted, but he found it hard to give up the idea that the British constitution was the world's greatest bulwark of liberty when rightly administered; every effort to procure a just administration had to be exhausted before the irrevocable step toward which events were now rushing was taken. This may be seen in the words in which Cato took final leave of his readers:

When it shall clearly appear, that we can be no longer *free*, nor secure in our *rights* and *property*, in connection with Britain, or that we can be more secure in any other connection (and the time which will enable us to judge of this cannot be very remote) the author of these letters shall not then lisp a word against whatever measures the sense of the majority of this country, fairly taken, shall adopt for the common good; and he will be ready to give his best assistance for carrying them into execution. But he must ever bear his testimony against being surprized into public decisions, by misrepresentations, ungrounded suggestions, and delusive arguments; too evidently proceeding from prejudice, or pre-determination of a question, in which the happiness of a great continent is involved.

In a letter to Lady Juliana Penn on March 14, 1776, Smith wrote:

The Times are such that I have long declined all Correspondence in England. You will be pleased to make this Apology to Mr Baker, whose obliging Letter lies yet unanswered; but I propose soon to write to him, when I see what Situation Affairs are like to be in, upon the Arrival of the Commissioners expected from England. God grant that they may have proper Terms to offer, & Reconciliation may yet take Place— If the Terms are otherwise, I need not say what will be the Consequence— The Mouths of the most zealous Friends of Peace will then be shut—

Enough has surely been quoted to show that Smith maintained a consistent attitude throughout the troubled years preceding the Revolutionary War. From the beginning he hoped for a reconciliation with the mother country on terms which would preserve the just rights of the colonies; yet he made it clear that if the time should come when a choice had to be made between the preservation of these rights and continuance of union with Britain, he would willingly give up his hope of reconciliation. The only flaw in Smith's attitude was that the strength of his hope tended to make it difficult for him to recognize when the time for a choice had come. It is easier to appreciate the inevitability of any event after it has happened than before; Smith was not alone in failing to realize the inevitability of the American Revolution.

After independence had been declared, anyone who had spoken against breaking with Great Britain (no matter how long before) naturally was suspected of Toryism. Smith was no exception, but the very moderation of his views, which caused some to suspect him of being a Tory, led others to look upon him as a rebel. On December 29, 1776, Samuel Seabury complained to the secretary of the Society for the Propagation of the Gospel, after having praised the loyalty of himself and the New York clergy:

But the Conduct of the Philadelphia Clergy has been the very reverse. They not only rushed headlong in to the Rebellion themselves, but perverted the Judgments & the Tempers & inflamed the Passions of the People, by Sermons and Orations, both from the Pulpit & the Press. Their Behaviour hath been of great Disadvantage to the loyal Clergy. I have been many times asked by the Rebels, Why I could not join them as well as Dr Smith & Mr Duchè? However when the Army was in Motion towards Philadelphia, the Doctor refused to sign an Association in favour of the Rebellion, & was taken into Custody: Whether he hath since been released, I have not heard.

Seabury's statement is the only surviving evidence that Smith was taken into custody in 1776. In August of 1777, Smith was one of a number of Philadelphians asked by the Executive Council of Pennsylvania to promise not to do anything "injurious to the United Free States of North America, by Speaking, Writing or otherwise." He was not, however, taken into custody, and the following June he was discharged from this parole.

Although Smith was comparatively silent on public affairs after the publication of the Cato letters, there is no record that he in any way spoke or acted against the colonial cause. One does not need to look far for reasons for his silence. The course which he had advocated so often—reconciliation and a redress for grievances—became an impossibility with the Declaration of Independence. And during the critical period from 1779 to 1789, Smith was not living in Philadelphia, the center of political activity. The College of Philadelphia having been supplanted by the University of the State of Pennsylvania, Smith was compelled to seek a living for himself and his family wherever he could find it; he found it at Chestertown, Maryland, as parish priest and as first principal of Washington College. The very scarcity of his public utterances during the war period makes an examination of them the more desirable.

On December 28, 1778, Smith delivered a sermon to the Masonic lodges of Pennsylvania in Christ Church, Philadelphia, in the presence of George Washington. Whether or not the Masonic lodges served as nuclei for revolutionary activity (a question that is not germane to the present work), the fact that Smith was invited to preach on this occasion is proof enough that he was not regarded as a Tory by his Masonic brethren. Indeed, he was at this time holding the office of Grand Secretary of the Grand Lodge of Pennsylvania, and continued to hold the office even after his removal to Maryland. Smith preached from the text: "As FREE, and not using your LIBERTY as a Cloak of *Maliciousness;* but as the Servants of GOD" (1

Peter ii : 16). After describing an ideal character, he went on
to say:

Such, to name no more, was the character of a Cincinnatus
in ancient times; rising "awful from the plough" to save his
country; and, his country saved, returning to the plough again,
with increased dignity and lustre. Such too, if we divine aright,
will future ages pronounce to have been the character of a
********** [Washington]; but you all anticipate me in a
name, which delicacy forbids me, on this occasion to mention.
Honoured with his presence as a Brother, you will seek to
derive virtue from his example; and never let it be said, that
any principles you profess, can render you deaf to the calls of
your country; but, on the contrary, have animated you with
intrepidity in the hour of danger, and humanity in the mo-
ments of triumph.

It may be supposed that Smith preached appropriate sermons
in his parish church at Chestertown on the various days of fasting, mourning, and thanksgiving recommended by Congress
during the war. Of these sermons, only two have survived in
print, one of them a not very remarkable sermon preached on
May 3, 1781, a day of fasting. The other was a thanksgiving
sermon preached on December 13, 1781, from a text in Exodus:
"I will sing unto the Lord; for He hath triumphed gloriously."

At the close of the war, Smith preached "A Thanksgiving
Sermon, for the Establishment of Peace and Independence in
America." This sermon was never printed and cannot be exactly dated; it is known through being listed in a prospectus
issued in 1789 for a proposed edition of Smith's sermons.

The only other appearance Smith made after the war as a
speaker on public affairs was on July 4, 1790, when he preached
in Christ Church, Philadelphia, before the Society of the Cin-
cinnati. The society had chosen to hear a sermon rather than an
oration because the Fourth that year fell on a Sunday. Smith
spoke of the spiritual duties which devolved upon a free people,
of the necessity of remaining true to religious principles and of
extending them throughout the United States. Not a single

word could be construed by any twist into disapproval of American independence:

Be wise, then, be instructed, ye rising American States! Let it be your glorious contention which of you should stand foremost in making liberal provisions for the advancement and support of Freedom and Virtue; without which, neither the ordinances of Religion, nor the Laws can be duly administered; nor the civil duties of life fulfilled; nor the manners of a people improved; nor their happiness for any length of time secured. But by wise establishments for the instruction of youth, the advancement of the Arts and Sciences, the encouragement of industry, and the maintenance of Religion and Morality—this shall become a great and happy land!

In this sermon Smith referred to a Fourth of July service which had been included in a temporary Prayer Book of the Protestant Episcopal Church, but had been omitted from the permanent liturgy recently adopted, chiefly because it had been found that people did not go to church on the Fourth unless that day was a Sunday. "The external parade of shews and rejoicings" was more attractive. The interesting thing about this service is that it had been drawn up by Smith himself.

With the adoption of the Federal Constitution in 1789, a new era in American history was begun. Smith belonged essentially to an earlier period; the issues which had meant most to him were now settled. He continued to be interested in public affairs, but after losing his provostship and the influence that went with it, he had less opportunity—and perhaps less desire—for active participation.

VI

THE CHURCH

To A reader in the twentieth century, it may appear a little strange that a young man preparing to become an educator should have sought ordination as a clergyman. In the eighteenth century, the wonder would have been if the situation had been otherwise. Not only were most of the educators of the English and Scottish colleges and universities members of the clergy, but the university studies were largely directed toward the making of clergymen. When Smith specified that the principal of the College of Mirania should be a clergyman of the established church, he was following the practice of the English universities of his time. And he was only fulfilling his own requirement when he was himself ordained before returning to America to take up his duties at Philadelphia. As preparation for his entrance into orders, Smith had primarily, of course, the background of his Aberdeen education. He may have studied divinity privately, possibly with some help from his clerical friends, during his residence in New York from 1751 to 1753. It has been mentioned that he went to England in 1753 with the idea in mind of studying divinity at Oxford but did not pursue that intention. In any event, the Bishop of London must have been satisfied with Smith's qualifications before he consented to ordain him.

Upon his settlement in Philadelphia, Smith was frequently consulted on church matters by his fellow clergymen in the city and the surrounding territory, and occasionally preached in their churches. Nevertheless, when he was awarded the D.D. degree by Oxford and by Aberdeen in 1759, he was being honored, not for his clerical activities, but for his attainments as an educator. This may be seen in the language of the diplomas and, more particularly, in a recommendation of Smith which was sent to the University of Oxford. Signed by the Archbishop of Canterbury and five bishops, this document did not even mention Smith's services in the pulpit, although it spoke extensively of his work in the College and Academy of Philadelphia and in the schools for the Germans.

Shortly after his return from the visit abroad on which he became Dr. Smith, Smith engaged in more purely ecclesiastical concerns than he had previously. During the autumn of 1759 and throughout most of 1760, the Episcopal clergy of Philadelphia was experiencing a tempest in a teapot. The Reverend William Macclanechan was the cause of the trouble. It is enough to say here that Macclanechan, having left his parish in Virginia, stopped in Philadelphia on his way north and was invited to preach in Christ Church. In spite of the fact that the rector, Dr. Jenney, and most of the congregation were not favorably impressed by Macclanechan or his sermons, he managed to get a testimonial from some of the vestry supporting his application to the Bishop of London for appointment as an assistant at Christ Church. Smith supported Dr. Jenney's opposition to Macclanechan and wrote an account of the matter to the Archbishop of Canterbury. The affair is not important in itself, but it did have one interesting consequence: it brought about the first general meeting or convention of the Church of England clergy in Philadelphia and vicinity. The group, consisting of the rector and the two assistant ministers of Christ Church, Philadelphia, five Pennsylvania and two New Jersey missionaries, William Smith, and Macclanechan himself, came together on April 30, 1760. Dr. Jenney of Christ Church declined the honor of presiding over the meeting and suggested Smith. It was as the president of the meeting, then, that Smith delivered a sermon before the group on May 2, 1760. Smith's address was notable for a remarkable portrait of the ideal preacher, which he gave to his fellows:

SOME men there are who, in their preaching, betray a marvellous Littleness of Genius, and Barrenness of matter. They are ever upon minute distinctions, Party-Shibboleths, perplexing definitions, and nice modes; ten thousand of which, if put in the balance with true Religion, and the *weightier matters of the Law*, would not weigh a single grain, especially when attended (as they generally are) with Revilings and Cursings and *Anathemas* against all others differing the least in persuasion, to the breach of that HEAVENLY *Charity*, which is the very essence of *Christ's* Gospel, and height of religious perfection. We may well suspect such men to be but Smatterers in the Divine Science of Religion, much like those bold Pretenders in the other sciences, who finding it a work of hard labor to obtain a thorough knowledge of their profession, or, peradventure, not having the capacity for it, are therefore obliged to hide their own ignorance and supply the want of real skill, by arrogant pretensions to some new discovery, or an affected singularity in the treatment of some common points.

BUT not so the man of comprehensive knowledge. Not so the Preacher who has a clear and glowing view of his Master's religion in general. He will not endeavour to divide and perplex mankind by vain and insignificant distinctions, but to unite and animate them all in the exercise of true vital and evangelical piety. He will not multiply notions, or delight to dwell on trifles, that tend to sow animosities and create confusions among the same Species; but to enforce universal Virtue, and light up the lamp of heavenly Charity, to adorn and gild this gloomy vale of Life.

SUCH a one will first endeavour to obtain for himself, just and elevated notions of the supreme Being, together with a masculine devotion of heart, by approaching in frequent acts of contemplation to the fountain of all grace; and what he himself *is*, he will strive to make others *be*. When he steps into the pulpit, he will carry no schemes of views thither with him that are short of his Master's Glory. He will appear as one standing in the presence of the great Jehovah, glowing for the good of his species, and impressed with the vast consequence of eternity. On every subject, he will *speak* what he *feels*, and strive to make others *feel* what he *speaks*.

BUT, in his more solemn addresses, when he finds it more particularly necessary to reluminate the dying spirit of Freedom and Religion here on earth; or when the glorious prospects of a better world, or the awful mysteries of Redeeming Love, are his theme, he will then be great indeed! He will seem all on fire. His very face will speak a soul of rapture. He will be borne along with a winged ardor of Genius, pouring forth a torrent of sacred Eloquence, which some will call *En-*

thusiasm; but if it must be called so, it will be the noble *En-thusiasm* of Truth and Reason—a pure and transcendent flame, bearing all down before it, and burning still clearer and stronger to the very last—

THE fallen and sinful estate of man; the Grace and Good-ness of God; the wonders of his Love; *Christ crucified;* the Purity of his everlasting Gospel; Charity and Virtue; Right-eousness, Temperance and a Judgment to come, together with an eternity afterwards—who, my brethren, that has these sub-jects before him, would stoop to anything of trivial moment, or disgrace them by a crude and unworthy management?

MAY the God of heaven give all of us the grace of his holy spirit to manage them as we ought, and conduct us in every other part of our duty, "*for the edifying the body of Christ." May we strive, in our several spheres, with an earnest conten-tion of soul, for the establishment of genuine piety, according to the true Gospel-simplicity. May our Lives be a convincing argument to the Heathen around us, that our Religion is some-thing more than a name, and that we are in good earnest our-selves, concerning that which we would persuade them to embrace!

* Ephes. iv. 12.

Although Smith may have been glancing in the general direc-tion of Benjamin Franklin in the first paragraph and although his whole discourse could valuably have been applied to Mac-clanechan, he far outrose any local applications.

The convention of 1760 drew up addresses to the Governor and the proprietaries of Pennsylvania, the Archbishop of Canter-bury, and the Bishop of London. The address to the Arch-bishop stressed the difficulty under which the Church of England clergy was placed by the lack of a bishop in America. Not only was a candidate for orders obliged to cross the ocean twice (and perhaps four times) before he could be fully or-dained and serve a congregation, but the absence of a bishop also made it impossible to administer the rite of confirmation.

A little more than a year after Smith preached his sermon to the 1760 convention, he was again the speaker at an important occasion in the life of the church in Philadelphia, for he was chosen to deliver the sermon at the dedication on September

4, 1761, of St. Peter's Church, which had been built as a "chapel of ease" to Christ Church. As Smith explained in the introduction to the published sermon, the church could only be dedicated; in the absence of a bishop, the service of consecration could not be performed. Smith's sermon was in the simple and serious manner of his best style. One passage may be taken to show as well the genuine devotion that was his:

By this work of ours, we pretend not to confer any peculiar sanctity on particular places, or portions of inanimate nature. What we do is only declarative of our own fixed intention of endeavouring, through God's Grace, to sanctify ourselves in this place, in the full hopes of meeting the spiritual consolation of his Divine Presence therein; and entering into a solemn engagement, for ourselves and our posterity, of keeping it forever sacred to these pious uses, agreeably to the pure model of that most excellent Church, whereof we are members.

The affairs of the College of Philadelphia—and particularly the trip abroad to raise funds—completely absorbed Smith for the next few years, but by 1767 two different (though not altogether unrelated) church matters claimed a share of his attention and were to hold it for many years.

At a meeting of Church of England clergymen from New York, New Jersey, and Pennsylvania, held at Elizabethtown, New Jersey, in October 1767, a resolution was adopted "to appoint a committee to frame some plan of provision for the distressed widows and children of such of our clergy as should die in narrow or necessitous circumstances." Dr. Smith, Dr. Auchmuty, Dr. Cooper, and Mr. Cooke were the reverend members of the committee, which met at Perth Amboy on May 12, 1768, to draw up plans for the charity and drafts of its charter. It was decided to have the organization chartered in each of the three colonies, for the easier conduct of its business. Smith and Richard Peters were appointed a committee to forward the securing of a charter in Pennsylvania; their efforts were successful and the desired charter was granted on February 7, 1769. New Jersey followed in May, New York in September. Duly chartered, the Corporation for the Relief of the Widows and Children of Clergymen in the Communion of the Church of England in America held its first meeting in Christ Church, Philadelphia, on October 10, 1769. A sermon for the occasion was preached by Smith. Its effectiveness may be gauged by the fact that forty pounds and sixpence for the use of the charity was collected at the church doors after he had spoken. It is interesting to notice that the first treasurer for Pennsylvania (there was one for each of the three colonies) was Francis Hopkinson; another of Smith's former pupils, Jacob Duché, was a member.

During the Revolutionary period, the activities of the corporation were naturally disrupted, but after the restoration of peace, the work was resumed. From 1784, when the reorganization took place, until his resignation in 1789, Smith served as president of the society. For a number of years the corporation continued as one organization, but its growing size made desirable the formation of separate companies for the three states which were represented by the membership. Three separate corporations were accordingly formed in 1806 and the assets of the parent company divided among them. All three are still extant. By far the largest and most prosperous is the Corporation for the Relief of the Widows and Children of Clergymen in the Communion of the Protestant Episcopal Church in the Commonwealth of Pennsylvania. In 1934 its assets were estimated at over two million dollars. The New Jersey and New York corporations, although smaller, have continued their useful careers down to the present time.

When he published his sermon of October 10, 1769, Smith prefixed an account of the corporation and of its establishment. In so doing, he remarked that "everything relative to this design, from the beginning, has passed through my hands, assisted by a few others, appointed for that purpose." One readily agrees with the opinion of the most recent historian of the corporation, the Reverend Walter Herbert Stowe, that "this statement errs on the side of modesty. Like the chairman of a typical committee of today, he probably did most of the work."

The perennial problem of attempting to secure an episcopal succession for the Church of England in America precipitated in 1767 a considerable controversy, when a certain group in the church somewhat rashly sought to win public favor for the idea. The immediate cause of the commotion was the publication by the Reverend Dr. Thomas B. Chandler of *An Appeal to the Public, in Behalf of the Church in America;* this was itself the outgrowth of a meeting of the clergy of New York and New Jersey, at which Dr. Chandler had been appointed to publish such an appeal. To many members of other religious groups, the appeal served only to call attention to an idea that was repellent to them. A lively pamphlet warfare was soon under way and before long, in the genial custom of the eighteenth century, the fight was taken up by newspaper controversialists. Since he felt that Chandler's pamphlet was "an appeal *Coram non Judice,*" Smith did not enter the controversy at once, but his fighting spirit would not let him stay long on the sidelines. As he mentioned in a letter to the Bishop of London, "tho' I could have wished our side had not given any cause, yet they must not be left undefended, and I am determined now to contribute my mite, for great openings are given to detect their shameful misrepresentations."

Smith's mite consisted of a series of nineteen letters contributed to the newspaper war that was going on briskly throughout 1768 and the early part of 1769. "The Anatomist— No. I" appeared in the *Pennsylvania Journal* on September 8, 1768, and the other letters followed at weekly intervals. The series was gathered together in the second volume of *A Collection of Tracts from the late News Papers, & c.*, which John Holt published in two volumes in New York in 1768 and 1769. The titles of some of the other series reprinted there indicate the heated nature of the controversy: "The American Whig," "A Whip for the American Whig," and "A Kick for the Whipper." The Anatomist papers would have appeared in another collection—Smith's own collected works—if that project had ever been completed, for they were listed in the prospectus which Smith prepared a year before his death.

Smith was quite right when he told the Bishop of London that great openings had been given to a writer who wished to defend the proposal for introducing bishops into America. The opponents had laid stress upon the fact that bishops in England were also temporal lords and that they held "spiritual courts." Laud's persecutions were cited as examples of what might be expected if the foul institution of the bishopric were established on the virgin soil of America. These statements arose partly from a genuine fear, born largely in ignorance, and partly of course from mere partisanship and obstructionism. A fear that the Church of England might become too highly favored and might even attempt to drive out other denominations seems to have been felt strongly. Although Smith's articles were on the whole rather more temperate than those of his opponents, it must be admitted that he answered their arguments in kind; gentleness was not the mark of this or any other newspaper controversy of the day. The idea that bishops might have widespread power over the general population was the most frequently repeated argument of the opposition and the one he was most careful to deny. In his thirteenth letter, the Anatomist clearly stated that "a church establishment, and ecclesiastical courts, having jurisdiction over the laity, cannot by the common law of England, be introduced into America in the person of a bishop." All that was desired Smith set forth in one sentence in his fifteenth paper: "By the plan for an American Episcopate, which hath been fairly published, no other power is desired than that of ordination, confirmation, and such government of the clergy as is derived from the Church and the laws of canonical obedience." There was surely nothing in such a proposal to make anyone fearful. Yet it is easy to understand the apprehension of those opponents whose forbears had come to America, or who themselves had come, to escape religious persecution. Smith's articles were designed to reassure them. The controversy was unproductive at the time, since, after all, Parliament and the

Church of England, not the American people, could decide whether or not the desire for American bishops would be granted.

It was also in 1767 (or possibly late in 1766) that Smith began to occupy the pulpit of the church at Oxford, Pennsylvania, the charge having been vacated by the Reverend Mr. Hugh Neill. This was the first time that Smith had served a parish at all regularly. At first, he tried to be at Oxford once a fortnight; later he was able to preach there nearly every Sunday. Since a minister was necessary in order for the church to have a properly constituted vestry and to perform certain legal functions, Smith allowed the congregation in February of 1767 to enter his name upon its records as that of its minister. Actually, he did not have time to perform the full duties of ministering to a parish. In 1770 the vestrymen and wardens wrote to the Society for the Propagation of the Gospel, thanking the society for its interest in their charge and mentioning the services of "Dr. Smith who, notwithstanding his many Engagements, hath been very constant in his Attendance, and acted with much Zeal for the good of the Congregation." In the same year Smith was officially named by the Society for the Propagation of the Gospel as its missionary for the Oxford church, a title which he held for the next five years.

On October 14, 1772, Smith, Richard Peters, and Jacob Duché reported to the Reverend Dr. Burton, secretary of the Society for the Propagation of the Gospel, that they had by turns supplied the church at Bristol, Pennsylvania, during that summer.

With his removal to Maryland in 1779 began the most active period of Smith's career as a churchman. There were two very good reasons for this. Smith was now the rector of the parish of Chestertown, in Kent County, and thus had a direct part in the day-by-day life of the church. Moreover, this was the period in which the reorganization of the American church demanded by the Revolution was made.

It was due to the peculiar legal position in which the Maryland clergymen found themselves during the war as well as to the presence in their midst of that indefatigable organizer William Smith that on November 9, 1780, three of the six clergymen remaining in Maryland (Smith, Samuel Keene, and J. J. Wilmer) and some two dozen prominent laymen of the church gathered in convention at Chestertown and addressed a petition to the General Assembly of Maryland, asking for the passage of a law that would provide "for the support of public religion by an equal assessment and laws" and would also allow the various parishes by pew rents and otherwise to raise money for their own support. At this meeting the name Protestant Episcopal Church, suggested by Wilmer, was first applied to the body which could no longer be known as the Church of England.

Conventions of the Maryland clergy were also held in 1781 and 1782, but nothing of particular moment was accomplished at them. Meanwhile, Smith went on with the performance of his parochial duties and those pertaining to Washington College. After the establishment of peace in 1783, the Episcopal clergymen of Maryland met in convention to consider what the position of their church would be under the new political order. One thing was evident: the necessity of having American bishops. The risk and expense of ocean voyages were as great as ever, and there was now the added difficulty that the English ordination service included a vow of loyalty to the king, which could hardly be asked of an American candidate and which, if taken, would certainly have deprived him of any influence at home. To solve the immediate question of how to provide enough men to fill the parishes of the state, the convention appointed six of its members—three from each shore—to act as examiners of any young men who wished to enter orders. Each acceptable candidate was to become a lay reader in a vacant parish, under the supervision of the nearest neighboring clergyman, who would administer the sacraments and perform other functions limited to ordained clergymen. The action taken by the Maryland convention toward a permanent solution of the problem before it may best be seen in a letter which it addressed on August 16, 1783, to the Bishop of London:

Maryland—Annapolis—
Augt 16th 1783.

My Lord,

Whereas the good People of this State, in Communion with the Church of England, have long laboured, and do still labour under great Difficulties, through the Want of a regular Clergy, to supply the many Parishes that have, for a considerable Time, been vacant.—

To prevent, therefore, and guard against such an unhappy Situation for the future, We, the Convocation, or Meeting of the Clergy of the Church of England, have made Choice of, and do recommend, our Brother, the Reverend Doctor William Smith, as a fit and proper Person, and every Way well qualified to be invested with the sacred Office of a Bishop, in Order to perpetuate a regular Succession of Clergy among us. We do, with the greater Confidence, present unto your Lordship this godly and well learned Man to be ordained and consecrated Bishop; being perfectly satisfied that he will duly execute the Office whereunto he is called, to the edifying of the Church, and to the Glory of God.

Your Lordship's well known Zeal for the Church, and Propagation of the Christian Religion induces us to trust that your Lordship will compassionate the Case of a remote and distressed People, and comply with our earnest Request in this Matter. For, without such a Remedy, the Church, in this Country, is in imminent Danger of becoming extinct.

That your Lordship may long continue an Ornament to the Church, is the hearty Prayer of,

My Lord,

Your very dutiful and
most obedient
Servants,

the twenty-two clergymen of the Maryland convention. The fact that the original letter is still preserved in the Smith Papers is sufficient proof that it was never presented to the Bishop of London.

Smith was undoubtedly flattered at being recommended to the bishopric, but he realized the practical difficulties then in the way of obtaining consecration. What steps, if any, he took

in 1783 toward this end are not known. He probably consulted
with other church leaders and decided to await a more favorable
time for presenting the recommendation. A little later Samuel
Seabury, selected likewise to be a bishop by the Connecticut
church, proceeded to England and was unable to obtain consecration from the English bishops because they did not feel that
they had the legal authority to omit the oath of loyalty. Unwilling to give up, Seabury went to Scotland and was consecrated
there by the successors of the nonjuring bishops, who were in
a measure independent of the English church. The English prel-
ates were naturally eager to keep the church alive in America
and were instrumental in obtaining the passage in 1787 by
Parliament of a special act which permitted them to consecrate
not more than three bishops in such places in the world as were
not under the political reign of the king and where the oath of
allegiance could not obtain. Three being the number of bishops
required by canon for the consecration of another bishop, it
was necessary to provide for the consecration of three American bishops in order to insure the perpetuation of a succession.
Under the authority of this act, William White was consecrated
Bishop of Pennsylvania and Samuel Provoost Bishop of New
York on February 4, 1787. The question naturally arises: "Why
was not William Smith consecrated Bishop of Maryland on this
same occasion?"

Bishop White himself, in an autobiographical letter to the
Reverend Dr. John H. Hobart, gave a clue to the answer:

In the beginning of the organising of our Church, I thought it
my duty to oppose myself to his [Smith's] being recommended
by the General Convention to the episcopacy, to which he had
been elected by the convention of Maryland; and to me his
failure was principally owing. My reasons are not detailed,
partly because there has been no reproach cast on me on that
account, and partly because, in our frequent collisions, I ought
not to claim the commendation of an impartial narrator. During his subsequent years, we were on very amicable terms.

This statement, it should be remembered, was made in 1830,
when White was eighty-three years old and was speaking of

events which had taken place more than forty years earlier. Of course, he may have been entirely correct in his remarks; all that one can say is that the available records (taken from the Bishop White manuscripts, incidentally) do not show that he was the principal mover against Smith.

At a General Convention of the church, held at Wilmington, Delaware, on October 10 and 11, 1786, White and Provoost, together with David Griffith of Virginia, were recommended for consecration. It so happened that Dr. Griffith's ill health prevented his going to England. Smith apparently applied to the same convention for a recommendation for consecration. Although no names were mentioned, Smith must have been the person referred to in a letter that Dr. Griffith wrote to Dr. White on October 20, 1786:

I have rec^d your Letter, dated since your return from Wilmington, and am greatly obliged to you, as well for the information it contains, as for your kind attention to the business of the Testimonial.—

The discussion of the Maryland affair must have been very painful, and I feel myself happy in having been absent on such an occasion, yet most heartily approve of the conduct of the Convention in a matter of so much importance to the reputation, and, consequently, to the usefulness of the Church. I should hope and expect that, after so publick and general a censure on his conduct, the Gentleman and his Friends will desist from any further attempt to obtain Consecration. . . .

The mystery surrounding Smith's failure to obtain consecration is only deepened by this letter, but the explanation is to be found in reports of the 1786 Maryland state convention of the church, which met at Annapolis on October 24. Rebuffed by the General Convention, Smith turned to the state meeting in the hope that he might receive a confirmation of its former recommendation, which might in turn produce a favorable vote at the next General Convention. To the Maryland convention he went armed with a testimonial from the vestry and warden of his parochial charge at Chestertown. This document stated that the signers knew of no cause or impediment "touching his sufficiency in learning, soundness in the faith and purity of manners" which should or could prevent his consecration, and further declared that he had for six years been regarded by them "as an orthodox, learned and truly evangelical preacher, yielding us both satisfaction and edification by his ministry, doctrine and conversation." Even a testimonial couched in such glowing terms did not prove sufficient to overcome the charge which was made against Smith. The nature of this charge comes out in a letter from Dr. Thomas Craddock, a lay delegate to the Maryland convention, to the Reverend Dr. John Andrews of Philadelphia:

Balt⁹ 27ᵗʰ Octʳ 1786

Revᵈ & Dʳ Sir.

Your favour was given me on my way to our Convention, & I take pr post the opportunity of giving you the earliest notice of the steps I took respecting Dʳ Smith—

Mʳ Johnson was the only Lay delegate there besides myself; him with Dʳ West I consulted, & the conclusion was, that Mʳ Johnson & myself address'd Dʳ Smith upon the subject.— He persever'd in his resolution—denied the Charge & insisted upon the information you gave to be laid before the Convention, (which was, in fact, intended) that a proper investigation might be made & his innocency prov'd— The matter stands thus at present.— He will insist upon your *proving* the Charge of intoxication & it is necessary to be done (as it is so strenuously required) before the next Convention, when the matter will again be taken into consideration. . . .

The Mr. Johnson referred to is undoubtedly the gentleman who signed himself "Samˡ Johnston" when writing to Dr. Andrews from Baltimore on October 31, 1786, saying among other things:

From what I have lately heard, I am persuaded, that an account of Our late proceedings, in the Convention of this State, will be acceptable to you.

On Tuesday last a small number of the Clergy, & no layman but myself, attended; Doctor Smith was not arrived, and therefore as we were few we adjourned to the next Day; at which time the Doctor, and Doctor Keen—with a few others that were then in Town not exceeding twelve in all—attended,

& received information of the alterations made in General
Convention, as to the Church Service and of the intelligence
from the Arch Bishops.

In the afternoon Doctor Craddick came, & before the meeting of the Convention after Dinner, shewed me your Letter;
which Doctor West & Doctor Clagget also saw: We were by
that time satisfied, that D S was determined to bring on the
affair, relative to his being recommended as a Bishop, before
the Convention; and therefore thought it best, to let him see
your Letter: Doctor Craddock & myself, were obliged to perform this very disagreeable Task, hoping it would prevent the
necessity of any notice being taken of it in Convention; but
in that we were disappointed.

D: S: produced to the Convention a Testimonial or Certificate from the Vestry & Church Wardens of his Parish;
strongly recommending him for his very great Services, in the
character of their Minister; which he desired to be entered on
the minits of the Convention; this Certificate mentioned the
Recommendation which the Clergy had Signed some Years
since. Doctor Clagget in a very respectful manner to D S informed the Convention, that he was obliged at that time to
mention what Dr Wharton had informed him, relative to D S^s
being much intoxicated, when at New York with Convention;
D^r. Craddick produced your Letter: and Dr West mentioned
what he heard from Col: Rogers of this Town, & requested
that his Name to his recommendation might be struck out,
which D S refused as the Charge was not made out. D S then
moved that an enquiry should be made into the truth of these
Charges; which was accordingly ordered by the Convention:
so that the truth of the Facts alledged, is now to be supported
by Evidence in those different Places, or by Persons of Character, who were present at the time; those gross Acts of Immorality (if established) will certainly silence the warmest
Friends of that Gentleman: many of whom are of the Clerical Order: It is much to be lamented that things are in this
critical Situation; the prospect is gloomy on every side. Should
the Doctor be so fortunate, to shew himself innocent of the
charges against him; and be recommended to the Bishoprick;
Yet the strong prejudices against him will greatly lessen that
reverence & respect, which will be always paid to that dignified
Station, when the Person, who holds the same, is of acknowledged Piety and Moral Rectitude: Should the Charges be made

out, we shall loose the Services and assistance of a very able Man; who will certainly withdraw himself. thus the Church here, is likely to suffer, be the Case as it will: But we must do what is right and trust to Providence for the rest. . . .

The letters from Johnston and Craddock, along with one he had received from the Reverend Dr. William West, Dr. Andrews sent on to William White at London, explaining that he knew White was probably "curious to know how Dr. Smith made out with the Convention of Maryland" and that by enclosing these letters he could give his correspondent full information and himself little trouble.

Although one school of biography might hail such an episode as evidence of the essential humanity of the subject, it surely represents a tragedy in the life of Smith—and a tragedy not only for him but for the American Episcopal Church, which thus lost the services as bishop of a man who, with no disrespect to William White or Samuel Seabury, able men both, was a far greater organizer and driver than either of them or than any of the other men active in the councils of the church in its formative years in the United States. Smith apparently never asked for recommendation again; he probably realized that to press the matter would be to open old wounds and to harm the church.

From all available information it appears that the inquiry ordered by the Maryland convention was not prosecuted and that the charge was dropped. Whether or not Smith could have cleared himself, one cannot say; there is little more than hearsay evidence on which to base a judgment. Ezra Stiles once wrote of Smith that he was "a jovial Priest," an epithet which might mean almost anything, and at another time that he was "a contemptible drunken Character!" Stiles was forced to admit, however, that "I know him personally, tho I am not a Witness to his Immoralities." Dr. Benjamin Rush of Philadelphia commented after Smith's death that "he early contracted a love for strong drink and became towards the close of his life an habitual drunkard. He was often seen to reel and once to fall in the streets of Philadelphia." Rush did not claim to have been an eye-witness of any of these incidents, and he did not reveal the source of his information. There were certainly people in Philadelphia who disliked William Smith enough to touch up and pass on any bit of gossip about him that came their way. An indulgence in hard liquor and a persistent looking upon the wine when it was red (and white, too) were characteristics not entirely unknown among Scotsmen and, for that matter, among eighteenth-century Church of England clergymen. But it is ridiculous to suppose that Smith could have been habitually intemperate, or more valid evidence would be found in con-temporary accounts. His tremendous energy and accomplish-ment, his many positions of honor and trust, and the testimony of his own parish all weigh heavily in rebuttal. The judgment which decided that Smith was disqualified to hold an Amer-ican bishopric, unfortunate as it may have been, is one that can-not now be argued to any useful purpose.

Smith's views on temperance may be seen in his writings and sermons. On May 8, 1768, in one of his sermons as chaplain *pro tempore* to "the XVIIIth, or Royal Regiment of Ireland," then stationed at Philadelphia, he spoke very strongly against in-temperance and concluded by repeating "The Speech of a Creek Indian," on the same subject, which he had published some fourteen years before. Smith made a tolerant distinction in this sermon which his ecclesiastical colleagues of 1787 may have failed to make:

I do not include here, those occasional excesses which men of gay and social spirits (enemies to all habitual intemperance) may sometimes be innocently and unguardedly led into; (though these ought to be avoided with a strict and watchful care) . . .

It is pleasing to note that Smith remained on friendly terms with both Dr. White and Dr. Andrews after the Maryland af-fair and continued to serve the church.

In 1784, the year after his election as bishop, Smith presided over a convention of the Protestant Episcopal Church of

Maryland at Annapolis from June 22 to 24. With William West and John Andrews of the clergy, and Richard Ridgely, Joseph Couden, and Dr. Thomas Craddock of the laity, Smith was appointed to a committee which was to digest and print the proceedings of this convention and those of the preceding year, and "to confer and treat with any *Committees* that may be appointed in the *Sister-States,* for considering and drawing up a Plan for such Alterations in the Liturgy of the Church, as may be necessary under the *American Revolution* for *Uniformity of Worship,* and *Church Government.*"

Smith, the sole delegate from Maryland, also presided over a general meeting of the church at New York in October 1784. If this meeting did not accomplish anything of especial consequence, the same cannot be said of the general meeting which was held in September of the following year at Philadelphia. William White of Philadelphia was president of this convention. Smith was appointed chairman of a committee to consider and report back to the convention such alterations in the liturgy of the church as were necessary following the Revolution, and such other alterations as it might seem advisable for the convention to recommend to the various churches for adoption. In the absence of any formal organization and constitution of the American church, this convention could not of its own motion adopt any changes in liturgy, but could only make recommendations to the individual churches.

Smith's committee made the obvious recommendations that the prayers for the royal family be omitted and that the prayer for the high court of Parliament be changed to one for the Federal Congress. It also made a large number of rather minor recommendations concerning other parts of the liturgy, perhaps the most important of which were the omission of the Athanasian and Nicene Creeds and the omission of the words "He descended into hell" from the Apostles' Creed. During the convention, a service according to these changes was held in Christ Church, with Smith preaching the sermon of the day. Most of the revisions were acceptable to the convention, and

Smith, William White, and the Reverend Dr. Charles Wharton of Newcastle, Delaware, were appointed a committee to publish a new Prayer Book incorporating the recommendations of the convention. The committee was to make any necessary verbal and grammatical changes, an authority which it interpreted very generously as time went on. Its work began immediately after the adjournment of the convention in October 1785, and continued until the new book was finally printed toward the end of April 1786. The deliberations of the committee were conducted almost entirely by mail, chiefly between Smith and White, with occasional letters to and from Wharton. Almost the entire body of this correspondence has been preserved and is now in the three volumes of Smith Papers and the three volumes of White Papers deposited by the General Council of the Protestant Episcopal Church in the New York Historical Society. The material, a large part of which is concerned with trivial matters of phraseology, is more pertinent to a history of the Protestant Episcopal Church or to a life of Bishop White (whose career was more exclusively devoted to the church) than it is to a life of William Smith. One interesting fact revealed in the letters is that Francis Hopkinson was applied to for assistance with the hymns and psalm tunes, and composed several new pieces for inclusion in the book.

For a number of reasons, this "proposed book," as it came to be called, did not win widespread acceptance and was never adopted by the church. Certain revisions which it made were not understood by all the laity and were definitely repugnant to some of the clergy. The omission of the Athanasian and Nicene Creeds and the change in the Apostles' Creed were regarded with great disfavor by the English bishops, who held a sort of veto power over any changes proposed during the reorganization of the American church, by virtue of their ability to withhold consecration from the American bishops-elect. To some persons, the 1785 convention seemed to have exceeded its authority in ordering the publication of the new book, although that convention and the committee it appointed had rightly intended the book as a recommended rather than a prescribed revision. The 1786 General Convention, in accordance with the desire of the English bishops, replaced the Nicene Creed and "He descended into hell." It was at this convention that William White, Samuel Provoost, and David Griffith were recommended to England for consecration as the first American bishops in the English succession.

The next general meeting of the church was not held until 1789, after the first two of these gentlemen had been consecrated. It will be recalled that Samuel Seabury, elected Bishop of Connecticut, had not waited for the action of the convention of 1786 or the passage of an act of Parliament but had boldly gone abroad to seek consecration and finally obtained it from the nonjuring bishops of Scotland. Many churchmen looked with disapproval upon this consecration and some, including especially Bishop Provoost, were inclined to doubt its validity. The 1789 convention had as one of its most critical problems the resolving of the dissension over Seabury, in order to bring the church in New England and the church in the middle and southern states into accord. The story of how this was accomplished again belongs more in a history of the church than in a biography of William Smith, but it must be mentioned that William Smith and William White by their personal influence were able to bring the opposing sides harmoniously together, and thus helped in a large measure to assure the unification of the church. The convention met in Philadelphia on July 28, 1789, for its first session. Bishop Provoost, who was expected to preach the opening sermon, did not appear, and on a single day's notice Smith substituted for him, delivering a sermon which was a model of the humility with which such a task as that facing the convention should be approached. On Saturday, August 8, Smith again preached to the members of the convention, but on a much sadder occasion—the funeral services for David Griffith, bishop-elect of Virginia, who had died the preceding Monday. It soon became apparent that the business of the convention could not proceed until the differences between Seabury and

Provoost had been settled; since more time was needed to accomplish this, the convention adjourned to September 29. The meetings which began in Christ Church, Philadelphia, on September 30, 1789, and were moved to Independence Hall on October 2 were perhaps the most important in the history of the Protestant Episcopal Church. The Book of Common Prayer was revised and adopted, and a form of church government was established. Both have remained substantially unchanged to the present time. When the convention resolved itself into the House of Bishops and the House of Clerical and Lay Deputies, Smith was elected president of the lower house and presided over its meetings.

Smith was elected to the same position at the next triennial meeting of the church, held in New York City in September 1792. At this time he was further honored with an invitation to preach the sermon on the occasion of the first consecration of a bishop to take place in America, that of Thomas John Claggett as Bishop of Maryland. Three bishops deriving consecration from the English line (Dr. James Madison had by this time been consecrated in England as Bishop of Virginia) and one from the Scottish line took part. It is a considerable testimony both to the members of the convention and to Smith that this invitation was given and that it was accepted by the man who had himself at one time been the Bishop-elect of Maryland. On September 17, 1792, Smith responded with a powerful sermon, glorying in the establishment of a line in which "we see the whole Episcopate of the land from whence many of us sprung, the English and Scots, happily united" and prophesying a great future for the church thus endowed.

The events of the convention of 1792 were almost exactly repeated in 1795, when Smith was again elected president of the House of Clerical and Lay delegates and again preached the consecration sermon for a new bishop. Dr. Robert Smith was elevated to the bishopric of South Carolina on September 13, 1795, in Christ Church, Philadelphia. Likewise, when Edward Bass was consecrated Bishop of Massachusetts and New Hampshire in Christ Church May 7, 1796, Smith was called upon for the sermon of the day. To have preached the sermons at the consecrations of the first three bishops consecrated in this country was indeed an honor for any churchman. Once more, in 1799, Smith presided over the lower house of the General Convention, but in 1801 he felt obliged to decline the office because of the state of his health.

That Smith was called upon so many times to deliver sermons before important gatherings of his fellow churchmen is an indication of the regard in which they held both him and his preaching. This regard was widely shared, as one can see from the many invitations which came to him to speak before other bodies. Enough quotations from his sermons and orations have been given to show that they were written with a keen appreciation of the requirements of oral delivery. He must have been a compelling speaker. Bishop White said that Smith was always heard with earnest attention and great satisfaction, though "he had no uncommon advantage of voice; and of action, absolutely none." Even Dr. Benjamin Rush had to admit that as a preacher Smith was "solemn, eloquent and impressive in a high degree." Surely more than once Smith's auditors were "sensibly affected," to use the words employed by the *Pennsylvania Gazette* in reporting one of his sermons. For the most part Smith's sermons were of the order that is sometimes called evangelical: that is to say, they were inclined to be hortatory and admonitory, directed toward the arousing of the congregation to some act, if no other than the general act of leading better lives. They were not discourses upon abstruse points of doctrine or theology; they did not bristle with appeals to the fathers or theologians. An occasional quotation was employed, but it was likely to come from Burnet or Bishop Newton or another of the more popular theological writers. In an examination of Smith's sermons, only one instance has been noticed in which a scholarly reference to the original meaning of a word was made. Speaking from that text in which St. Peter advised the soldiers to "use no violence," Smith remarked of one type of violence:

This is that violence more immediately meant in the text; the original word there, signifying the shaking or terrifying a man, so as to force money from him through fear.

Smith's theology was the orthodox theology of the Church of England in the eighteenth century. He shied away from Enthusiasm and held to sanity as an essential of true religion. Preaching to the convention of the Maryland church on June 23, 1784, he said:

A devotion worked up by fervour, whatever proceeds from the mere force of animal spirits, *is of the Earth, earthy;* in no manner like to that true Spirit of Regeneration which is of the Lord from Heaven, and begets the divine life in the souls of men.

Smith emphasized particularly the comfort of religion. His preaching was not like that which won for Gilbert Tennent, one of the early Presbyterian preachers in Philadelphia, the sobriquet of "Hell-Fire." It has been seen that he spoke of the rewards of virtue rather than of the punishments of sin in his Fast sermon of July 20, 1775 (pp. 174–175, *supra*). An even more explicit statement in this vein is to be found in a sermon he preached on the fourth Sunday in Advent of 1765, a manuscript copy of which is preserved in the University of Pennsylvania Library:

In this World of Suffering & of Woe, in which man as the sad Consequence of his fall, is doom'd to wander a Pilgrim & Stranger— In such a World, the Sound of Comfort & Joy must be inexpressibly sweet. But above all the Sound of Spiritual Joy, Words of Comfort nay of eternal Comfort spoken to the Soul, & declared to be Words from Heaven, by the Prophets of the most high God; and at last confirmed by the Mouth of God himself—this my B[rethre]n must surely be welcome to the Ears of Men. And therefore it is with the highest Propriety that the Gospel of Jesus is called Good Tidings, a Message of Love and Joy and Peace!

Smith's humanism (in the less restricted meaning of that word) shines out through such a statement as this:

Nor am I fond of ascribing every striking dispensation of Providence, to any particular Interposition of its power. It is sufficient for us that we consider ourselves always under its general government—and that we look upon our own fortunes as suspended at all times in the uplifted hands of the Almighty!

At times, however, Smith displayed a gift for a more florid and oratorical style of preaching, examples of which will have been noted in other quotations. The roll of time can be felt in these words from his sermon to the Masons of Philadelphia on December 28, 1778:

These are fundamental Principles, and Practices of immutable Obligation in our Society. Flowing from the Fountain-head of Antiquity, they have roll'd down to us, in pure and uncorrupted Streams, through the Channels of Time; and, we trust, will still roll, broader and deeper, until the *dread Order* of this TERRESTIAL FABRICK shall be consumed in the *endless Order* of ETERNITY.

Despite the number of sermons which Smith delivered and his undoubted prominence as a pulpit orator, it was not as a preacher that he was of greatest service to the church. His organizing ability and his ready pen were of far more use. It must be admitted that Smith left behind him no great contribution to the doctrine of the church, no outstanding body of divinity. But it would be foolish to argue from that fact that he was himself spiritually shallow and interested only in the formal organization of the church. His sermons and his letters clearly show that he was possessed of a sincere devotion to the principles of Christianity as he conceived them. It is true that he was not interested in the refined abstrusenesses of the logicians; such matters were folderol fit only for the amusement of little minds which could not find better employment. This judgment may have been prejudiced, but it was the judgment of a strong-minded man whose hard common sense offered no soil for mysticism or mistiness—indeed, they were one to him. As might be expected from such a character, Smith possessed a wide measure of tolerance. Petty distinctions of creed or doctrine did not seem to him worth fighting about. He did not worry about them and could not understand why anyone else should. At the same time, he was fiercely proud, even to a point approaching intolerance, of the broad basis of his own belief. For what lay beyond that he had little use. Although he later admitted that his youthful expressions against the Roman Catholics had been too severe, he shared the general feeling of the eighteenth-century Church of England on the subject of "Popishness." The fact that for some years the enemies on the frontier of Pennsylvania were French Catholics tended to confuse the political and religious aspects of his opposition to them.

It is trite to remark that all sorts of men are needed to make up a church, but it is a truth sometimes forgotten. There are times when men with deep spiritual insight are especially necessary, men who can satisfactorily adjust inherited creed to changing world conditions of action and thought. There are also times when men of wide vision are required, men who can formulate bases of organization upon which an institution can be assured of perpetuation and increase. William Smith belonged essentially to the latter type of humanity and churchmanship. To him and to William White, who was of much the same cast of mind, the Protestant Episcopal Church largely owes the broadness of its foundations.

VII

LAST YEARS

With his retirement, albeit unwilling, from the College and Academy of Philadelphia in 1791, William Smith at the age of sixty-four might have expected to spend the remainder of his days in quiet pursuits befitting a clergyman and retired educator. A large family of children was now nearly full grown, and some of them were already beginning to present him with grandchildren. Above all else, Smith must have considered as the greatest blessing of his retirement the opportunity of spending more time with his wife. Forced to leave Rebecca Moore shortly after their romantic courtship and marriage, Smith had several times undergone long periods away from home in pursuit of his duties. On April 19, 1764, just before sailing from Falmouth after his two-year money-raising expedition, he wrote to Mrs. Smith:

In a few Hours I expect to be under Sail in the Halifax Packet, a fine new Ship; & I am happy in the Hopes of clasping you to my Heart in a few Weeks; & I am resolved that Seas nor Lands, nor any earthly Circumstance shall ever separate between us again, till Death comes & makes our Separation final.

Smith's resolution, the sincerity of which it is impossible to doubt, he was unfortunately not able to keep to the letter. For one thing, the trustees of the College of Philadelphia decided in 1771 that the Provost should undertake another money-raising campaign, this time in South Carolina. From Charleston on February 11, 1772, Smith wrote to his wife:

Believe me, my ever dearest Life, that I am fully sensible my frequent Absences have subjected you to many Pains & Sollicitudes and Inconveniencies wch if God ever brings us together again, it shall be the Business of my Life to attone for by the Continuance of every Instance of Tenderness that can contribute to your Happiness. May God keep you & our dear Children by Night & by Day—

208

Certain factors, however, made the prospect of a pleasant and comfortable retirement unlikely of fulfillment. Foremost among these was financial stringency. Smith had received a far from princely salary in his teaching positions, and he was now left with his one-hundred pound annuity and whatever else the generosity of the trustees might bestow upon him. Moreover, much of what money he had was tied up in land, in which he had been speculating for years. Land speculation was part of the spirit of the age, of the expansionist feeling of the times. Everybody in America with a shilling to spare was putting it into land, with the hope of a vast return. Even while he was still tutoring in New York, Smith had dabbled in land deals. He first took an interest in Pennsylvania lands shortly after his removal to Philadelphia. As early as 1757 he began the acquisition of land at Falls of Schuylkill, where he later built his home. In 1762 he bought the first of many tracts in western Pennsylvania, and during the next thirty years he gradually acquired more and more land until he was the holder of nearly seventy thousand acres, the largest groups of which were located in the Bedford and Huntington districts. The intricacies of his transactions, however shrewdly conducted, are of little concern here; what matters is that Smith was interested in western lands and that in 1791, though somewhat relieved from the pressing poverty of his early days, he may still be described as land-poor. Occasional preaching could hardly add enough to his scanty income to be of any real help.

Some assistance was soon forthcoming from the state government. On April 13, 1791, Governor Thomas Mifflin approved "An Act to provide for the opening and improving sundry navigable Waters and Roads within this Commonwealth," Section IX of which called for the governor to appoint "agents of information," who should advise about proposed improvements. The following month Mifflin appointed William Smith, William Findley, and David Rittenhouse agents of information. The act specified that the agents were "to be paid . . . accordingly as the services of such agents shall be especially directed and employed, of which the governor shall have discretionary power to determine." Smith could not, however, have received a large sum for his services, since the act limited to five hundred pounds the total amount that could be paid to the agents in any one year. Extensive travel throughout the state had qualified Smith for the work. In earlier days he had inspected sites for schools and missions; later he had visited his own and other land holdings; all this now came to good use. Just how long Smith held the position of agent of information cannot be determined.

Perhaps this small taste of public employment whetted Smith's desire for public office, or perhaps the small income it afforded led him to look around for a more remunerative service. On September 13, 1791, he wrote the following interesting letter to the Honorable Richard Peters, speaker of the state senate and a nephew of Smith's old friend and associate, the Reverend Richard Peters:

Sir

As a Member of your Body has done me the Honour to give my Name a Chance of being run in the proposed Election of a Senator for the United States, in your House this Day; Give me Leave, by your Means, to acquaint the House, that as I have solicited no Vote of any Member, so I trust no one will think Himself neglected by Me on this Occasion. The private Solicitation of Votes, in all such Cases, I have always judged to be indelicate & improper.

The Mention of my Name, I believe, has arisen from what passed among some of my Friends in the Western Counties who hearing that there were Candidates on the East Side of Susquehannah and in the Neighbourhood of Philadelphia, express'd a Wish that if any Person in that Quarter were set up, it might be myself, or some Person of Abilities, having an Estate & large common Interest with them in the Western Counties, acquainted with their Circumstances, and a Friend to the Improvment of their Roads & Navigation, & what is called the Susquehannah Interest. I beg Leave to add that if I should have the Honor to be elected (of which I have no very sanguine Expectations) I shall exert my utmost Abilities in the Service of this State & of the United States in General. This I

request you to communicate, in my Behalf, & with all possible
Respect to the Senate. I have the Honour to be—
Sir
Your most obed^t humble Servant
WILLIAM SMITH

Smith's judgment of his chances was realistic; no call to serve
in the United States Senate came to him. He returned, apparently, to attending his private concerns. Timothy Matlack and
Jonathan Mifflin wrote to Governor Mifflin in November 1791
that "the plan of sluice navigation mentioned in the proposal
made by the Reverend Doctor William Smith in behalf of his
son and others, design'd by the commissioners who lately
viewed the Aughwick Falls, appears to be practicable and we
have no doubt but if well executed will answer the purpose
intended." On December 14, 1791, Smith was named in the official records as one of the sureties on a bond of £4,040 for
some canal work.

Perhaps most men age slowly and unnoticeably, but with
William Smith this was not true. It is possible to say of a certain
brief space in his life that he entered it vigorous and active and
emerged from it an old man. This was at the time of the 1793
yellow fever epidemic in Philadelphia—one of the great natural
calamities that claims a place in history along with the London
plague. Hardly had Smith's daughter Rebecca recovered from
the fever when another Rebecca, his wife, was stricken. The
course of her disease is told in a series of letters which Smith
wrote to Dr. Benjamin Rush, the family's physician. Rush was
himself ill and unable to attend Mrs. Smith, but sent his assistants.
Smith's notes asked for help or described symptoms to aid Rush
in making his decisions on the case. Unfortunately most of the
letters are not dated, so that one cannot follow so closely as he
might wish the exact sequence of events. On October 14, 1793,
Dr. Rush wrote to his wife, who was out of the city, that "Mrs.
Dr. Smith is ill and attended under my direction by Dr. [Wood-
house] and Ed. Fisher. The poor Dr. alone remains with her."
Several times during that week Smith wrote asking Rush's help.

At three o'clock on Saturday afternoon, Smith was able to say that Mr. Fisher thought that Mrs. Smith had "no alarming Sympton." He added, however, that "she does not think so herself, & that from her great Debility she thinks she cannot recover." Mrs. Smith was a better judge of her own condition than her physician, and the next day Dr. Rush sent word to his wife that "This day poor dear Mrs S breathed her last." The whole melancholy story Smith poured out in a letter to Rush, opening his heart as perhaps he had never done before:

My dear Friend—

Indeed my only Friend, whose own Distresses, have permitted them to mingle their Cordials of Consolation in my bitter Cup of Affliction— How shall I thank you for your many Sympathies—worthy of a *Physician*—and (what is above all) worthy of a *Christian!* The severest Dispensation of Providence is now past with me, & blessed be God who has enabled me to sustain it— That Dispensation which shall lay me by the Side of my dear departed inestimable Treasure in *this Life,* will be but *little felt;* as I trust, thro the Mercies of my God and Saviour, it will call me to share with *her,* her Treasure in another & *better Life,* where, as you so well express it, according to the sacred Oracles, "Death and the Grave & Hell itself shall be swallowed up in Victory; the genuine Friendships of this Life shall be revived, and Love—and Life—and Light and Truth—reign forever & ever!"—

But, Oh! my dear friend! busy Recollection & Memory, asleep & awake, and the many tender Charities & Offices due to my breaved Family & Children, who *nearly adored* the heavenly Woman I have lost—the Sight of the Numerous Remembrances of her in this *lonesome* House—the Letters and written Charges which she has left me with the Delivery of her *Keys* to me, by the faithful little black Girl after her Funeral—*judge* my dear Sir—nay *feel* for your *Feelings* are tenderly alive—how these Circumstances thrill my Nerves, wch were never strong, & keep my Heart & Limbs & whole Body in such a *Palpitation* & Trembling, that I fear the Consequences— The Scene of her *Funeral* & some preceeding Circumstances can never depart from my mind— On my Return with my Wife from a Visit to our Daughter, whom we had been striving to console, on the Death of Mrs. Keppele, who

was long familiar and dear to both of us, my dear Wife passing the Gate of Christ-Church *Burying Ground*, which then
stood daily open, led me through it, to the Graves of her two
Children; and calling the old Grave *Digger*, markd a Spot for
herself, as close as possible to her Children & the Grave of D^r
Ph. Bond, whose *Memory* she adored—by the side of her *Spot*
we found Room & chose also mine, as it was not permitted during the Sickness to open a Grave once closed for the immediate burial of another. We therefore directed the Grave Digger that this should be the Order of Our Interment and pledged
ourselves to each other that this order should be observed by
the Survivor— But let me not be tedious to you—it gives me
some Ease—as my Children are all absent & cannot come near
me in Town,—to *pour* these Circumstances into the Bosom of
a Friend.— In melancholy Mood we retur'nd to our House—
Night approach'd— I hoped my dear Wife had gone to rest,
as she had chosen, since her Return from nursing her daughter thro the Fever, to sleep in a Chamber by herself, thro Fear
of Infection to her Grand Child & me— But it seems she
closed not her Eyes, sitting with them fixed thro' her Chamber
Window on Mrs Keppele's house (who had died that Day),
till about Midnight, she saw her *Herse* & follow'd it with tear-
ful Eyes as far as it could be seen— Two days afterwards M^rs
Rogers her next & only surviving intimate Friend was carried
past her Window, & by no Persuasion could we draw her
from thence, nor stop her *Sympathetic forebodeing* Tears, so
long as her Eyes could follow the Funeral, wch was, down
Arch street, thro' two squares, from 4th to 2^d Street, where
turning the Corner to the Baptist Church the Herse disap-
peard— She threw herself on her Bed—and requested me
who had stood by her Side during the Time of the funeral
Procession, to leave her to her own Reflexions for a few Mo-
ments, and she would soon be with me in my Study, where I
was writing Letters to my Friends and Family, on Business
to the Westward— She took her Pen, & assisted me in Copying some of them— It was Saturday, & we had persuaded our
Daughter to sett out for Norristown next Day— My Wife, tho
she informed me on Saturday Evening that she was indisposed,
and I am persuaded was sure of the Nature of her Case, yet
She charged me not inform her Daughter, and sent me to
hasten her out of Town on Sunday Morning, with an Apology
that she could not see her before she set out, finding it neces-

sary to take a little Physick for a slight Indisposition, and that
if she would send the Carriage back in two or three Days, we
hoped to follow her to Norristown— While I was getting my
Daughter ready & seeing her a few Miles out of town, w^{ch}
was not till 2 o'Clock on Sunday, my dear Wife, with her own
Hand—her last Hand to you—had written the *Note* which
you must have in your Possession—the Contents of wch or her
Apprehensions express'd in it—I can only guess— You know
the Rest—and my Situation thro' the Week following till Sunday evening, at 6 o'Clock, when in Much Agony, by a sudden an unexpected Turn (after I had fondly written to all my
distant Family, & to my dear Brother, that we believ'd her
out of Danger) she *breath'd her last*, compos'd & patient, her
Countenance appearing to brighten, as her Pangs & Groans
ceased, into the Countenance of an Angel—

Decently as the Time would permit, my Mournful Family
assisted only by a worthy & pious *Black—Richd Allen*, she was
laid in her Coffin. I approached with my dear Grand Child in
my Arms as near as the Black Man would allow, to take my
last *View*— *Silent*, but more awful and instructive than all the
funeral Pomp in the World—and short the Distance we had
to go, I follow'd her (accompanied only by the Coffin Maker,
& by *Richard* Allen, & my own weeping & faithful black Boy)
to the Spot she had chosen, about nine o'Clock in the Evening, neither Moon nor Torch Light, but Light sufficient thro'
the Gloom of the Evening, to deposit all that was *Mortal*—

Severe was the Task that remain for me Yesterday— To
write to my Daughter & other Children, & to good Mrs. Cadwalader who lov'd her Aunt as her own Parent— When these
letters were finish'd and an Express dispatch'd to my Son W^m
to take all possible prudent Measures to support his Sister in
her Affliction— My Messenger having taken his Course up one
Street, & my anxious dutiful Son having enter'd another, came
to my Door, while I was visiting the Grave to see if it had been
decently cover'd in the Night— My black Boy met my Son at
the Door of my House and was obliged to answer his Enquiry
concerning his Mother— *That she was no more.* I soon came
from the Ground & saw my dear Son leaning against the *Wall*,
for he would not enter the House, nor amidst the distressing
Scene could we exchange a Word, but my Desire & his ready
Obedience to fly to his Sister & overtake the Messenger, w^{ch}
he did at 8 M. Distance from Town— I have heard no more,

and I dread to hear from a Daughter, who lov'd & knew the Value of such a Mother— But much remains for me yet— My Son Charles & his Wife—My Brother & his Wife—my son Richard at Huntingdon—in whose Bosoms she was equally precious, as to us all— I can find no Conveyance, and hard will be my Task to write, if my Spirits & Health can be supported so long—

For that Reason only, & a few more Family Matters not yet arrang'd, especially a Codicil Which my dear Wife's Death makes necessary to my Will—if it will please God—I would pray for a few Days Continuance of Health—then as to Worldly Matters I shall be *prepared*, and thro the Goodness of God, I trust I am preparing, tho we can never, never be fully prepared (except in his Mercy) in our *Spiritual* Matters—.

If God continues me longer, my Worldly concerns will lie in a small Compass—his Goodness having given me Time to distribute a sufficient Inheritance to my Children, acquired I trust honestly & industriously without Injury to any Man—and I hope & believe from the Goodness of all my Children in whom I consider myself blest, they will use it accordingly— For the rest of my Days, few & they cannot be many—I would willingly devote them to discharge some public Engagements, by assorting & leaving to the World some Sermons & other Writings—but if they cannot have my last Hand, my Executors in my proposed Codicil, to wch I must now hasten, must suppress all, except what I have already publish'd and avowd.

My Friend Mrs Cadwalader & Mr Bond, press me, with your Advice, to take *Calomel* & *Jalap* &c.—(I know Nothing of Preventatives—) and then to move out of Town—but I wish not remove to a Distance from You for some Days yet, nor till you advise— I trust you will soon be so restord that we may have a personal Interview If moving for a few Days to my Daughters will change the Scene a little, perhaps it may be of Use— Thus my good Friend, I have pour'd into your bosom, *confidentially*, what may be of Use to my Family, for to none of them have I had Leisure nor would it be *yet* proper to say so much— The Name & Memory of my dear Wife, I must commit to your friendly hand, who knew her Virtues so well, to say to the *public* what may be necessary; but of this nothing yet, as I would not, & must notify Mr Brown thereof, unless you can do it for I say would not have her Name announced among the *Dead*, till I can find Means first to notify my distant Family— Alas! how shall I live well without Her? I never had a *Joy* w.ᶜʰ became a *Joy* to me till she shared it. I never had a Sorrow w.ᶜʰ she did not alleviate & participate— I never did an Action which I could consider as truly good till she confirm'd my Opinion— For my many Failings & Infirmities she had a friendly Veil— Her Conversation was enlighten'd, & that with her Correspondence by Letter, during my many Absences, have been my Joy for 35 Years and more— My Tears now stop my Hand—& will relieve You from reading more from

Your obliged and affectionate
Wᵐ SMITH

Excuse Inaccuracies, Omissions of Words &c for I cannot read over or correct what has flowed from my Heart & Pen—

Octʳ 22ᵈ 1793—
Dʳ Rush—

The ravages of the fever, however, were not over for Smith's family. In a letter dated merely "Wednesday Noon," but probably to be ascribed to October 23, 1793, Smith wrote to Rush that his sister, who had long lived in his household, was "seized with the Malignant *Disorder*." When, on Friday evening, Smith next wrote to Rush about his sister's condition, he added that "On Account of my dear Grand Child, as well as on my Account, I have been three Days at my Daughter's House in Market Street." This removal did not have the desired effect and Smith was himself stricken by yellow fever. In a very shaky hand, which becomes more legible as it proceeds, he wrote to Rush:

I am axtremly seiz'd with the Fever— Last Night I had a Chill after going to for about three Hours; but then fell a-Sleep for a few Hours if Sleep it might where my Imagination the living Images of my dear Wife and Mʳˢ Rogers my Da——r Blodget sitting by me & talking but when I ask'd Question they vanish'd in Air— I wak'd it immediately in a Fit of the Night— This Morning at Sunrise I was seiz'd wt a violent Trembling, wch soon brought on my present— My Body cool, no great Headack, my Pulse I see to have . . .

Wm SMITH

My Hand shake much at Intervals—
Monday Morning 28th Oct^{r}—

What shall I do with my Grand Child I cannot remove back to my own House—

Smith recovered from his attack of fever, but he was never the same man physically that he had been before.

In view of his own debility and the great blow that he had suffered, it is all the more remarkable that Smith should be found at the close of the year 1793 and in the first months of 1794 delivering a series of sermons in Christ Church, Philadelphia, "on the great visitation by the epidemical sickness, commonly called the Yellow Fever." The nine sermons of this series were all preached on Sunday mornings, the first on December 1, 1793, and the last on March 9, 1794. Smith also preached in Christ Church on Thursday, December 12, 1793, the day set aside by the Governor of the state as one of general thanksgiving for deliverance from the pestilence. Naturally, Smith's sermons were of a somber cast. He stressed the errors which had called down the vengeance of the Lord upon the country and the need for reformation, but more especially the comforts that religion afforded in such dark hours. One can readily understand that during the delivery of the first of these sermons Smith, as he recorded in his *Works*, never "lifted his eyes from his notes, which were drenched in tears."

Smith was, of course, less able to engage intensively in public or private pursuits after 1793. But he gradually began to regain his interest in some of his old activities. He occasionally preached in Christ Church or elsewhere, though his pulpit appearances became less frequent with the years. On June 24, 1795, he again celebrated the anniversary of St. John the Baptist by delivering a sermon to the Masons of Philadelphia. His mind must have gone back to that date exactly forty years before when he had spoken in the same place, on the same occasion, and under the same auspices.

Land speculations and particularly canal companies continued to attract Smith and led him to publication once more. As a young man in Pennsylvania, he had been the most facile writer in the political quarrels between the proprietary party and the Assembly. He now presented with much of the same facility the claims and advantages of various land and canal schemes. Although his name did not appear on the title-pages of these writings, Smith usually signed the preface or in some other way indicated his authorship. In 1795 there was published from his pen *An Historical Account of the Rise, Progress and Present State of the Canal Navigation in Pennsylvania*. The following year he compiled *An Account of the Proceedings of the Illinois and Oubache Land Companies*, and in 1798 an *Account of the Conewago-Canal, on the River Susquehanna*. The last-mentioned publication contains evidence that Smith did more than merely write up the account of the Conewago Canal company; he was also active in it. For example, when John Hall, acting under appointment from Governor Mifflin, made the official inspection of the canal on November 21 and 22, 1797, Smith "attended as a committee on the part of the Canal-Company."

In the capacity of chairman of the stockholders of the Delaware and Schuylkill Canal company, Smith sent a letter to the city councils of Philadelphia on December 19, 1797, concerning the city's need of a new water supply. A response came on January 31, 1798, when a joint committee of the select and common councils of Philadelphia issued a report in which it was agreed that the canal afforded the best way of providing that "supply of water . . . now thought essential to the health of the community, and one of the means most effectual to prevent or mitigate the return of the late contagious sickness," that it would also be of great value to inland navigation, and that the work on it, which had been stopped, should be continued. B. Henry Latrobe, the engineer for a rival scheme of supplying water to Philadelphia, was rash enough to publish some remarks about the unsoundness of the canal company's plans and to refer slightingly to the knowledge of engineering which might be expected of a doctor of divinity. This was a challenge Smith could not let pass, and early in 1799 he issued his *Remarks On a second Publication of B. Henry Latrobe, Engineer*. His remarks on Latrobe show that the passage of the years had in no way dulled the edge of Smith's satirical power.

In the last years of the eighteenth century, Smith was also reaping some of the honors which come to a man who is held in esteem by his fellows. After serving as vice-president of the St. Andrew's Society of Philadelphia from 1789 to 1796, he was elected president in 1797 and held the office until 1802. The American Philosophical Society, of which he had earlier been a secretary, elected him a vice-president in 1790, and from that time until 1801 he served either as a vice-president or a councilor.

Beside everyday business matters, Smith seems to have had two major concerns during his last years. Both are expressed in his letters, especially to members of his family. The first was to get his estate in good order and to provide for its distribution among his children. The second, of greater general interest, was to prepare a collected edition of his writings. He had published much, a great deal anonymously, and he felt a desire to gather everything together. The nearest approach that he had ever had to a collected edition was the *Discourses on Public Occasions*, of which two editions had appeared, in 1759 and 1762, neither complete even then. In 1789 he planned an edition of his sermons "in four or five octavo volumes." The General Convention of the church in that year passed a resolution testifying to Smith's "soundness in the faith, and eminent abilities for such a work." The members of the convention further showed their approbation of the project by subscribing to it. A large number of other subscriptions was obtained and a prospectus was printed, listing ninety-eight sermons. Other interests prevented Smith from going ahead with the project, and the distress he underwent in 1793 left him incapable of the task for some time. About 1800 he began work on a complete collection of his writings, and by 1802 he had progressed far enough for a prospectus to be issued. The sixty-four-page pamphlet, entitled *The Works of William Smith*, contained notices and reviews of some of Smith's earlier publications, an introduction written by Smith, and sample pages from the proposed series, including the tables of contents of the first two volumes. The most important thing about this prospectus, however, is that in it Smith listed the works which he planned to publish in the collection. The list is an invaluable guide to Smith's writings, since many of his anonymous publications are established as his only because of their inclusion in it.

The first two volumes of Smith's collected works—and the only two ever to be published—appeared in 1803. They sold well, if one may assume from the number of variant title-pages surviving that there were several printings. The library of the Historical Society of Pennsylvania contains a copy of a section of what must have been intended as the third volume of the series. It is called *Select Sermons of William Smith, D.D.*, and the title-page is either a half-title or a working title-page for a volume still in the course of preparation. The latter seems the more likely, for the printing is badly centered on the page. The section consists only of pages 65 to 196 and contains ten sermons, numbered from V to XIV. The fact that the folio signatures are numbered with the roman numeral III makes it evident that these sheets were intended as part of the third volume of the collected works.

But William Smith did not live to see the publication of even the two volumes of his *Works*. Early in 1803 his already weakened health began rapidly to suffer a further decline. A letter written from his home at Falls of Schuylkill on February 17 to his son Charles stated that "I get weaker every Day, and am wholly confined to my Bed Chamber." The course of his illness, like that of his wife, it is possible to follow through the letters which he sent from time to time to his physician. On March 9, 1803, he wrote to Dr. Benjamin Rush:

My dear Doctor—
The Medecine you sent to infuse in a Pint of Madeira Did no more Service than if I had infused so much Chaff. . . . these two Nights past my Asthma is returned with so much Malignity, that I could gasp a little for Breath, with the help of two Persons to keep in an erect Posture, and what is strange to me, the approach of the Morning Sun, relieves me much.
. . . Write me a Line by the Bearer, & try to send me Something by my good Girl & Nurse, to give me a little Breath till then— I am ever yours

Wm SMITH

Smith continued to grow worse. He sent a pitiable description of himself to Rush on April 4, and complained in the same letter that he thought his nurses had made some mistake in the administration of his medicine: "They cannot read, nor can I your small Hand." Ten days later, Rush received this note:

Dr Rush, Come and see a *friend* and, he hopes, a *resign'd Christian*, DIE!

Wm *Smith*

Come *soon*—you will see me at the best—W Smith
Don't let m^{rs} Blodget know I wish he to be at Lacanter first —W S.
14 Ap^r 1803

During this month of April, Smith was taken from his home at the Falls to that of his son William Moore Smith at Fifth and Chestnut streets in Philadelphia. His son had gone to England earlier in the year, but his daughter-in-law attended him constantly.

On May 11, 1803, Smith's son Charles wrote to Dr. Rush, expressing his concern over his father's condition and regretting that he could not be with him, since he had to be in attendance on the court in circuit until June 12.

Charles Smith's concern for his father was justified. On May 14, 1803, Dr. Rush entered in his commonplace book the notation that "Died this day at four o'clock the Rev. Dr. William Smith, formerly Provost of the College of Philadelphia, in the seventy-seventh year of his age." Unfortunately no account of

Smith's last days exists except that given by the rather unfriendly hand of Rush himself, who apparently could not overcome the shock of having a patient curse at his doctor once and at his nurses more than once during his final illness. Yet one can piece together from Rush's story and from certain of Smith's last letters and from a few other sources the general outlines of what happened in that dark and trying time. A reference which Smith made in his 1802 prospectus to the kindness of his publisher in attending with the proofs makes it possible to verify Rush's statement that Smith's sight gradually grew weaker until he finally lost all effective use of his eyes. From the pain and near-blindness of his last days, Smith could hope for only one relief, that which came to him at four o'clock on the afternoon of May 14, 1803. Circumstances prevented any of his children from being with him in the days and hours preceding his death, but his daughter-in-law stayed at his side. He was buried in a vault on his estate at Falls of Schuylkill.

It was a far cry from Aberdeenshire in 1727 to the Philadelphia of 1803, and Smith had experienced his full share of vicissitudes during that seventy-six years. He was in every sense a man of action; his nature would not let him exist in idleness. This tremendous energy accounts for the variety of his interests and the zeal he lavished upon them. Political quarrels and land speculations were side issues in the general sum of his career, yet he put into them the same driving force that established the most progressive system of college education in America.

Important as were his contributions to the Church of England in America and its successor, the Protestant Episcopal Church, William Smith was above all else an educator. Dr. Rush himself admitted Smith "possessed genius, taste and learning. As a teacher he was perspicuous and agreeable." Smith was not an especially original or deep thinker, but he was a great teacher. Although he left several sons and daughters, from whom a large and occasionally distinguished progeny has sprung (Richard Penn Smith, the playwright, being one of the most renowned), his greatest legacy to the world was through the young men whom he taught. The youth in his charge he inspired with a love for his own ideals and for the pursuit of truth and knowledge. He made no attempt to form his students into one mold, but inspired each of them to seek out and develop his own particular talents. How well he succeeded one can judge from the careers of three of his most gifted students: Benjamin West, Thomas Godfrey, and Francis Hopkinson.

No less gifted an administrator than a teacher, Smith did more than any other man to set up and endow the college which was later to become the University of Pennsylvania. Indeed, the College of Philadelphia was the living counterpart of his Mirania. The curriculum which he established became the model for American colleges for over 150 years.

In the history of that great movement which was the transplanting of learning and the arts from western Europe to colonial America, surely the teacher who guided and encouraged the first creators of the three arts of drama, music, and painting in America, and the educator who laid the foundations for one of the great American universities deserves a high place.

APPENDIX

DISPUTED POINTS

Horace Wemyss Smith, in his *Life and Correspondence* of Smith, stated that William Smith was born September 7, 1727, and baptized "in the old Aberdeenshire Kirk" on October 19, 1727. The office of the Registrar-General for Scotland, which now holds all extant parish registers of the Established Church of Scotland, has stated that no such church ever existed in the Established Church of Scotland and that no record of the birth of William Smith can be found in any of the records in its care. The present Episcopal Bishop of Aberdeen and Orkney is authority for the statement that no such church was ever known in the Episcopal diocese of Aberdeen. The Episcopal registers for that early period have been lost or destroyed. On the day of Smith's death, May 14, 1803, his physician, Dr. Benjamin Rush, noted in his commonplace book that Smith was "in the seventy-seventh year of his age, being seventy-six on the 20th of the preceding April." An obituary notice in the *American Daily Advertiser* for May 21, 1803, also gives Smith's age as seventy-six. Since his seventy-sixth birthday would not have come until September according to H. W. Smith's date, that given by Rush seems the only one allowable.

GRADUATION FROM ABERDEEN

The question of Smith's graduation from Aberdeen is perplexing. In the recommendation which the Archbishop of Canterbury and several other English bishops sent to the University of Oxford in 1759, requesting the D.D. degree for Smith, he is referred to as holding the M.A. degree from Aberdeen, and the Oxford diploma itself thus refers to him. Some of the title-pages of his early works (before his receipt of the D.D. degree) credit him with the M.A. degree, but the Aberdeen D.D. diploma of 1759 makes no reference to any previous degree having been granted there and, as stated in the text, the present University of Aberdeen has no record that King's College ever gave Smith the M.A. degree. This degree, it should be stated, was the one then customarily granted at the conclusion of the undergraduate curriculum. Smith's D.D. diplomas from Aberdeen, Oxford, and Dublin are preserved in the Brinton Collection, but there is no M.A. diploma in the collection.

In order to establish Smith's authorship of this poem, it is necessary to look some distance ahead of 1752. Smith in 1768 preached a series of sermons as chaplain *pro tempore* to a regiment which was then stationed in Philadelphia. To one of these sermons, both in its delivery and in its published form in his collected works (1803), Smith appended "The Speech of a Creek Indian" on the subject of temperance. In the *Works*, Smith stated that his possession of this speech and how he came to publish it "in London among some other writings of my own fifty years ago" were explained by the introduction to a republication of the "Speech" in the *Columbian Magazine* for June 1790. According to this introduction, the first draft of the speech had been taken down in shorthand at a council of the Creeks in 1748 and had come into the hands of a deputy of Sir William Johnson, Secretary for Indian Affairs, who had given his notes to a gentleman then living in New York ("who has long been honourably distinguished in the republic of letters, in Pennsylvania"), who first published the "Speech" in the New York *Gazette* and republished it in London in 1754, "with some other Indian compositions." A footnote to this last statement explained that the other compositions were:

> Viz. This Speech of a Creek Indian; a letter from Yariza, an Indian maid; Indian Songs of Peace; and an American Fable.

It so happens that these items form the exact contents of a volume published in London in 1754 under the title of *The Speech of a Creek Indian, . . . To which are added, 1. A Letter from Yariza, . . . 2. Indian Songs of Peace. 3. an American Fable. . . .* In the same year another edition of the work was published as *Some Account of the North-American Indians*. But in 1752 the letter from Yariza and the songs of peace were published in a twenty-seven-page pamphlet in New York, under the title of *Indian Songs of Peace*. Smith's authorship of these various works thus seems indisputable. And since the "American Fable" included in the 1754 volume was "The Mock-Bird and Red-Bird," it is easy enough to assign that poem to Smith. A statement in the "Advertisement" to the

1754 volume, implying that the "Speech" and the remainder of the volume were by different hands, does not seem to be more than polite persiflage, and is not borne out by Smith's own later statements.

BIBLIOGRAPHICAL NOTE

To LIST the manuscript sources for a biography of William Smith is a pleasant task, since every time one names a person or institution holding Smith material, he is recalling the name of someone who has been gracious and generous in making that material available. Easily the most outstanding group of manuscripts is the Brinton Collection of Smith Papers, owned by the Honorable Jasper Y. Brinton of Alexandria, Egypt, a direct descendant of Smith, and by him placed on deposit with the Historical Society of Pennsylvania. Another important source is the Smith Family Manuscripts, a collection presented to the Historical Society of Pennsylvania by William R. Smith. Other collections of that notable society also contain pertinent material: the Peters Papers, the Penn Papers (both Official and Private Correspondence), the Jacobs Papers, the Gratz, Etting, Logan, and Dreer Collections, and various miscellaneous collections.

The Smith Manuscripts and the White Manuscripts owned by the General Council of the Protestant Episcopal Church and deposited in the New York Historical Society are invaluable for a study of Smith's part in the affairs of the church. The early trustees' minutes of the College and Academy of Philadelphia, containing many references to Smith, and much other material are to be found in the custody of the Secretary of the University of Pennsylvania; the University Library has a number of Smith's letters in its collection of University Papers.

The letters Smith wrote to several individuals have been preserved in other collections, most notable among them the Rush Manuscripts in the Ridgway Branch of the Library Company of Philadelphia and the Franklin collections of the American Philosophical Society. The Hopkinson Papers, at present in the custody of Mr. Edward Hopkinson, Jr., of Philadelphia, contain Smith's letters to Francis Hopkinson. The Philadelphia Autograph Company owns an account book kept by Charles Smith in his capacity as an executor of his father's estate.

A number of important manuscript sources are located abroad. The Society for the Propagation of the Gospel in Foreign Parts has perhaps the largest and most important amount of material, but the collections of the Archbishop of Canterbury at Lambeth Palace and of the Bishop of London at

Fulham Palace provide considerable information of interest.

Smith's own works are, of course, the chief printed source for a study of his career. They are extensive, and the bibliography given in Sabin's *Dictionary of Books Relating to America* is practically complete and is satisfactory for all normal purposes. Lists in Smith's own handwriting in the Brinton Collection, together with the lists given in his 1789 and 1802 prospectuses, help establish a complete record of his works, the most important of which have been mentioned in the text.

The two best books on the early history of the University of Pennsylvania (including the College and Academy of Philadelphia) are Thomas H. Montgomery's *A History of the University of Pennsylvania from Its Foundation to A.D. 1770* (Philadelphia, 1900), and Edward Potts Cheyney's *A History of the University of Pennsylvania* (Philadelphia, University of Pennsylvania Press, 1940).

The magazines and newspapers of the period are invaluable sources of information. For the greater part of Smith's residence in Philadelphia, the *Pennsylvania Gazette* and the *Pennsylvania Journal* will be found most helpful. The *Pennsylvania Archives* and *Colonial Records* contain most of the official records of the commonwealth which in any way relate to Smith.

Of previous lives of Smith there have been two: Charles J. Stillé, a provost of the University of Pennsylvania, published in 1869 his *Memoir* of Smith. This was a brief account of Smith's life, dealing largely with his relations with the College and Academy of Philadelphia. Stillé's judgment of Smith's contributions to that institution was sound. In 1879 there appeared the first volume of *Life and Correspondence of the Rev. William Smith, D.D.*, by a great-grandson, Horace Wemyss Smith. The following year the first volume was reissued and the second volume published. These two large volumes contain much material, most of it from the Brinton Collection, the trustees' minutes, and Perry's *Historical Collections*. Unfortunately Horace Smith was completely inaccurate in many of his statements, often without apparent purpose. The impulse to show an ancestor to best advantage prevents his book from attaining any degree of objectivity in its treatment of William Smith.

A word might be said about available material on the lives

of the young men who constituted Smith's group. The only one about whom an adequate work exists is Francis Hopkinson; George E. Hastings' *The Life and Works of Francis Hopkinson* (Chicago, University of Chicago Press, 1926) is a thoroughly scholarly piece of investigation. The only full-scale biography of Benjamin West is still John Galt's *The Life, Studies, and Works of Benjamin West, Esq.*, a work no more recent than 1820. A complete life of West, with a catalogue of his works and some attempt at an honest appraisal of them, is needed. A more complete study of Thomas Godfrey, particularly of his relationship to William Smith and his group, may be found in A. F. Gegenheimer's article, "Thomas Godfrey: Protégé of William Smith," in *Pennsylvania History* for October 1942 and January 1943. An interesting account of Godfrey is that given by Archibald Henderson in the sketch prefatory to his reprint of the *Prince of Parthia* (Boston, 1917). A life of Jacob Duché would, the writer feels, be of interest; he hopes to have the opportunity of presenting such a volume at some future time. No adequate study of Nathaniel Evans has yet been made. Edgar Legare Pennington's *Nathaniel Evans, a Poet of Colonial America* is inaccurate and incomplete.

INDEX